SEVEN SEAS ENTERTAINMENT PRESENTS

Magical Angel Creamy Mami
and the Spoiled Princess

story and art by **EMI MITSUKI**   original concept by **STUDIO PIERROT**   **VOLUME 2**

TRANSLATION
Amber Tamosaitis

ADAPTATION
Ysabet Reinhardt MacFarlane

LETTERING AND RETOUCH
Jennifer Skarupa

COVER DESIGN
Nicky Lim

PROOFREADER
Stephanie Cohen, Dawn Davis

EDITOR
Jenn Grunigen

PREPRESS TECHNICIAN
Rhiannon Rasmussen-Silverstein

PRODUCTION MANAGER
Lissa Pattillo

MANAGING EDITOR
Julie Davis

ASSOCIATE PUBLISHER
Adam Arnold

PUBLISHER
Jason DeAngelis

Seven Seas press and purchase enquiries can be sent to Marketing Manager
Lianne Sentar at press@gomanga.com. Information regarding the distribution
and purchase of digital editions is available from Digital Manager CK Russell
at digital@gomanga.com.

Seven Seas and the Seven Seas logo are trademarks of
Seven Seas Entertainment. All rights reserved.

ISBN: 978-1-64827-245-5

Printed in Canada

First Printing: August 2021

10 9 8 7 6 5 4 3 2 1

W9-ADC-198

FOLLOW US ONLINE: *www.sevenseasentertainment.com*

READING DIRECTIONS

This book reads from *right to left*, Japanese style.
If this is your first time reading manga, you start
reading from the top right panel on each page and
take it from there. If you get lost, just follow the
numbered diagram here. It may seem backwards at
first, but you'll get the hang of it! Have fun!!

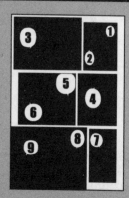

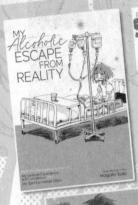
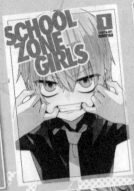
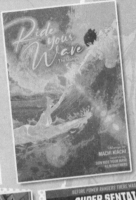
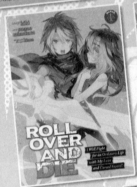
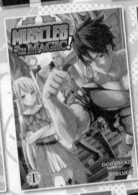
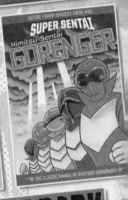
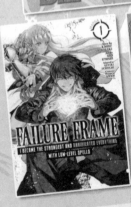
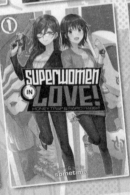
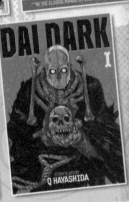

Magical Angel
Creamy Mami
and the
Spoiled Princess

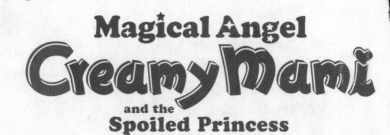

②

story & art: **Emi Mitsuki**
original concept: **Studio Pierrot**

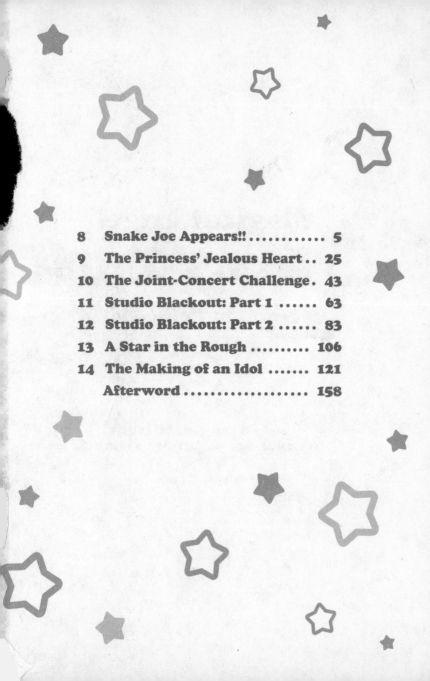

8   Snake Joe Appears!! 5

9   The Princess' Jealous Heart . . 25

10   The Joint-Concert Challenge . 43

11   Studio Blackout: Part 1 63

12   Studio Blackout: Part 2 83

13   A Star in the Rough 106

14   The Making of an Idol 121

     Afterword 158

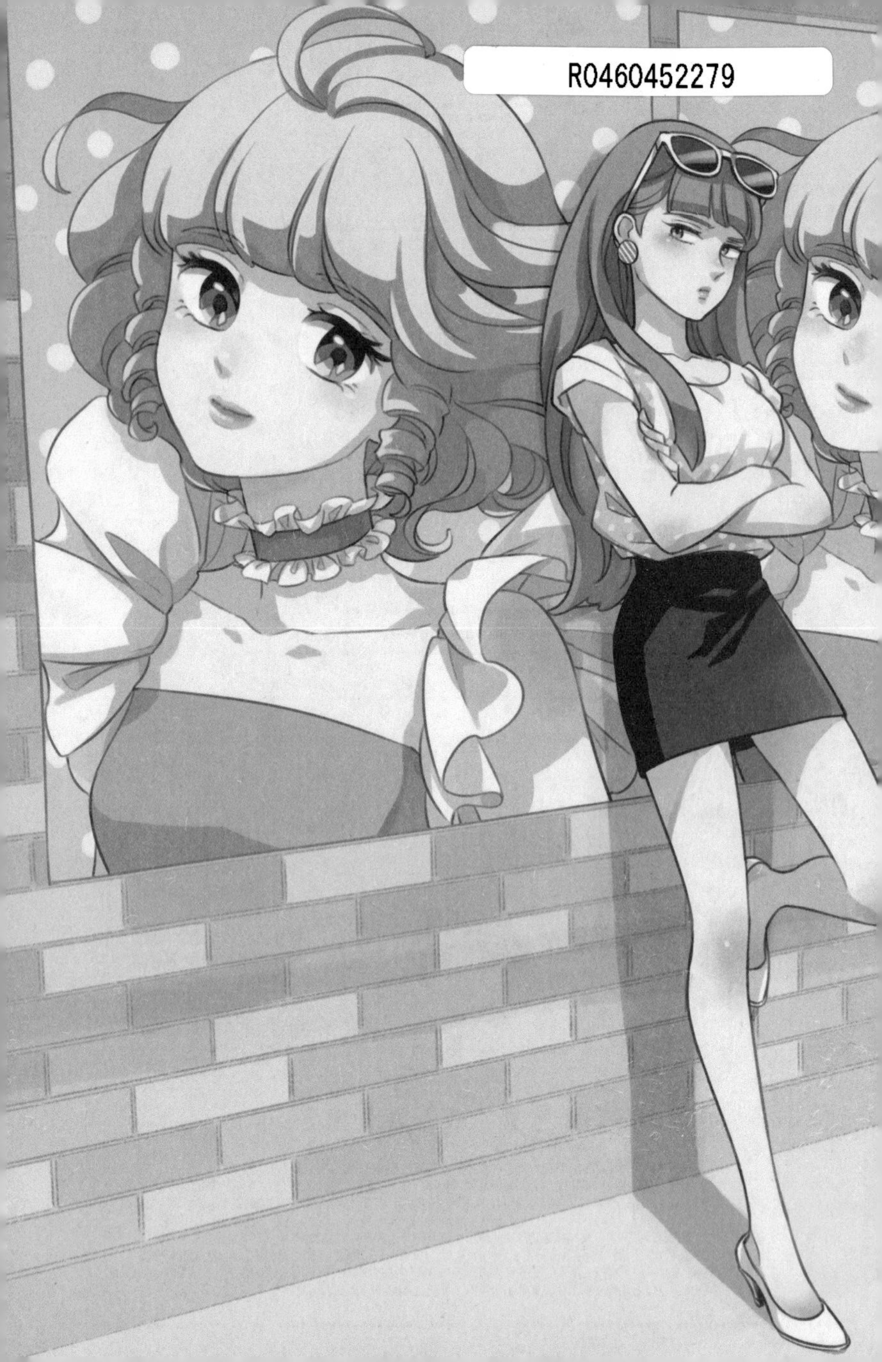

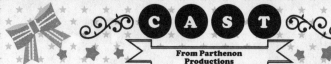

CAST

From Parthenon Productions

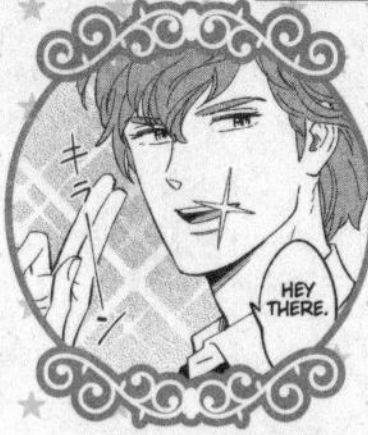

HEY THERE.

Tachibana Shingo

PARTHENON PRODUCTIONS' SECOND PRESIDENT. HE SCOUTED CREAMY MAMI AND GOT HER TO SIGN AN EXCLUSIVE CONTRACT WITH HIS AGENCY.

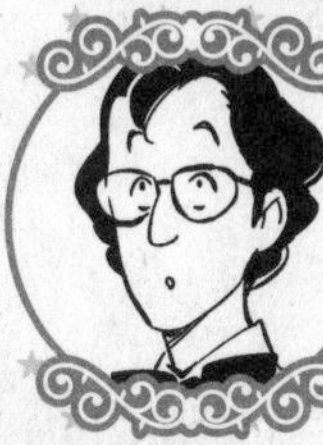

Kidokoro Hayato

A MANAGER AT PARTHENON PRODUCTIONS. HE STARTED OUT AS MEGUMI'S MANAGER, BUT HE'S NOW MANAGING CREAMY MAMI AS WELL.

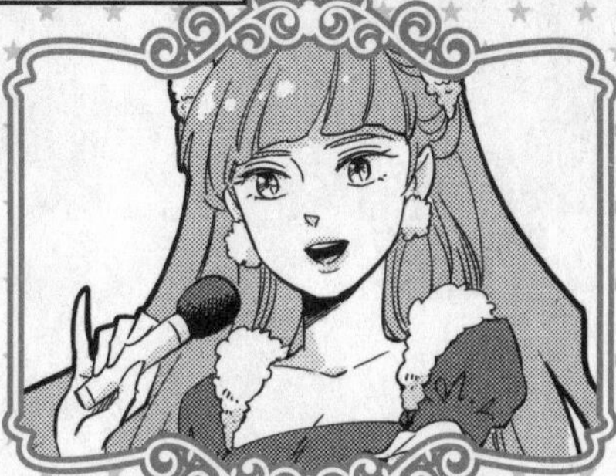

Ayase Megumi

AN IDOL SINGER REPRESENTED BY TALENT AGENCY PARTHENON PRODUCTIONS. AFTER SEEING A MYSTERIOUS LIGHT IN MAMI'S DRESSING ROOM, SHE BEGAN TO HAVE QUESTIONS ABOUT MAMI'S IDENTITY.

From Kurimigaoka

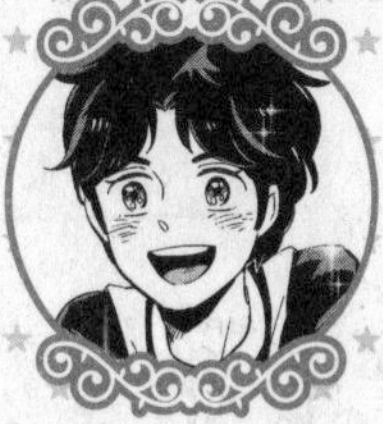

Ōtomo Toshio

THIS FOURTEEN-YEAR-OLD FRIEND OF YUU'S IS A MASSIVE CREAMY MAMI FAN.

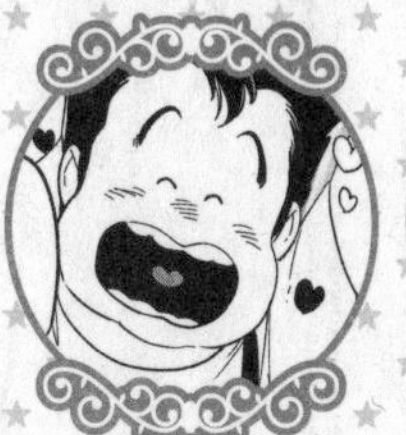

Kisaragi Midori

TOSHIO'S CLASSMATE AND BEST FRIEND. HE HAS A CRUSH ON YUU.

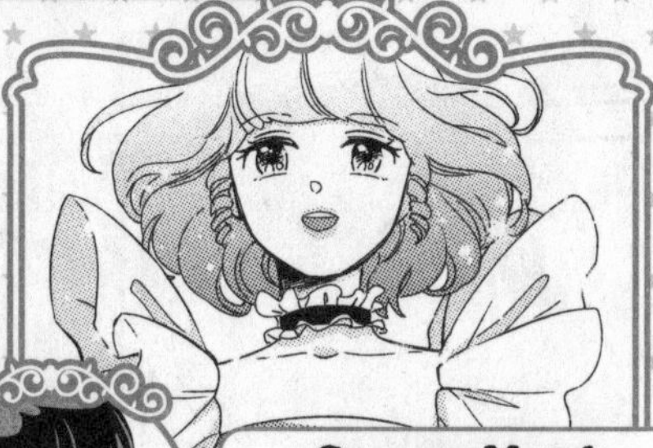

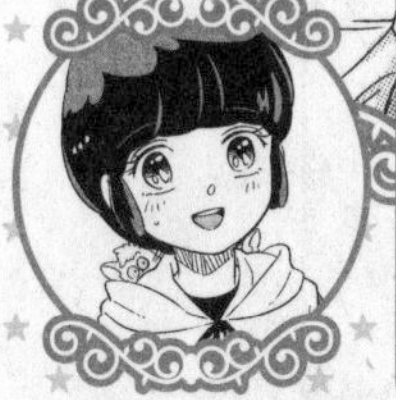

Creamy Mami
Morisawa Yuu

THANKS TO THE MAGIC SHE RECEIVED FROM THE ALIEN PINO PINO OF THE MAGICAL WORLD FEATHER STAR, TEN-YEAR-OLD MORISAWA YUU CAN TRANSFORM INTO CREAMY MAMI. AS CREAMY MAMI, SHE MADE HER DEBUT AS AN IDOL AND QUICKLY BECAME VERY POPULAR.

STORY

AS PARTHENON PRODUCTIONS' HEADLINER, AYASE MEGUMI'S IMMENSE POPULARITY HAD NEVER BEEN IN QUESTION...UNTIL THE DAY TACHIBANA SHINGO GOT AN UNKNOWN PERFORMER NAMED CREAMY MAMI TO FILL IN FOR HER. MAMI'S INITIAL APPEARANCE MADE A HUGE SPLASH AND SHE QUICKLY DEBUTED AS A SINGER. NOW, MAMI IS LAVISHED WITH ATTENTION AND CONSIDERATION AT THE AGENCY, WHILE MEGUMI IS TREATED MORE AND MORE POORLY. GRIPPED BY JEALOUSY AND THREATENED BY THIS UNEXPECTED NEW RIVAL, MEGUMI IS DETERMINED TO RECLAIM HER PLACE AT THE TOP.

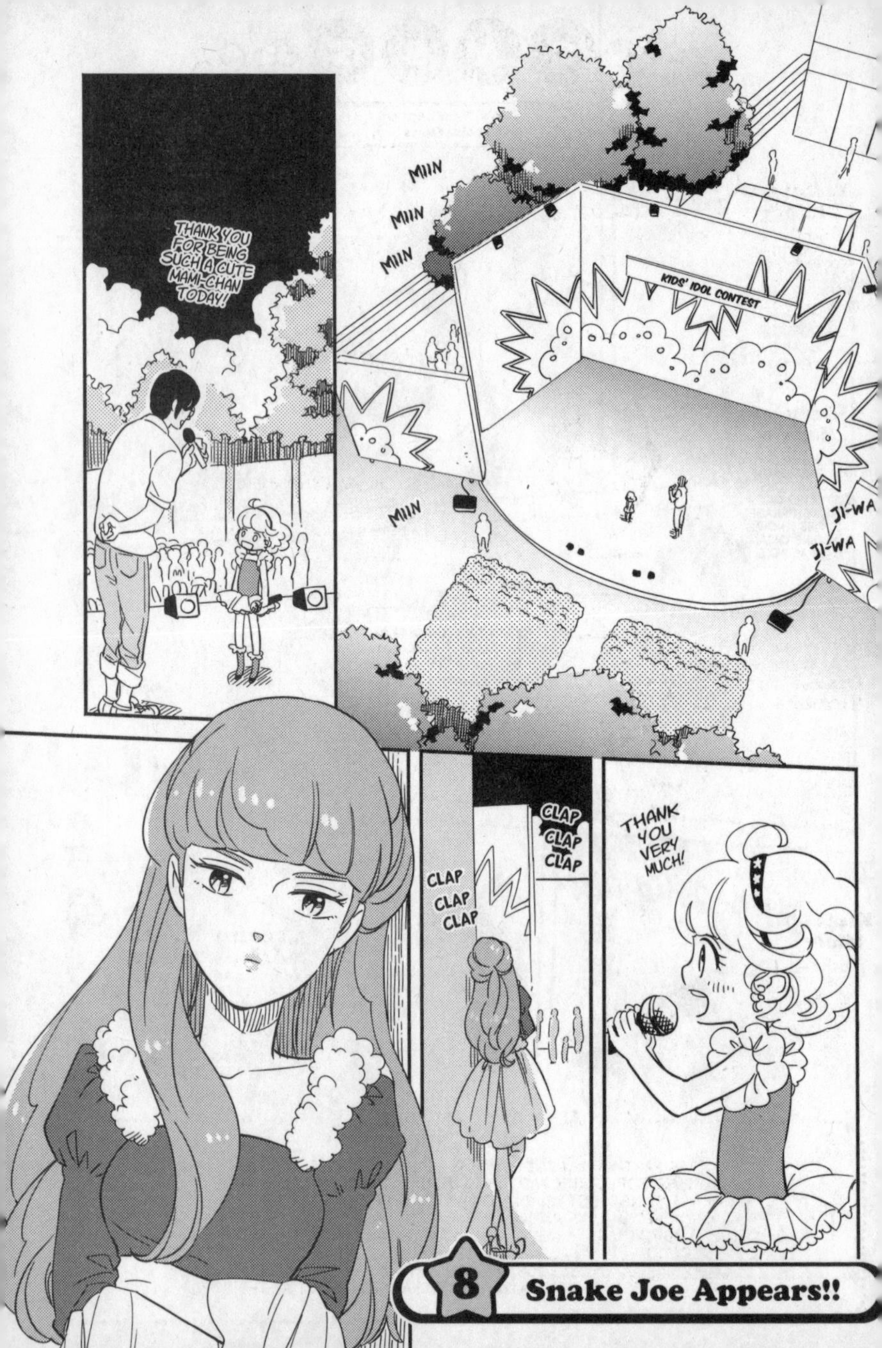
MIIN
MIIN
MIIN
KIDS' IDOL CONTEST
MIIN
JI-WA
JI-WA
THANK YOU FOR BEING SUCH A CUTE MAMI-CHAN TODAY!
THANK YOU VERY MUCH!
CLAP CLAP CLAP
CLAP CLAP CLAP
8 Snake Joe Appears!!

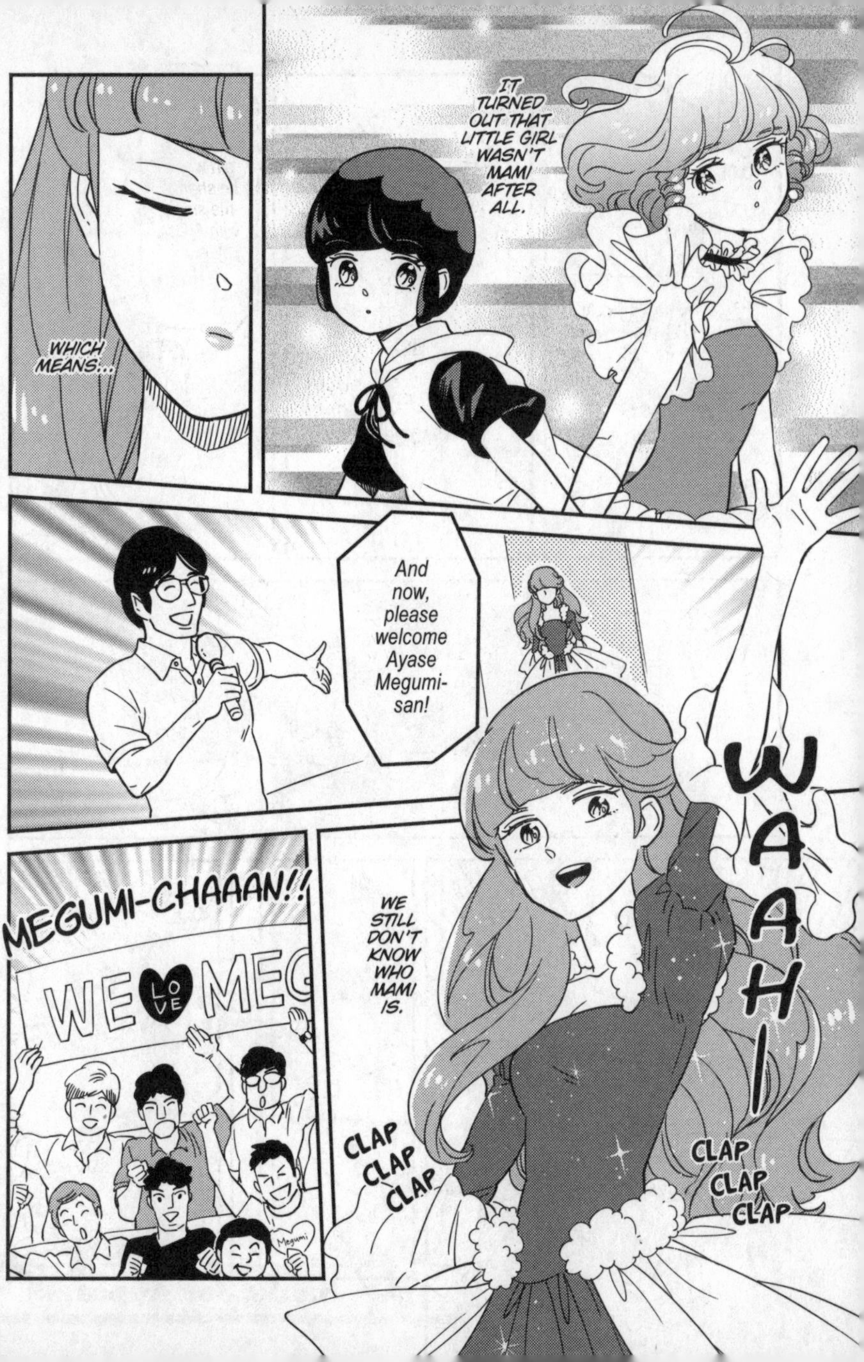
IT TURNED OUT THAT LITTLE GIRL WASN'T MAMI AFTER ALL.
WHICH MEANS...
And now, please welcome Ayase Megumi-san!
WAAHI
CLAP CLAP CLAP
WE STILL DON'T KNOW WHO MAMI IS.
CLAP CLAP CLAP
MEGUMI-CHAAAN!!
WE LOVE MEG
Megumi

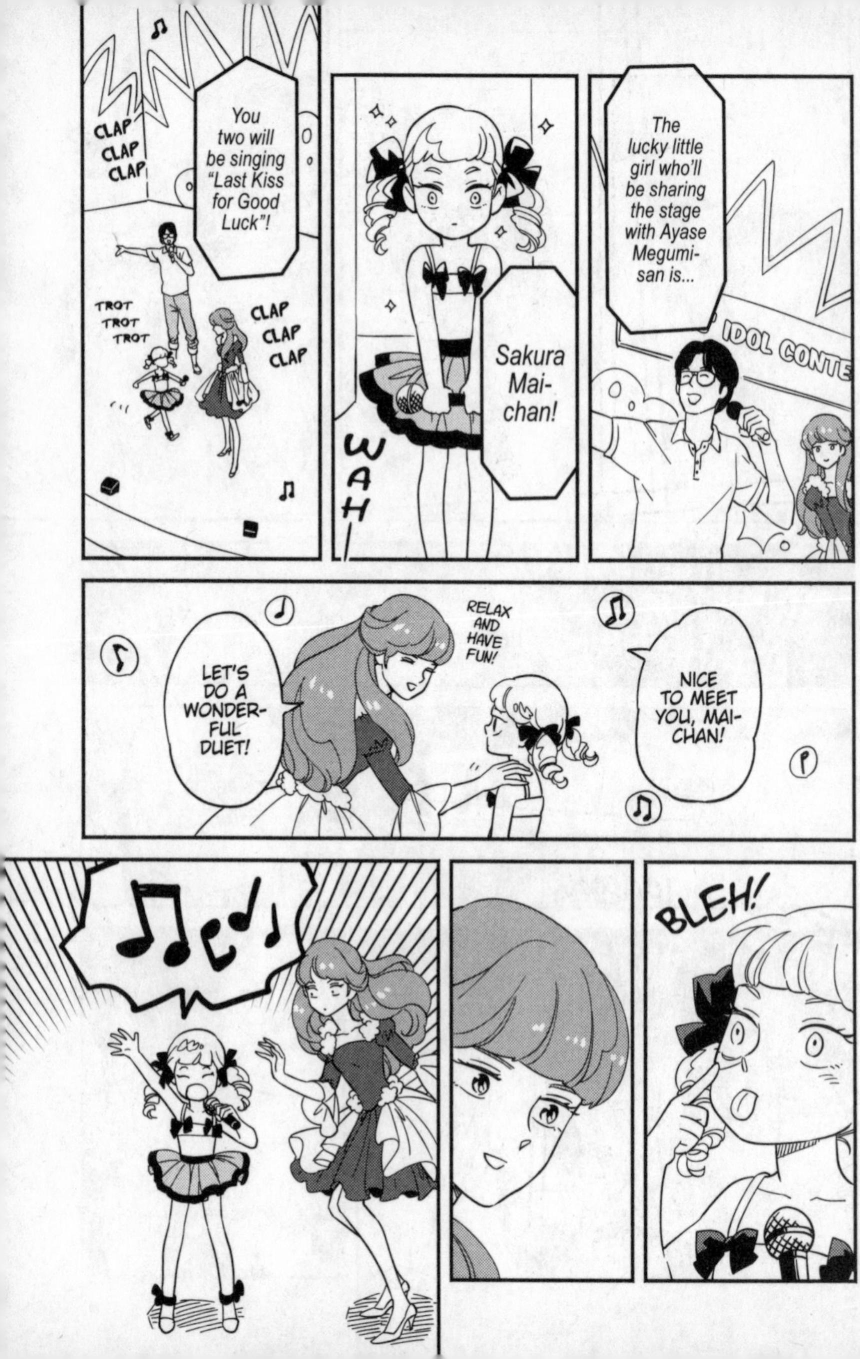
The lucky little girl who'll be sharing the stage with Ayase Megumi-san is...
IDOL CONTE
Sakura Mai-chan!
WAH
You two will be singing "Last Kiss for Good Luck"!
CLAP CLAP CLAP
TROT TROT TROT
CLAP CLAP CLAP
NICE TO MEET YOU, MAI-CHAN!
RELAX AND HAVE FUN!
LET'S DO A WONDERFUL DUET!
BLEH!

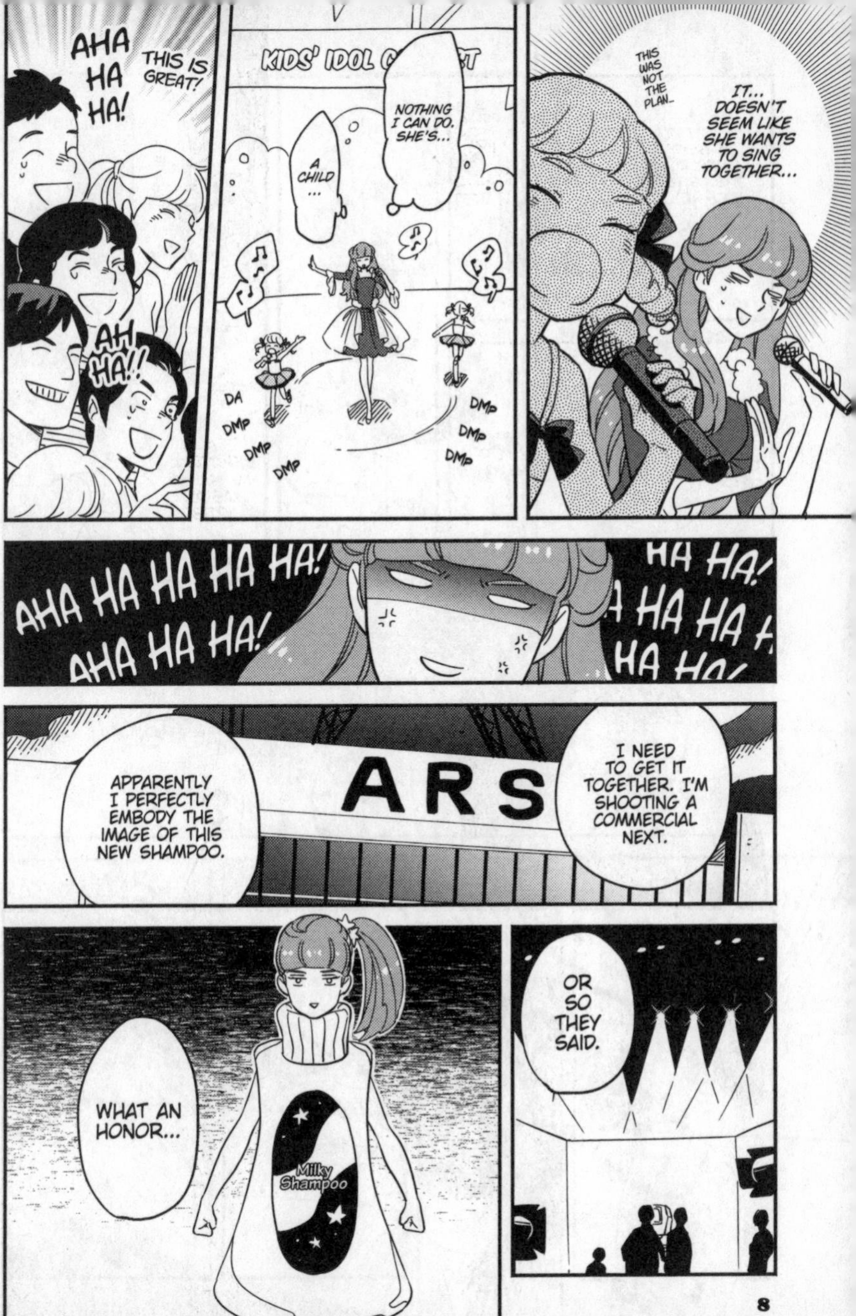
IT... DOESN'T SEEM LIKE SHE WANTS TO SING TOGETHER...
THIS WAS NOT THE PLAN...
KIDS' IDOL C
NOTHING I CAN DO. SHE'S...
A CHILD...
DMP DMP DMP
DA DMP DMP DMP
THIS IS GREAT!
AHA HA HA!
AH HA!!
HA HA!
A HA HA H
HA HA!
AHA HA HA HA HA!
AHA HA HA!
I NEED TO GET IT TOGETHER. I'M SHOOTING A COMMERCIAL NEXT.
ARS
APPARENTLY I PERFECTLY EMBODY THE IMAGE OF THIS NEW SHAMPOO.
OR SO THEY SAID.
WHAT AN HONOR...
Milky Shampoo

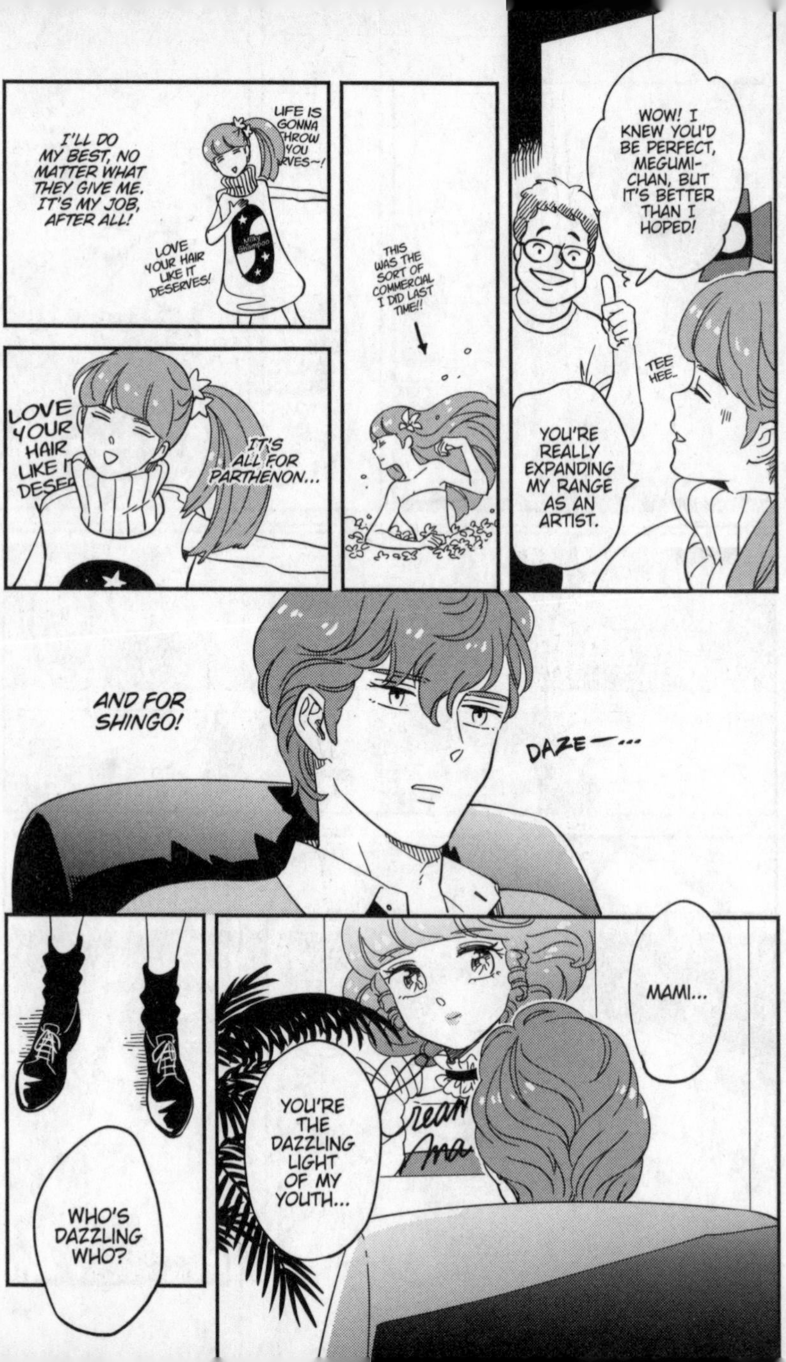
WOW! I KNEW YOU'D BE PERFECT, MEGUMI-CHAN, BUT IT'S BETTER THAN I HOPED!
TEE HEE..
YOU'RE REALLY EXPANDING MY RANGE AS AN ARTIST.
THIS WAS THE SORT OF COMMERCIAL I DID LAST TIME!!
LIFE IS GONNA THROW YOU RVES~!
I'LL DO MY BEST, NO MATTER WHAT THEY GIVE ME. IT'S MY JOB, AFTER ALL!
Milky Shampoo
LOVE YOUR HAIR LIKE IT DESERVES!
LOVE YOUR HAIR LIKE I DESE
IT'S ALL FOR PARTHENON...
DAZE—...
AND FOR SHINGO!
MAMI...
YOU'RE THE DAZZLING LIGHT OF MY YOUTH...
WHO'S DAZZLING WHO?

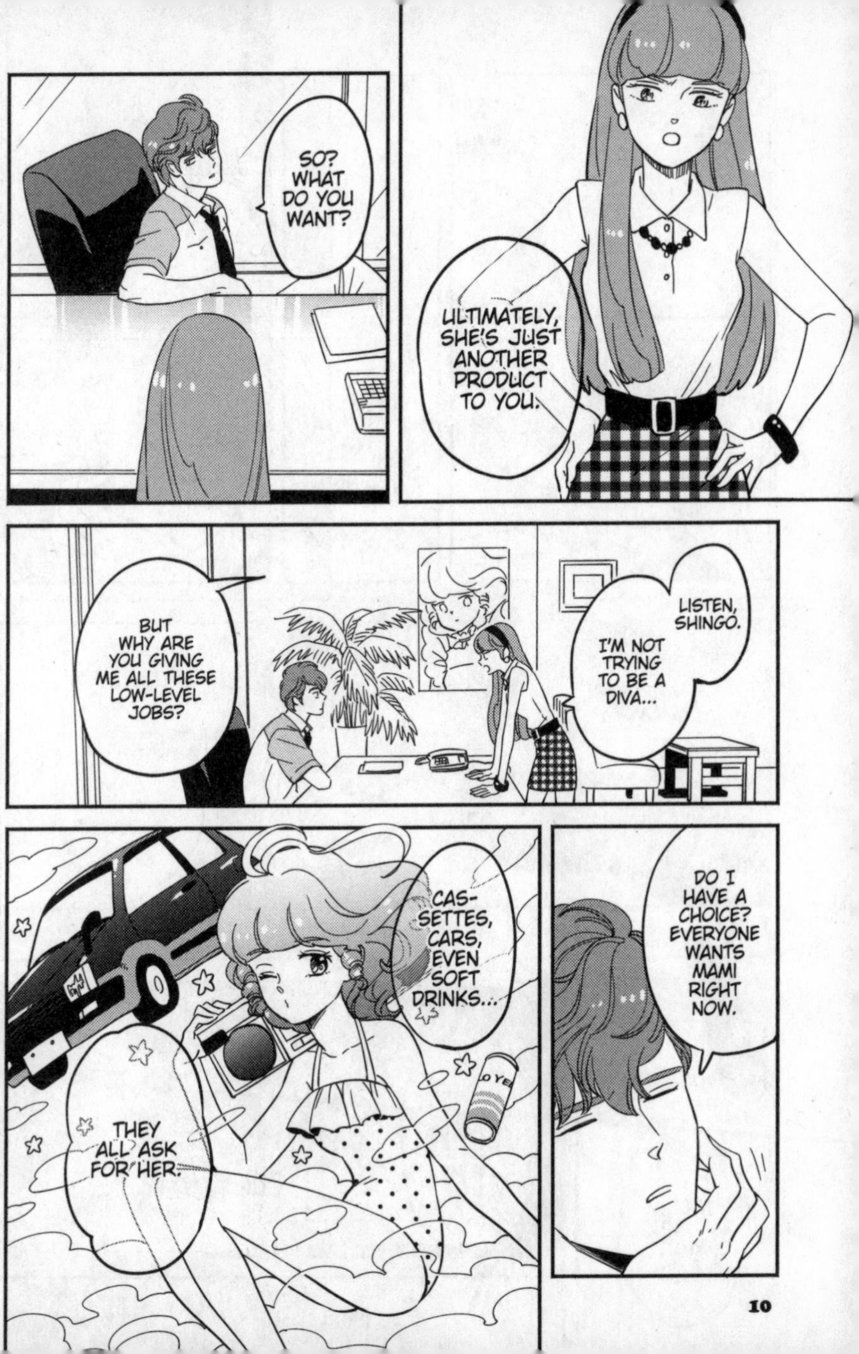
ULTIMATELY, SHE'S JUST ANOTHER PRODUCT TO YOU.
SO? WHAT DO YOU WANT?
LISTEN, SHINGO.
I'M NOT TRYING TO BE A DIVA...
BUT WHY ARE YOU GIVING ME ALL THESE LOW-LEVEL JOBS?
DO I HAVE A CHOICE? EVERYONE WANTS MAMI RIGHT NOW.
CAS-SETTES, CARS, EVEN SOFT DRINKS...
THEY ALL ASK FOR HER.

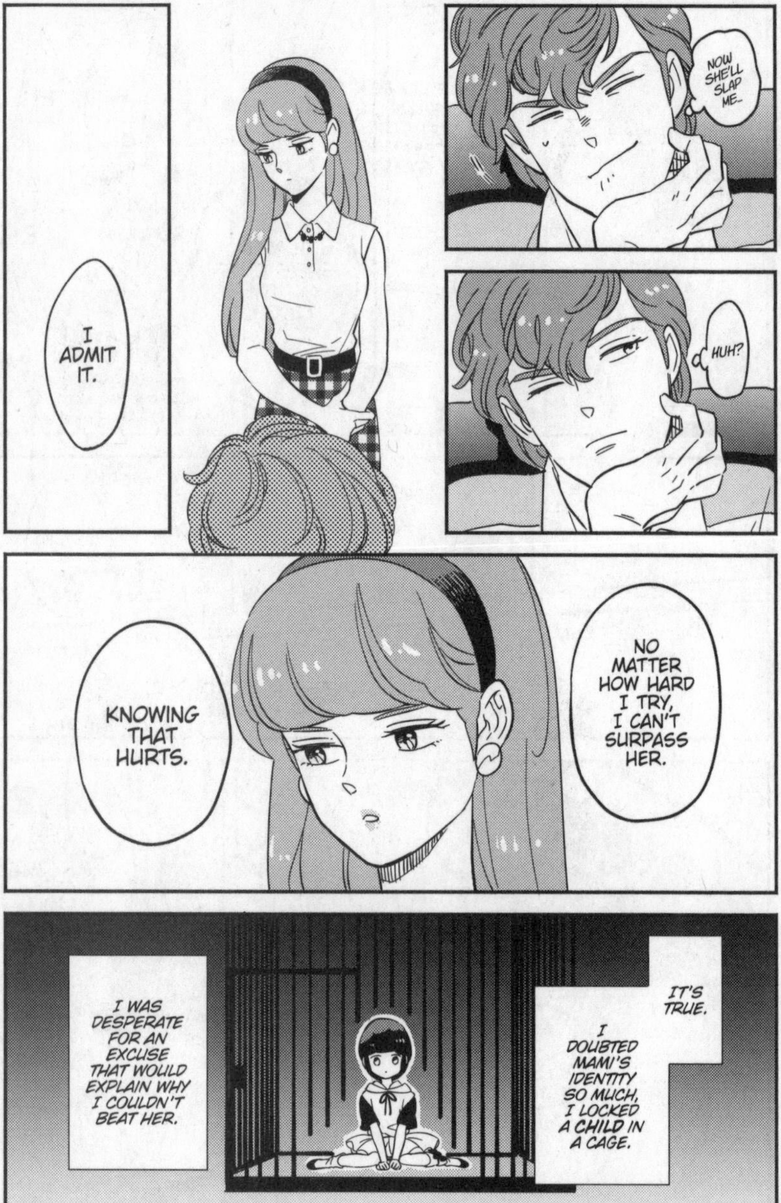
NOW SHE'LL SLAP ME..
HUH?
I ADMIT IT.
NO MATTER HOW HARD I TRY, I CAN'T SURPASS HER.
KNOWING THAT HURTS.
IT'S TRUE.
I DOUBTED MAMI'S IDENTITY SO MUCH, I LOCKED A CHILD IN A CAGE.
I WAS DESPERATE FOR AN EXCUSE THAT WOULD EXPLAIN WHY I COULDN'T BEAT HER.

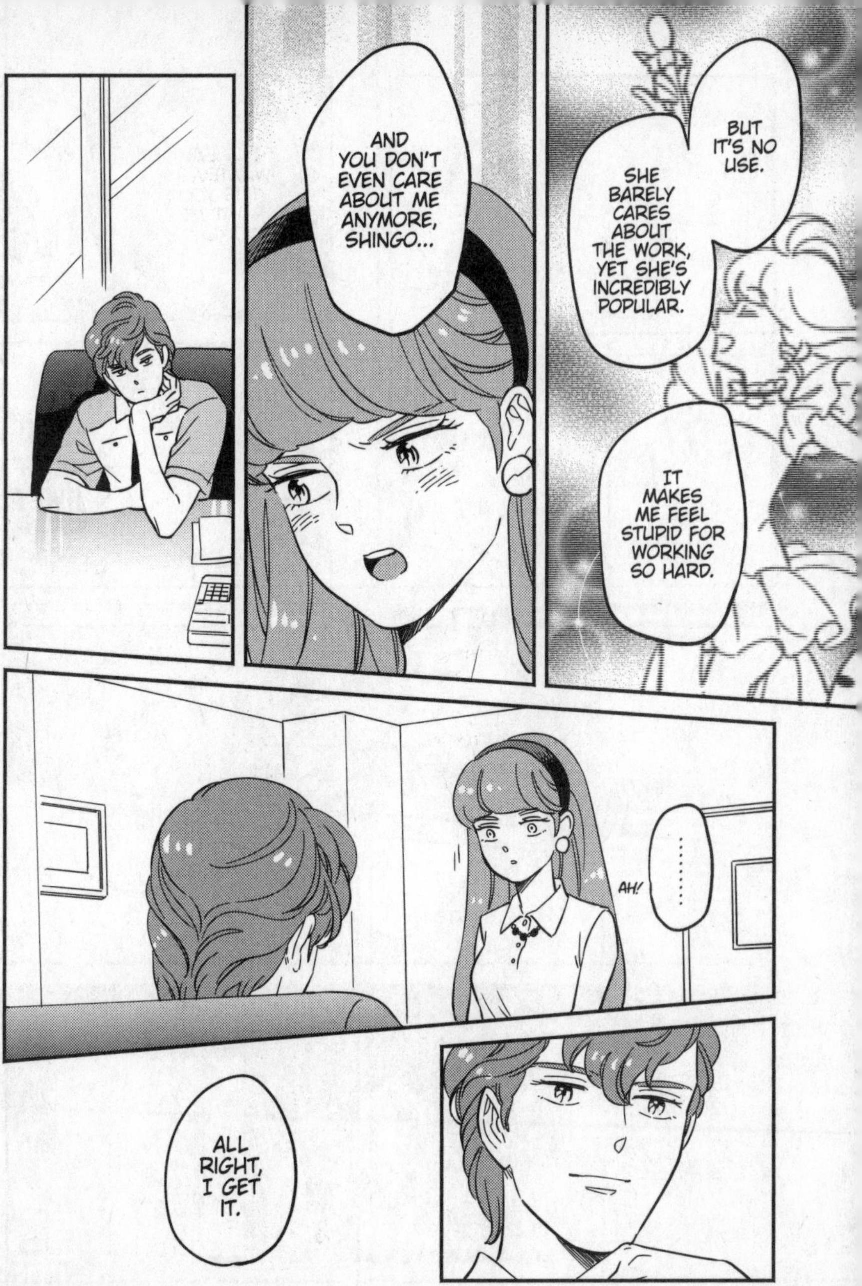
BUT IT'S NO USE.
SHE BARELY CARES ABOUT THE WORK, YET SHE'S INCREDIBLY POPULAR.
IT MAKES ME FEEL STUPID FOR WORKING SO HARD.
AND YOU DON'T EVEN CARE ABOUT ME ANYMORE, SHINGO...
......
AH!
ALL RIGHT, I GET IT.

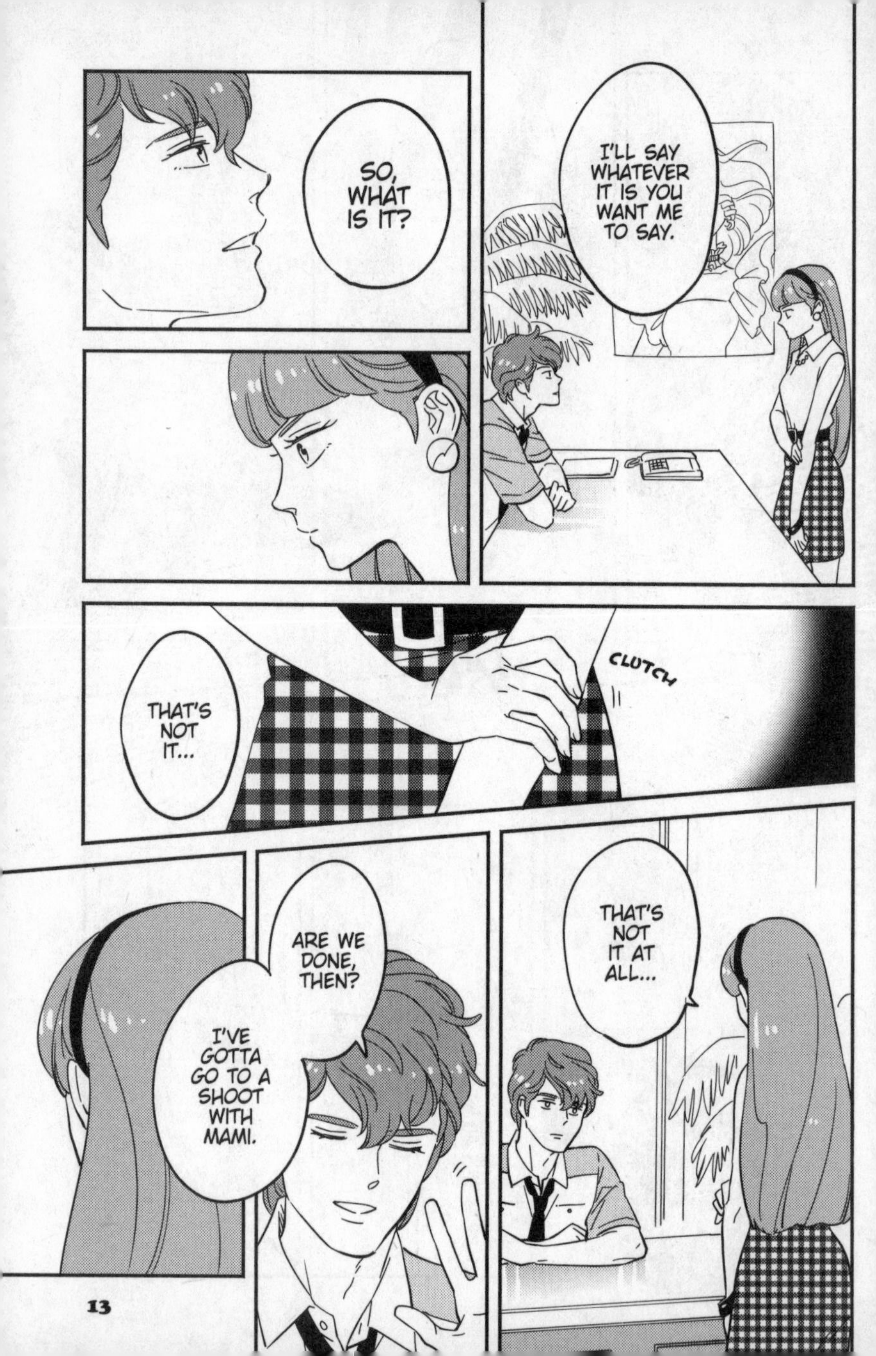
I'LL SAY WHATEVER IT IS YOU WANT ME TO SAY.
SO, WHAT IS IT?
CLUTCH
THAT'S NOT IT...
THAT'S NOT IT AT ALL...
ARE WE DONE, THEN?
I'VE GOTTA GO TO A SHOOT WITH MAMI.

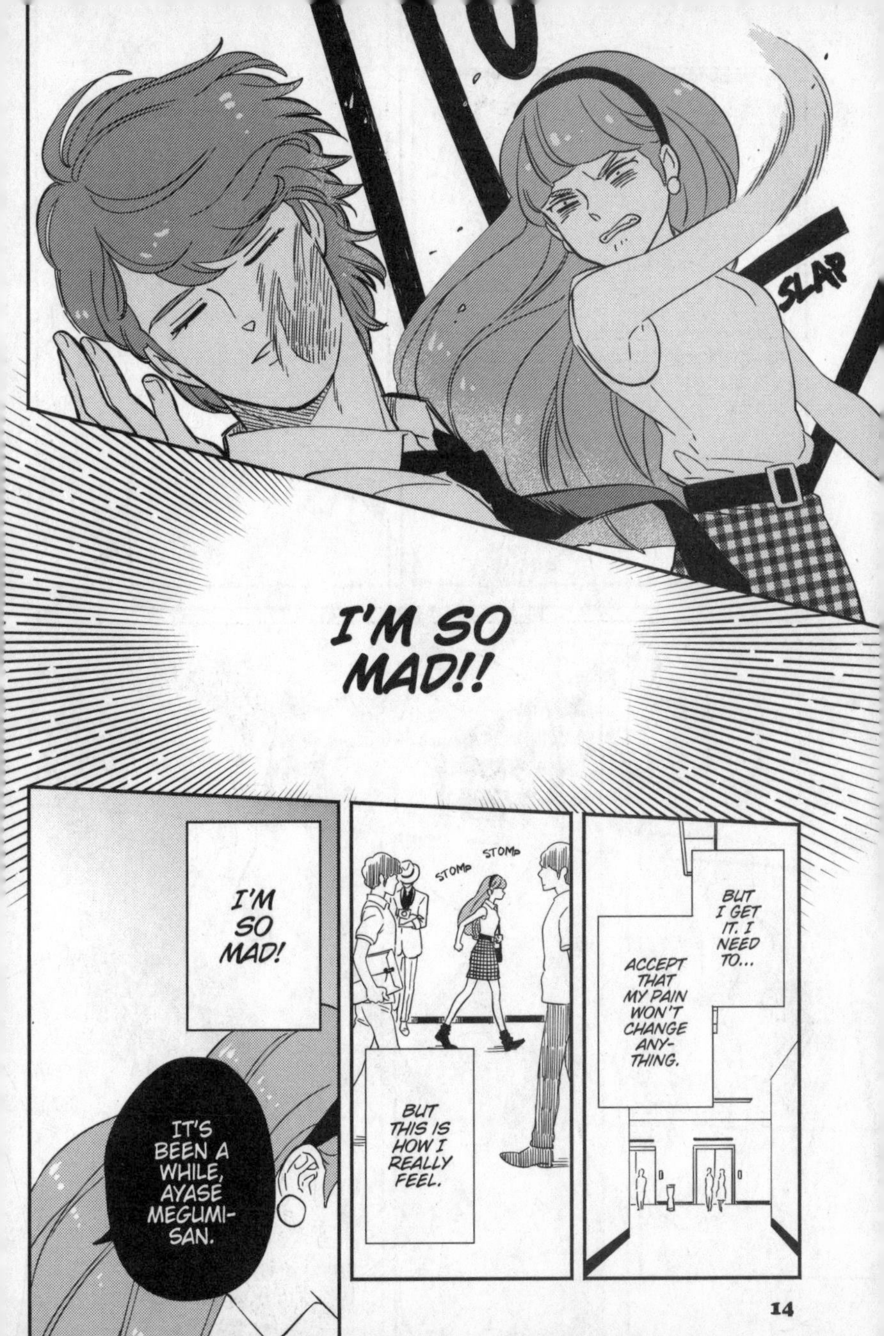
SLAP
I'M SO MAD!!
BUT I GET IT. I NEED TO...
ACCEPT THAT MY PAIN WON'T CHANGE ANY-THING.
STOMP
STOMP
BUT THIS IS HOW I REALLY FEEL.
I'M SO MAD!
IT'S BEEN A WHILE, AYASE MEGUMI-SAN.

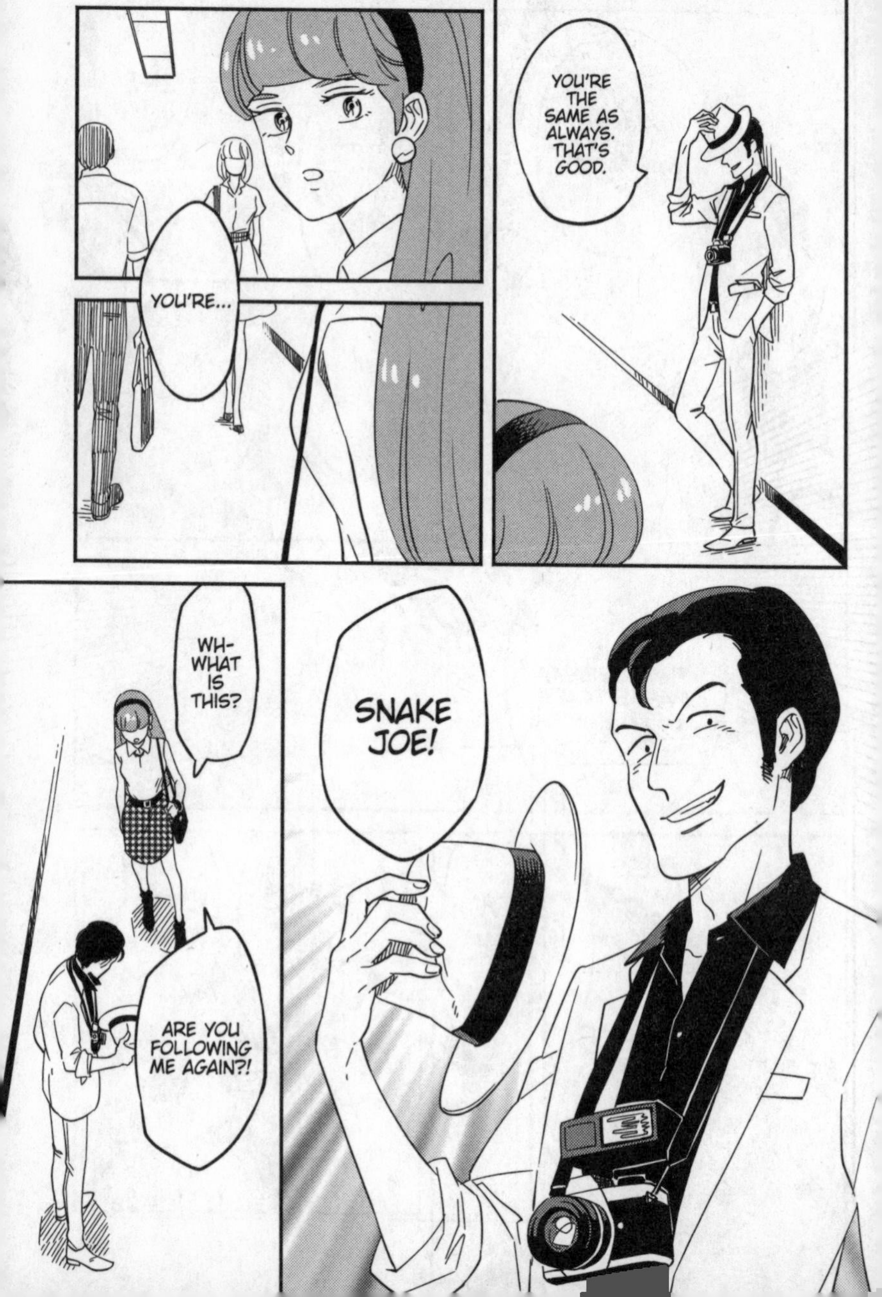
YOU'RE THE SAME AS ALWAYS. THAT'S GOOD.
YOU'RE...
SNAKE JOE!
WH-WHAT IS THIS?
ARE YOU FOLLOWING ME AGAIN?!

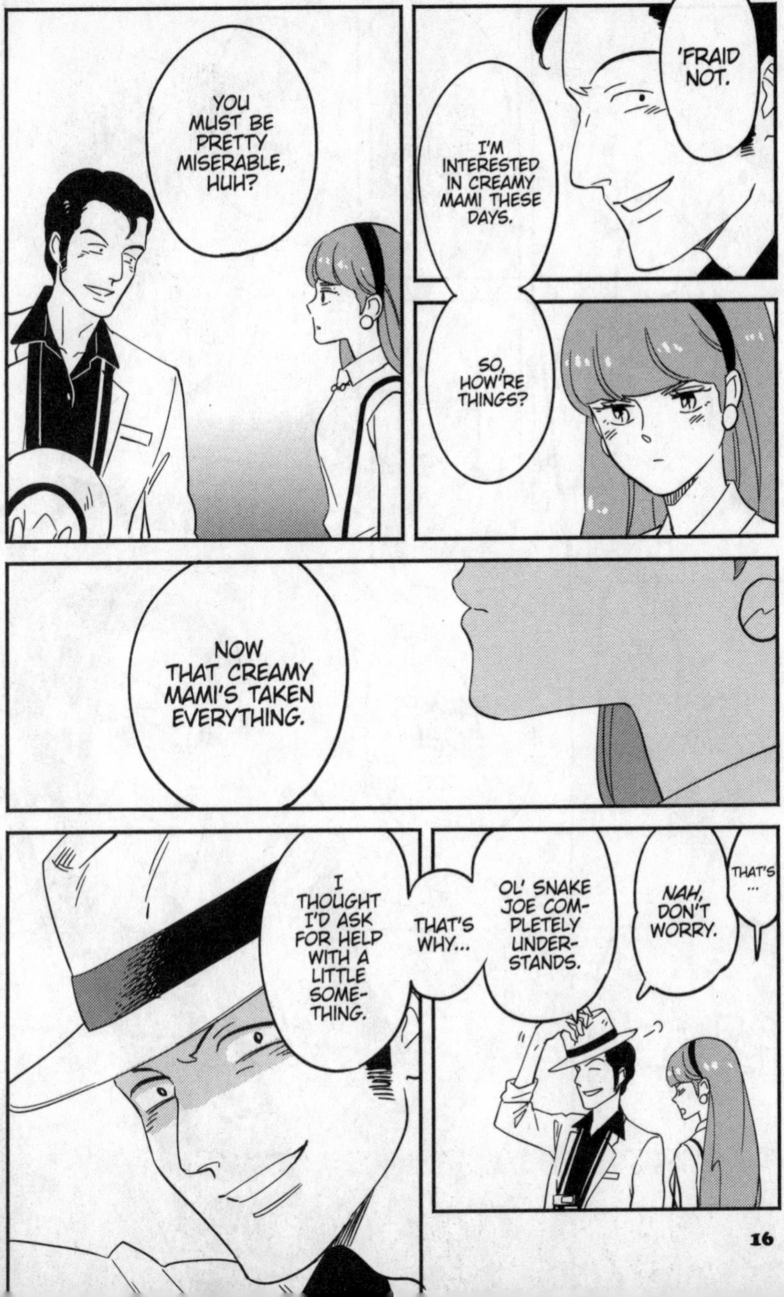
'FRAID NOT.
I'M INTERESTED IN CREAMY MAMI THESE DAYS.
SO, HOW'RE THINGS?
YOU MUST BE PRETTY MISERABLE, HUH?
NOW THAT CREAMY MAMI'S TAKEN EVERYTHING.
THAT'S ...
NAH, DON'T WORRY.
OL' SNAKE JOE COMPLETELY UNDERSTANDS.
THAT'S WHY...
I THOUGHT I'D ASK FOR HELP WITH A LITTLE SOMETHING.

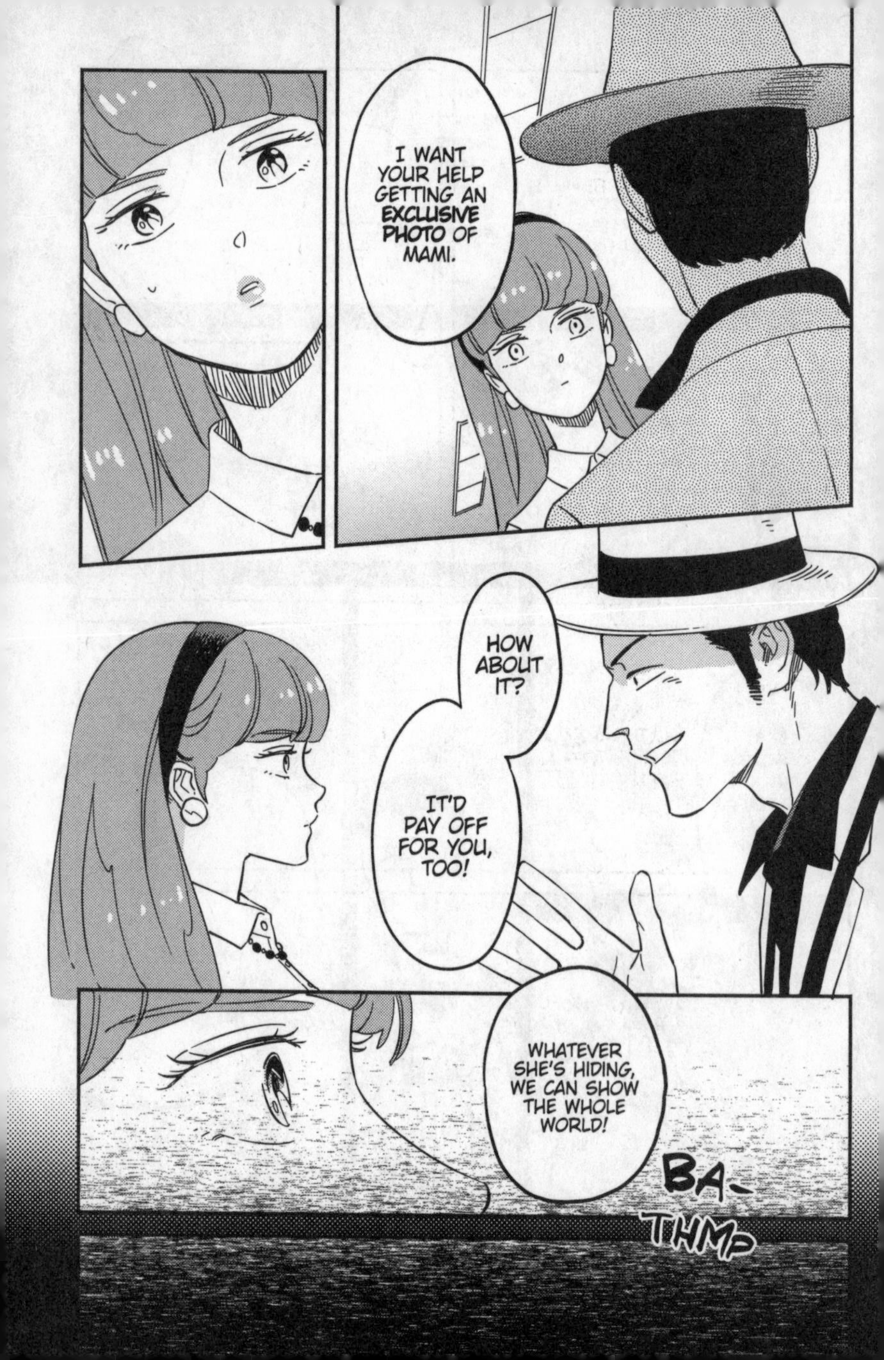
I WANT YOUR HELP GETTING AN EXCLUSIVE PHOTO OF MAMI.
HOW ABOUT IT?
IT'D PAY OFF FOR YOU, TOO!
WHATEVER SHE'S HIDING, WE CAN SHOW THE WHOLE WORLD!
BA-THMP

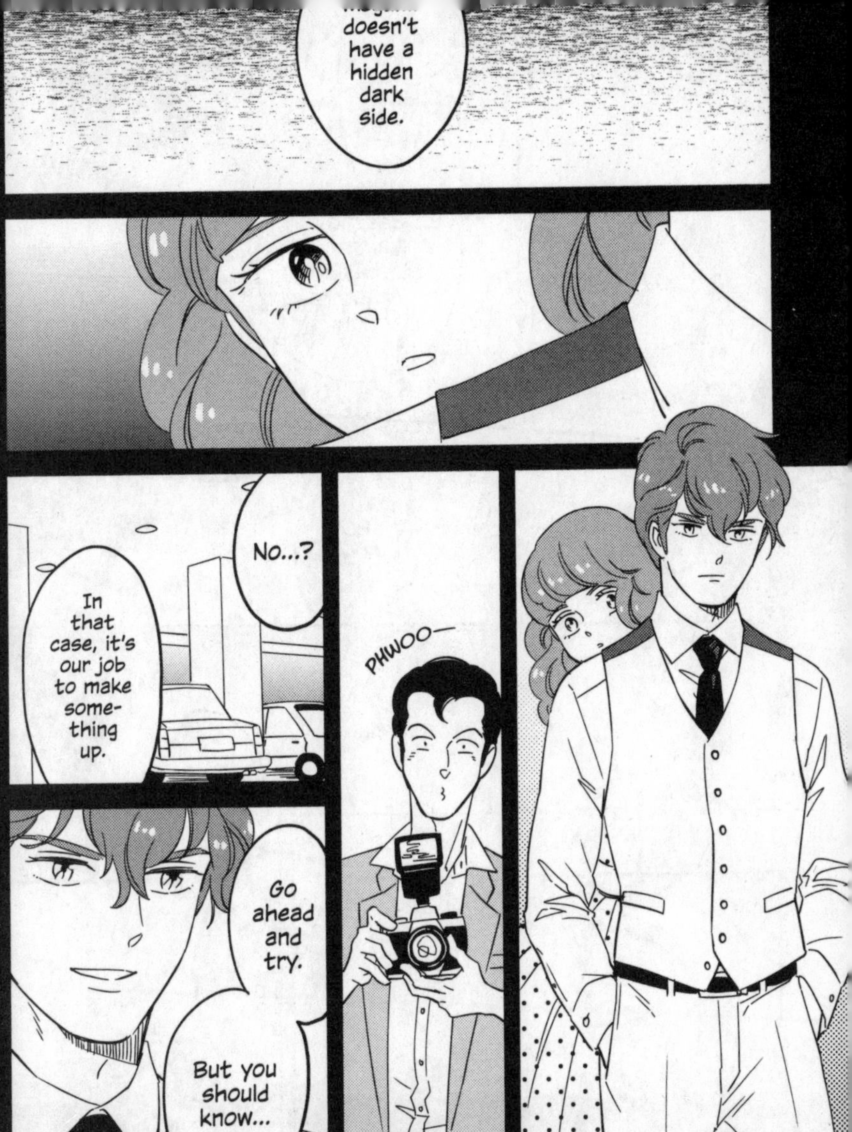
doesn't have a hidden dark side.
PHWOO—
No...?
In that case, it's our job to make some-thing up.
Go ahead and try.
But you should know...

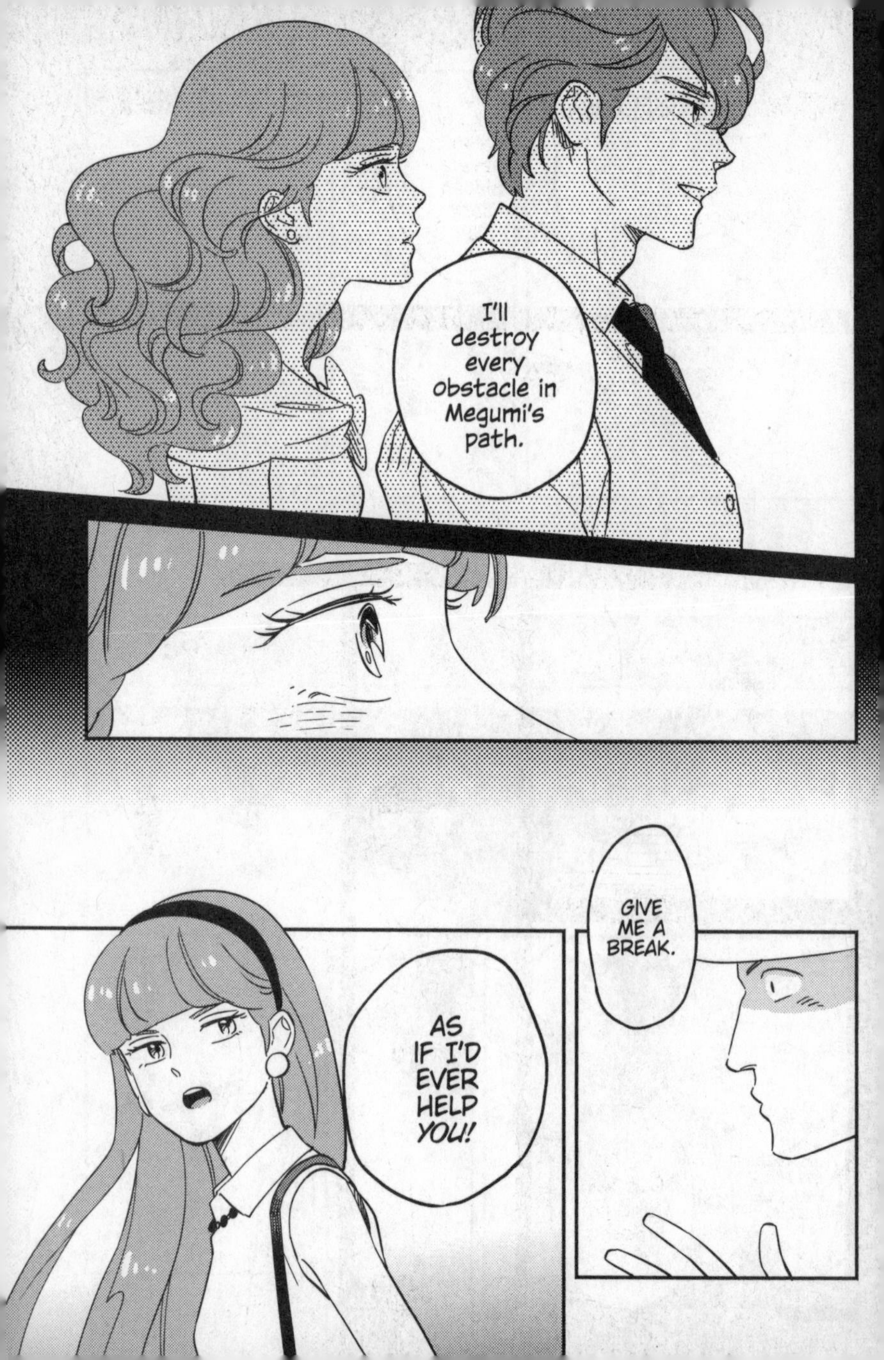

I'll destroy every obstacle in Megumi's path.
GIVE ME A BREAK.
AS IF I'D EVER HELP *YOU!*

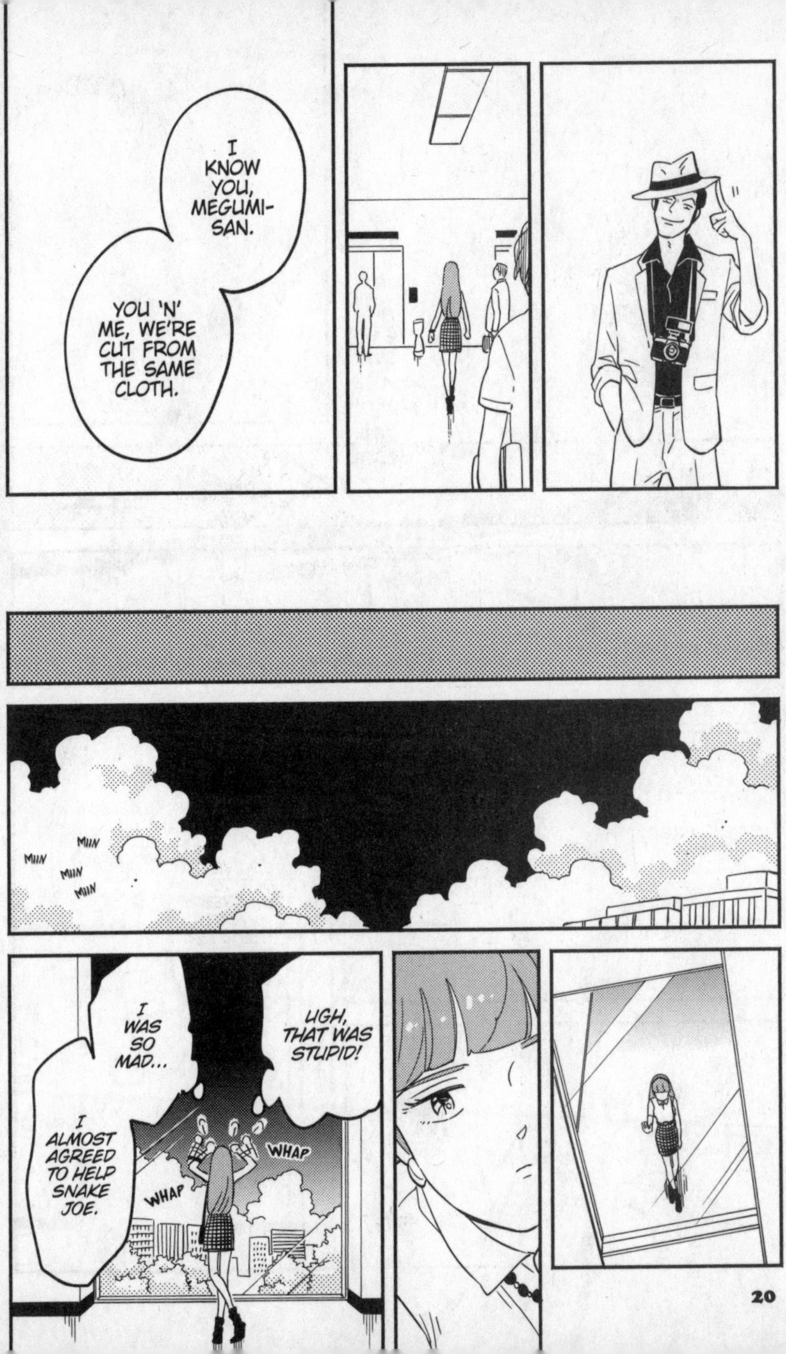
I KNOW YOU, MEGUMI-SAN.
YOU 'N' ME, WE'RE CUT FROM THE SAME CLOTH.
MIIN
MIIN
MIIN
MIIN
UGH, THAT WAS STUPID!
I WAS SO MAD...
I ALMOST AGREED TO HELP SNAKE JOE.
WHAP
WHAP

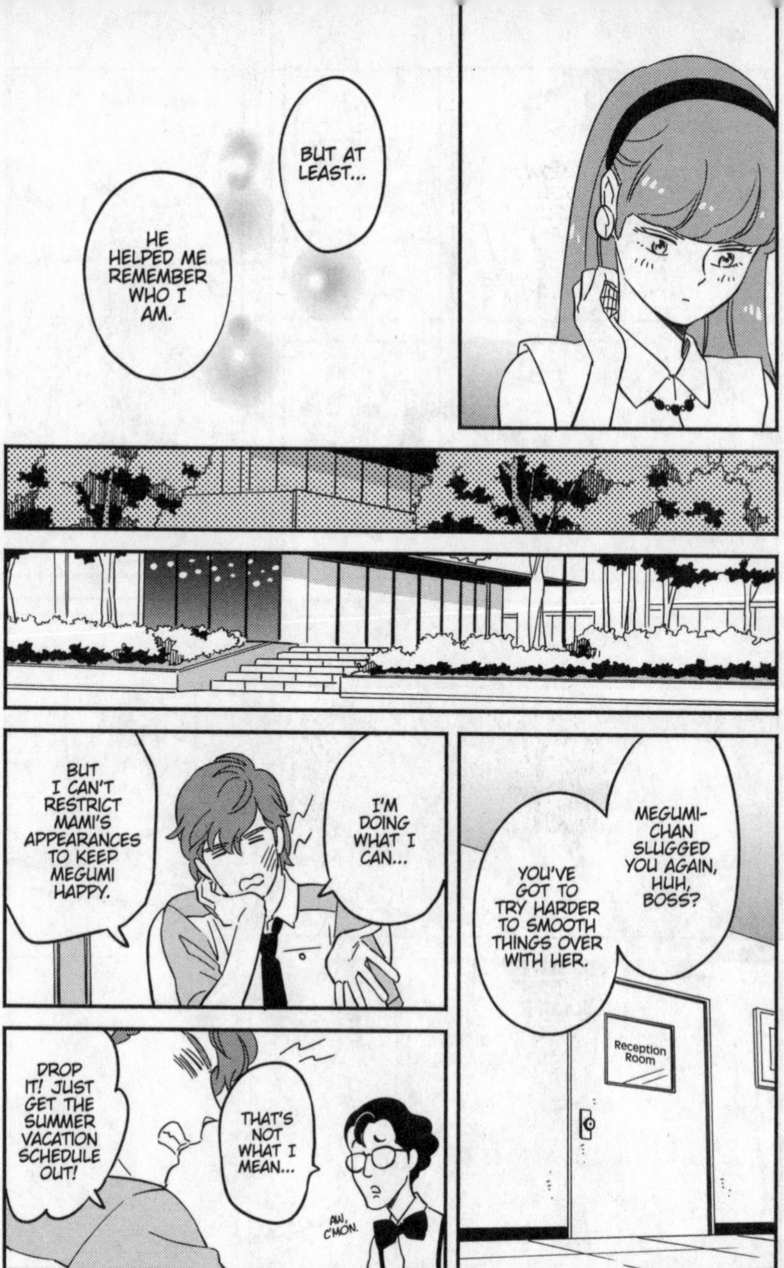
BUT AT LEAST...
HE HELPED ME REMEMBER WHO I AM.
MEGUMI-CHAN SLUGGED YOU AGAIN, HUH, BOSS?
YOU'VE GOT TO TRY HARDER TO SMOOTH THINGS OVER WITH HER.
Reception Room
I'M DOING WHAT I CAN...
BUT I CAN'T RESTRICT MAMI'S APPEARANCES TO KEEP MEGUMI HAPPY.
THAT'S NOT WHAT I MEAN...
AW, C'MON.
DROP IT! JUST GET THE SUMMER VACATION SCHEDULE OUT!

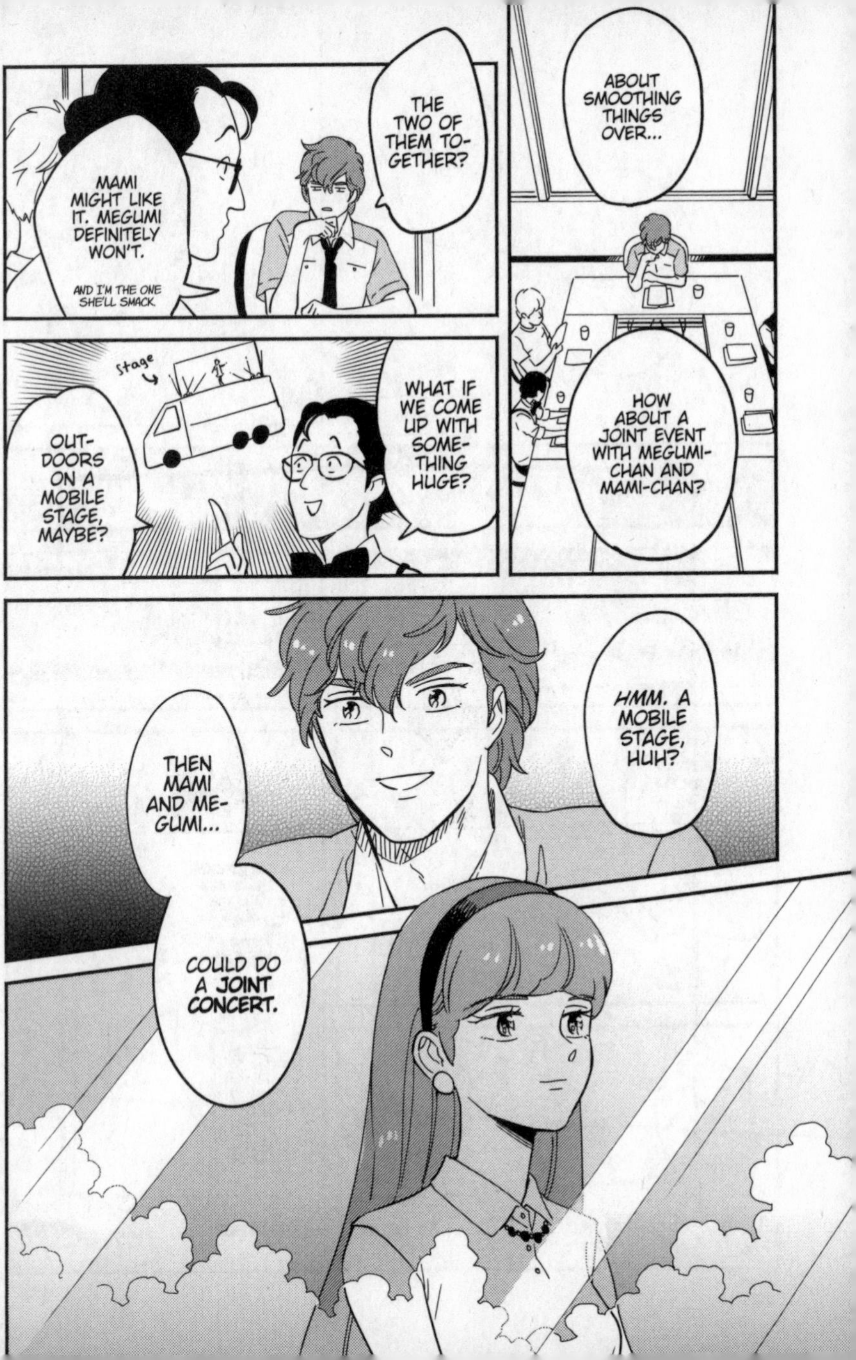
ABOUT SMOOTHING THINGS OVER...
HOW ABOUT A JOINT EVENT WITH MEGUMI-CHAN AND MAMI-CHAN?
THE TWO OF THEM TOGETHER?
MAMI MIGHT LIKE IT. MEGUMI DEFINITELY WON'T.
AND I'M THE ONE SHE'LL SMACK.
WHAT IF WE COME UP WITH SOMETHING HUGE?
Stage
OUTDOORS ON A MOBILE STAGE, MAYBE?
HMM. A MOBILE STAGE, HUH?
THEN MAMI AND MEGUMI...
COULD DO A JOINT CONCERT.

People of the '80s

I BOUGHT A PAGER.
A MUST-HAVE FOR BUSINESSMEN OF THE TIME.
THIS ONE HAS TWO DISTINCT SOUNDS.
IT SIGNALS YOU TO GO FIND A PHONE AND CALL THE PERSON TRYING TO CONTACT YOU.
THE FIRST IS FOR CALLS FROM THE OFFICE.
PI—
PI—
PI—
THE OTHER IS...
PI PI PI PI PI
UGH, IT'S FROM MEGUMI.
I CAN JUST IGNORE IT.
PI PI PI PI
IF YOU WON'T CALL HER BACK, WHY'D YOU ADD HER TO YOUR PAGER?
SO ANNOYING.

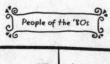

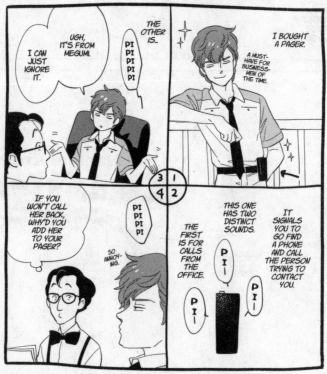

Magical Angel

Creamy Mami

and the
Spoiled Princess

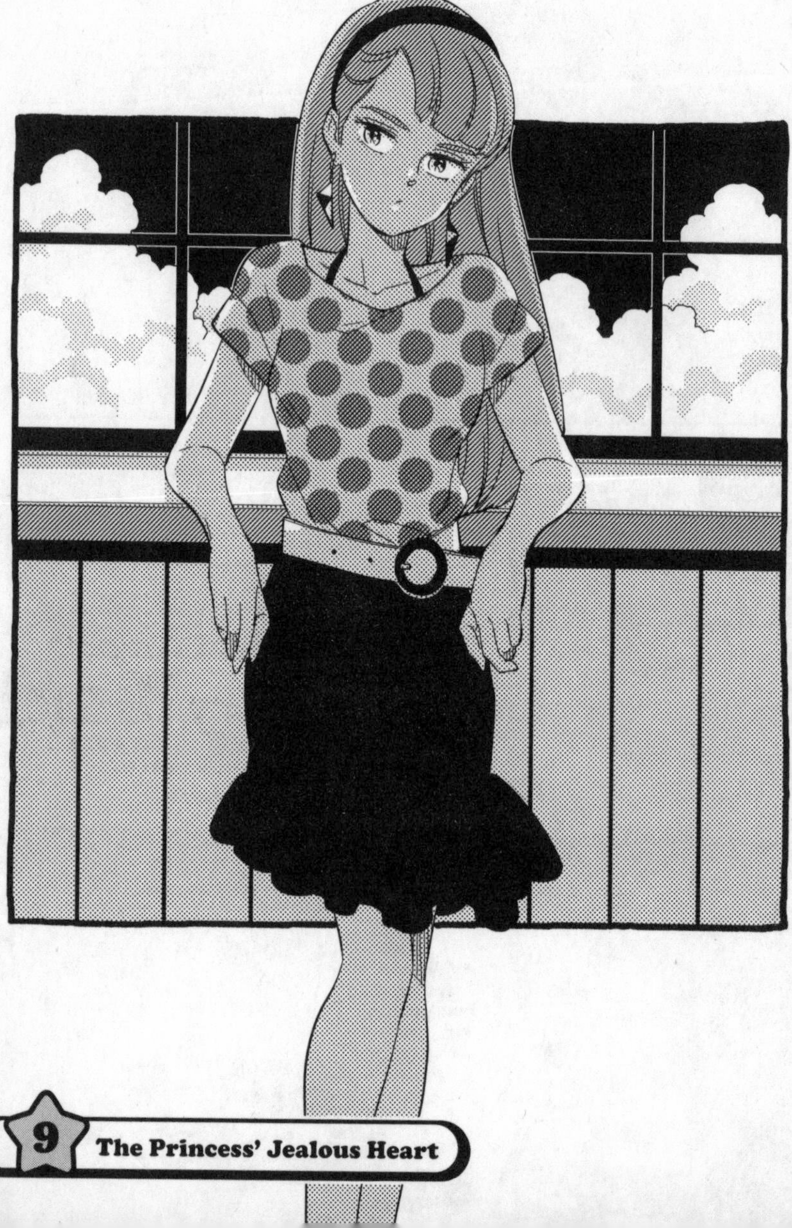

9 The Princess' Jealous Heart

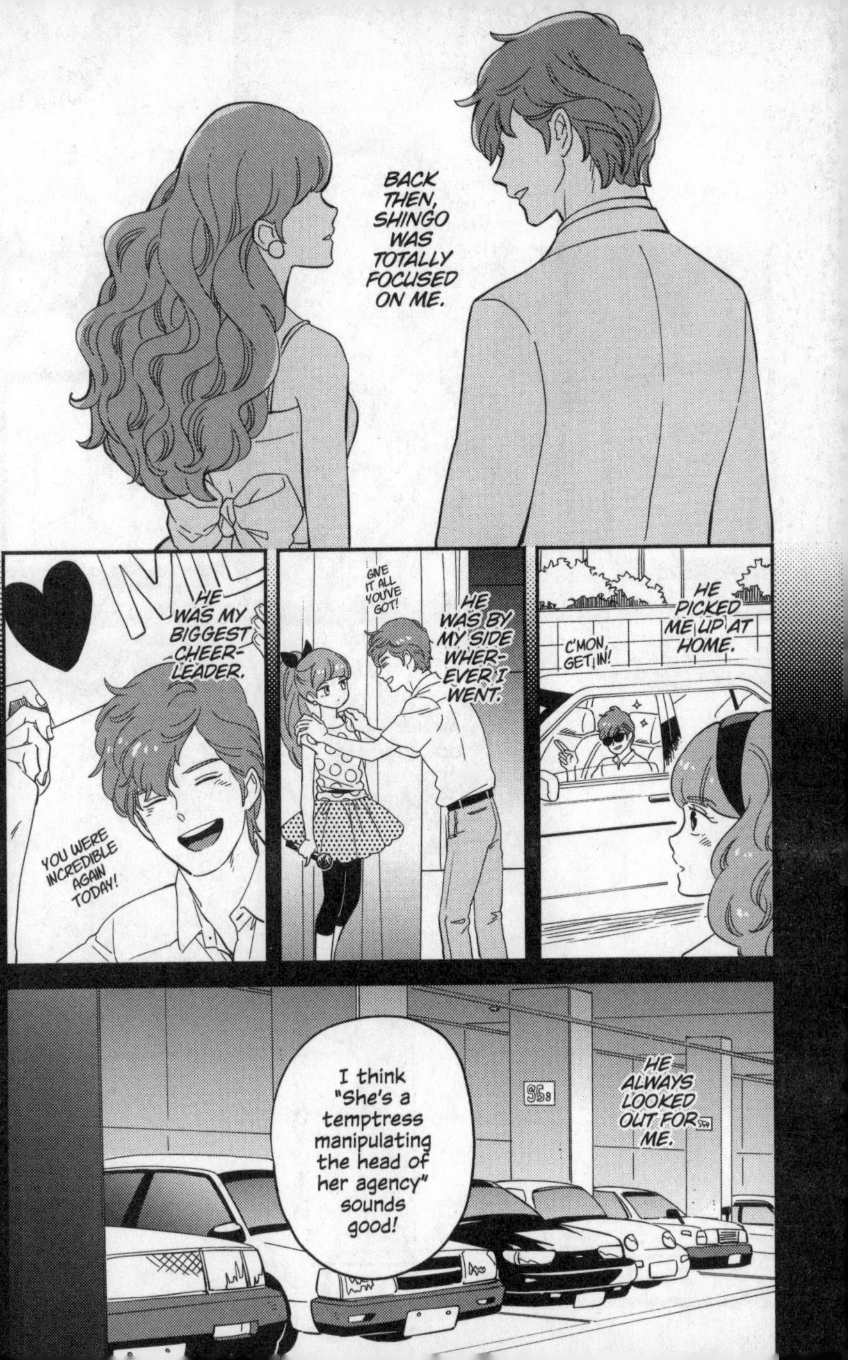
BACK THEN, SHINGO WAS TOTALLY FOCUSED ON ME.
HE PICKED ME UP AT HOME.
C'MON, GET IN!
HE WAS BY MY SIDE WHEREVER I WENT.
GIVE IT ALL YOU'VE GOT!
HE WAS MY BIGGEST CHEER-LEADER.
YOU WERE INCREDIBLE AGAIN TODAY!
HE ALWAYS LOOKED OUT FOR ME.
I think "She's a temptress manipulating the head of her agency" sounds good!

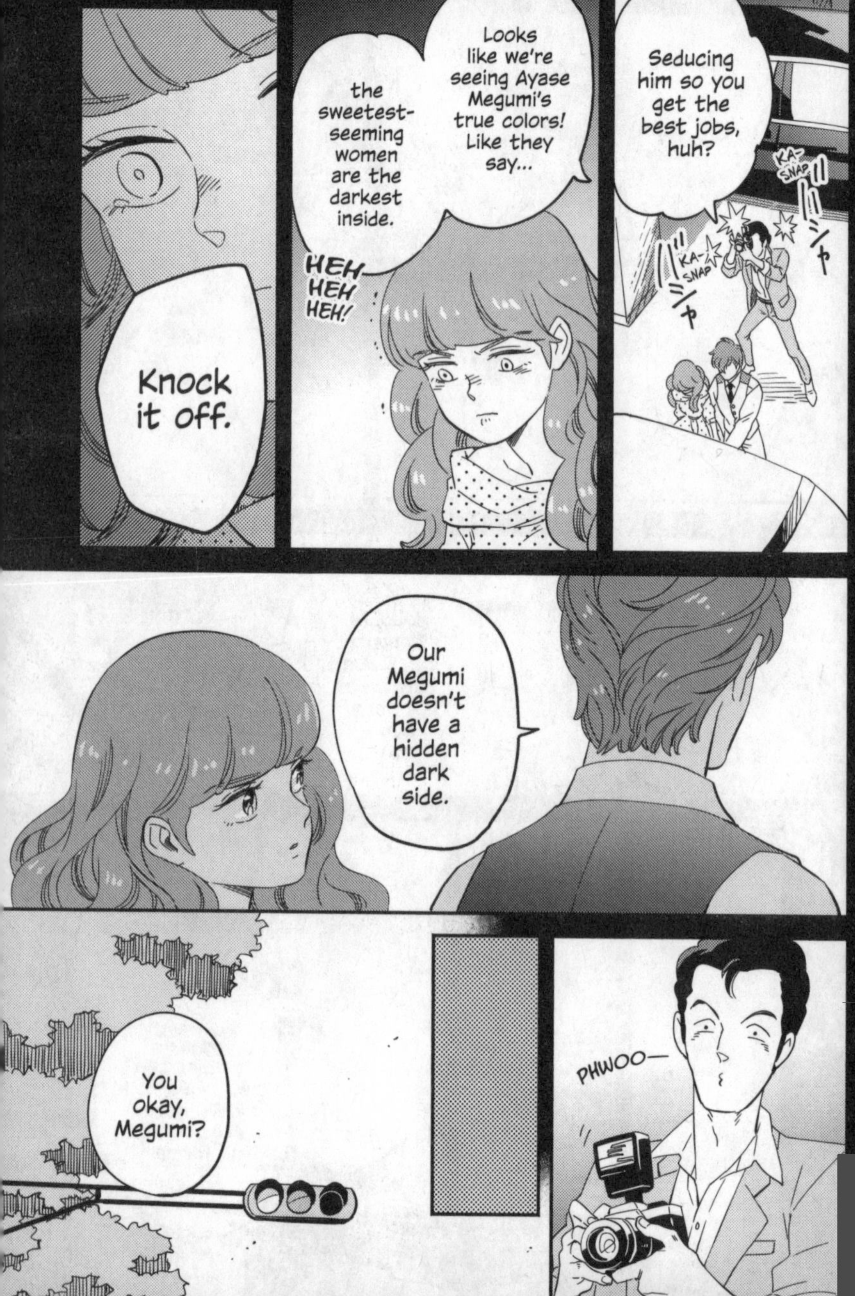
Seducing him so you get the best jobs, huh?
KA-SNAP
KA-SNAP
Looks like we're seeing Ayase Megumi's true colors! Like they say...
the sweetest-seeming women are the darkest inside.
HEH HEH HEH!
Knock it off.
Our Megumi doesn't have a hidden dark side.
PHWOO—
You okay, Megumi?

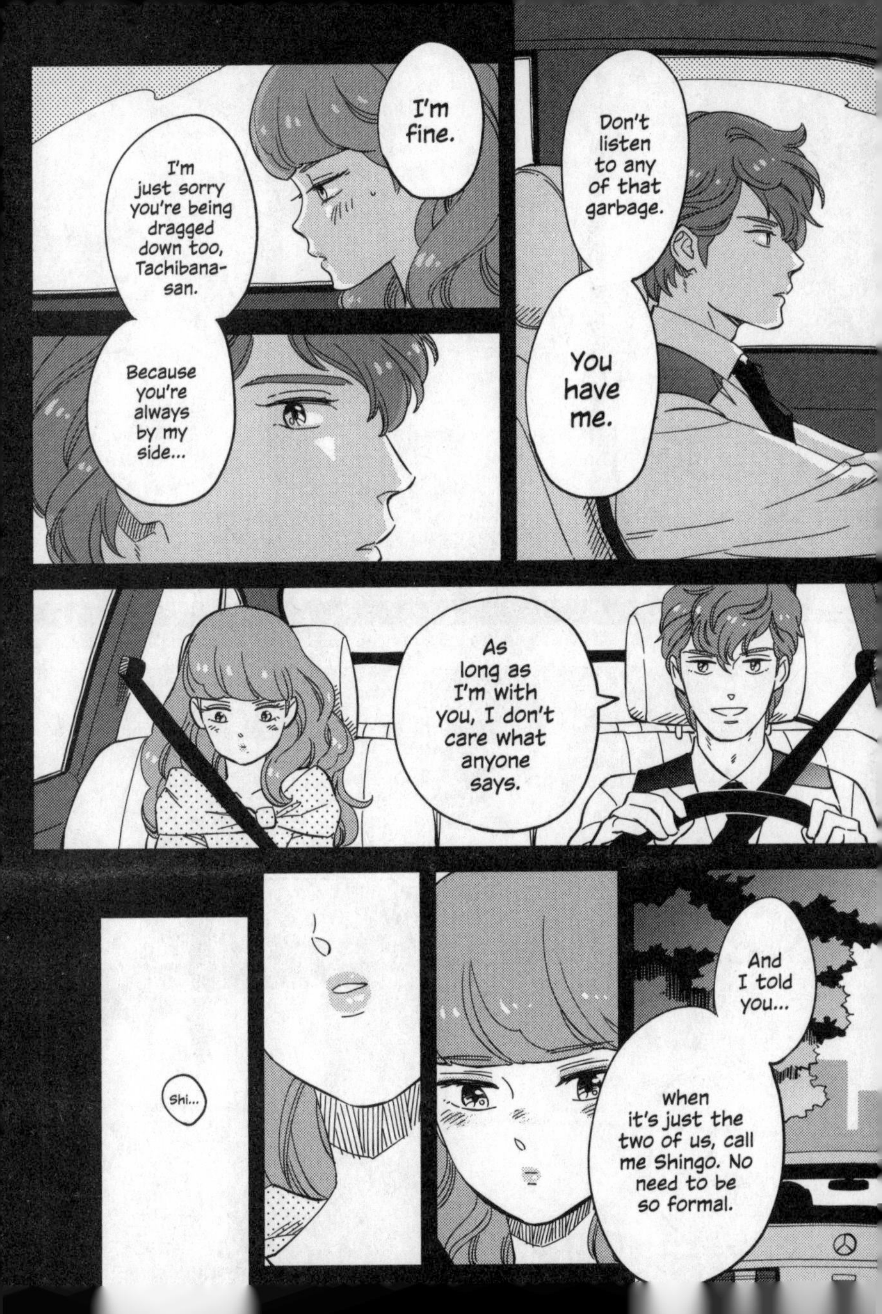
Don't listen to any of that garbage.
You have me.
I'm fine.
I'm just sorry you're being dragged down too, Tachibana-san.
Because you're always by my side...
As long as I'm with you, I don't care what anyone says.
And I told you...
when it's just the two of us, call me Shingo. No need to be so formal.
Shi...

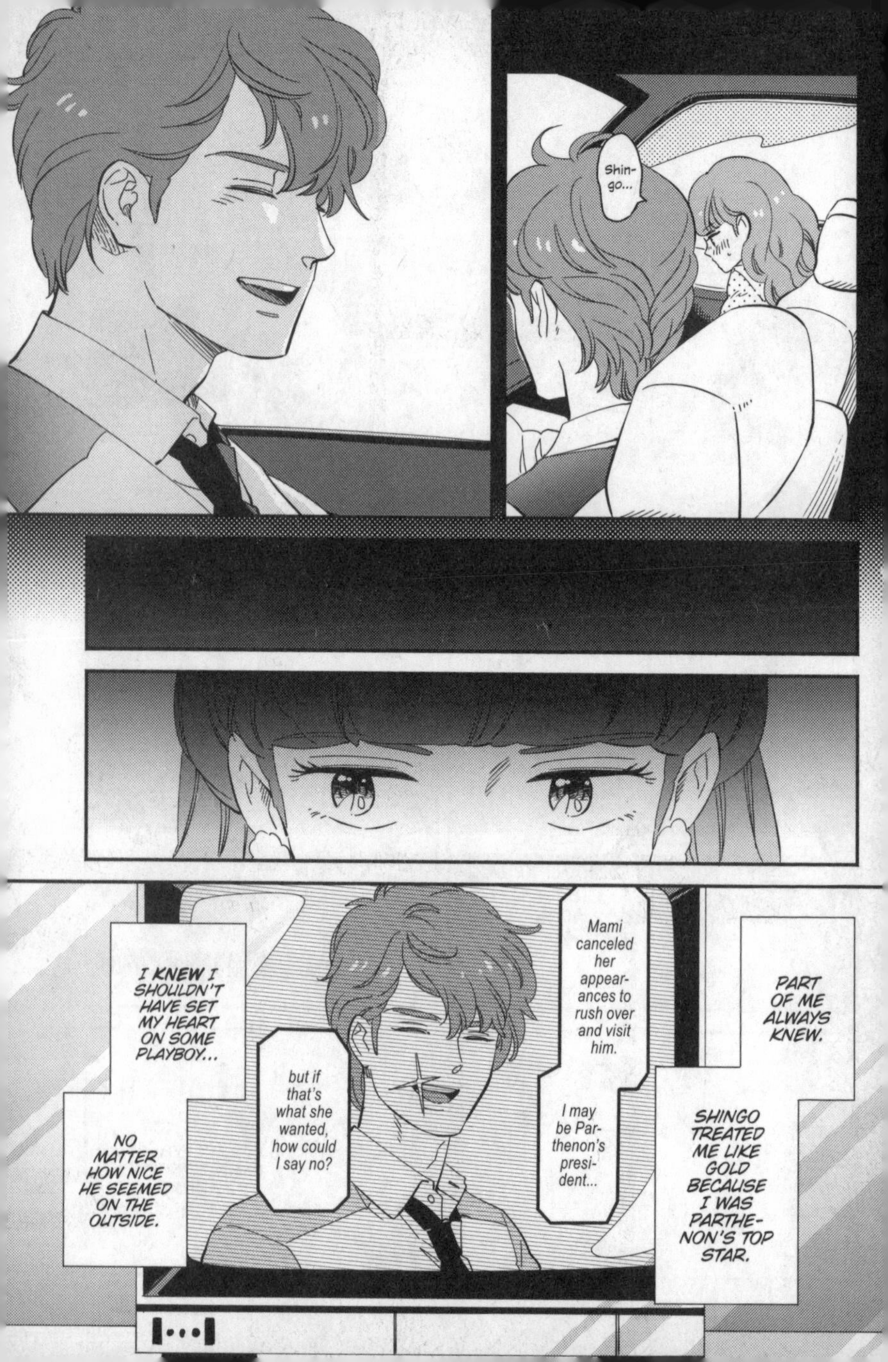
Shin-go...
PART OF ME ALWAYS KNEW.
SHINGO TREATED ME LIKE GOLD BECAUSE I WAS PARTHE-NON'S TOP STAR.
Mami canceled her appear-ances to rush over and visit him.
I may be Par-thenon's presi-dent...
but if that's what she wanted, how could I say no?
I KNEW I SHOULDN'T HAVE SET MY HEART ON SOME PLAYBOY...
NO MATTER HOW NICE HE SEEMED ON THE OUTSIDE.

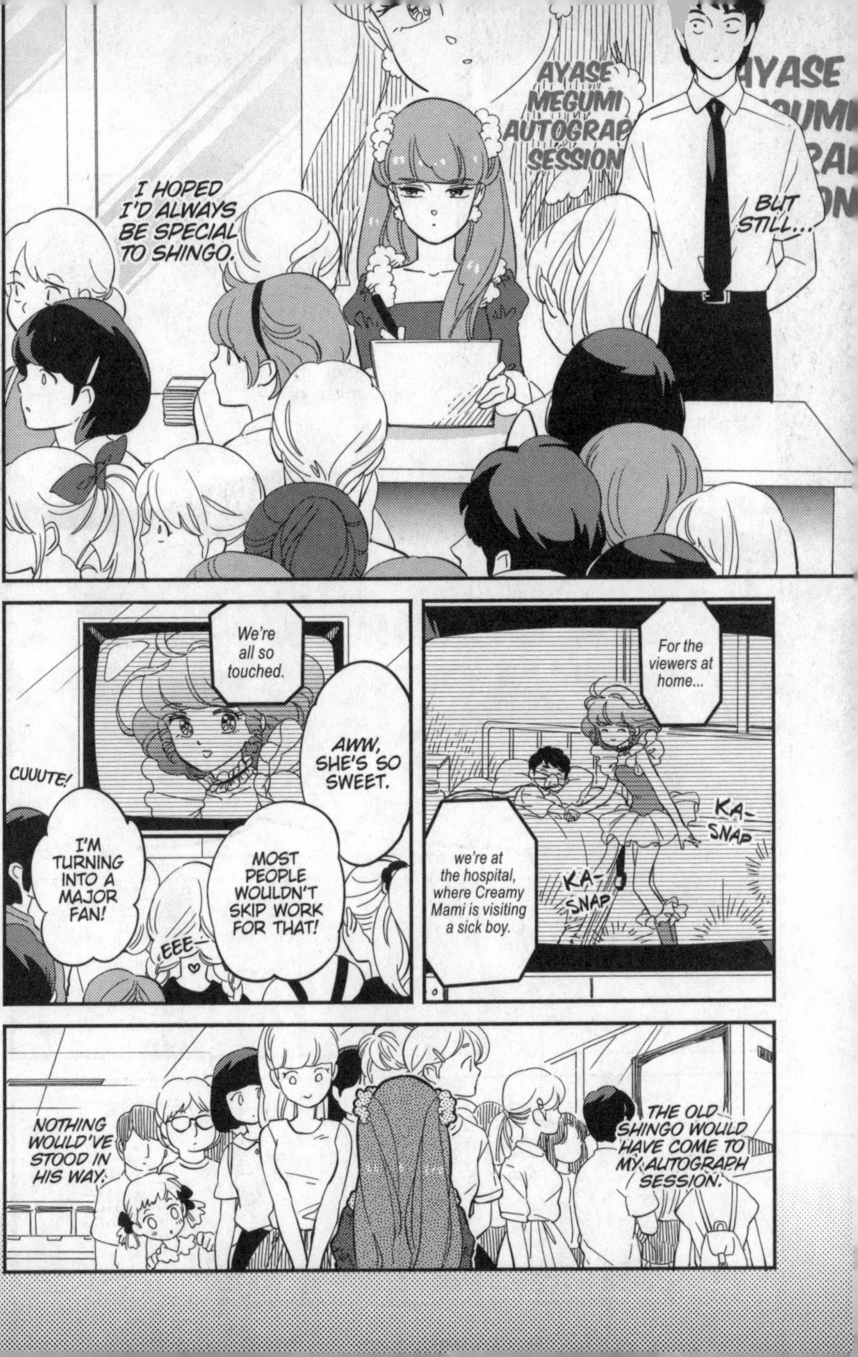
AYASE MEGUMI AUTOGRAP SESSION
BUT STILL...
I HOPED I'D ALWAYS BE SPECIAL TO SHINGO.
For the viewers at home...
we're at the hospital, where Creamy Mami is visiting a sick boy.
KA-SNAP
KA-SNAP
We're all so touched.
AWW, SHE'S SO SWEET.
MOST PEOPLE WOULDN'T SKIP WORK FOR THAT!
CUUUTE!
I'M TURNING INTO A MAJOR FAN!
EEE
THE OLD SHINGO WOULD HAVE COME TO MY AUTOGRAPH SESSION.
NOTHING WOULD'VE STOOD IN HIS WAY.

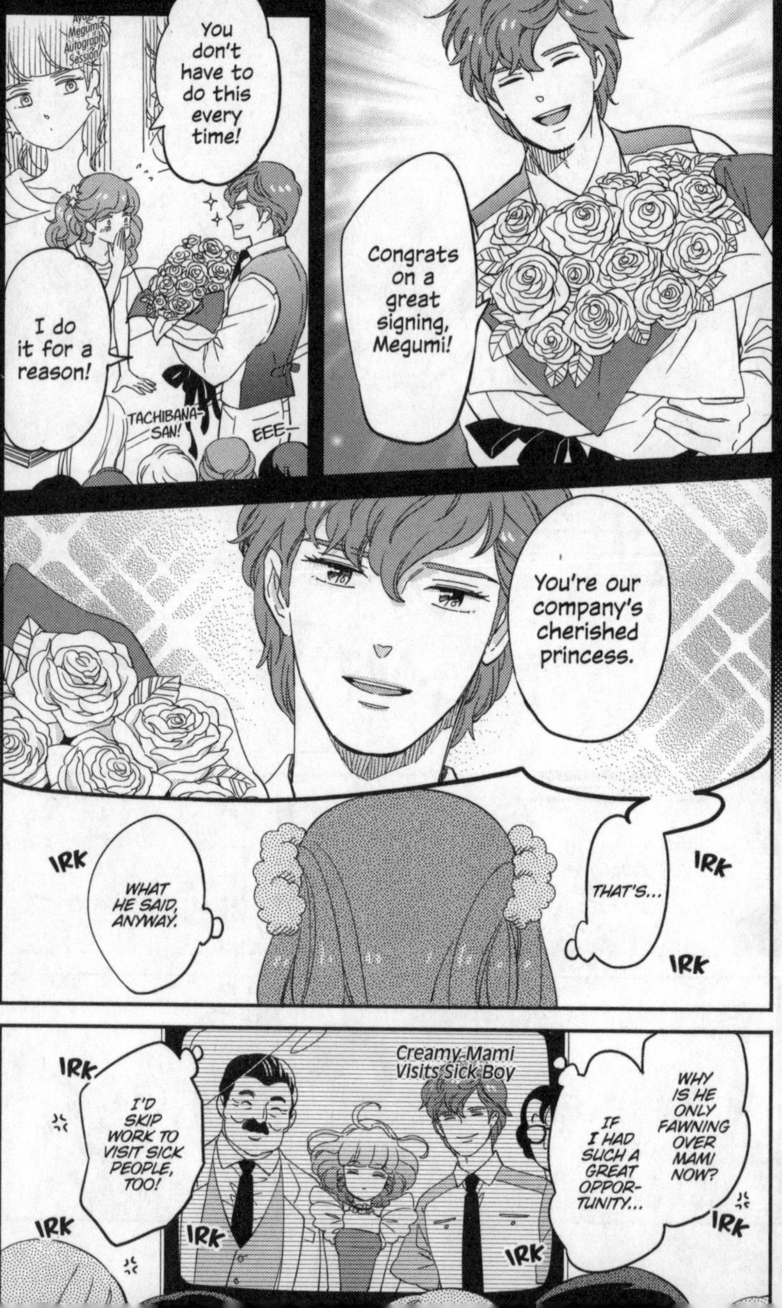
Congrats on a great signing, Megumi!
You don't have to do this every time!
Ayu Megumi Autograph Session
I do it for a reason!
EEE—
TACHIBANA-SAN!
You're our company's cherished princess.
IRK
THAT'S...
IRK
WHAT HE SAID, ANYWAY.
IRK
WHY IS HE ONLY FAWNING OVER MAMI NOW?
IF I HAD SUCH A GREAT OPPORTUNITY...
IRK
Creamy Mami Visits Sick Boy
I'D SKIP WORK TO VISIT SICK PEOPLE, TOO!
IRK
IRK
IRK
IRK

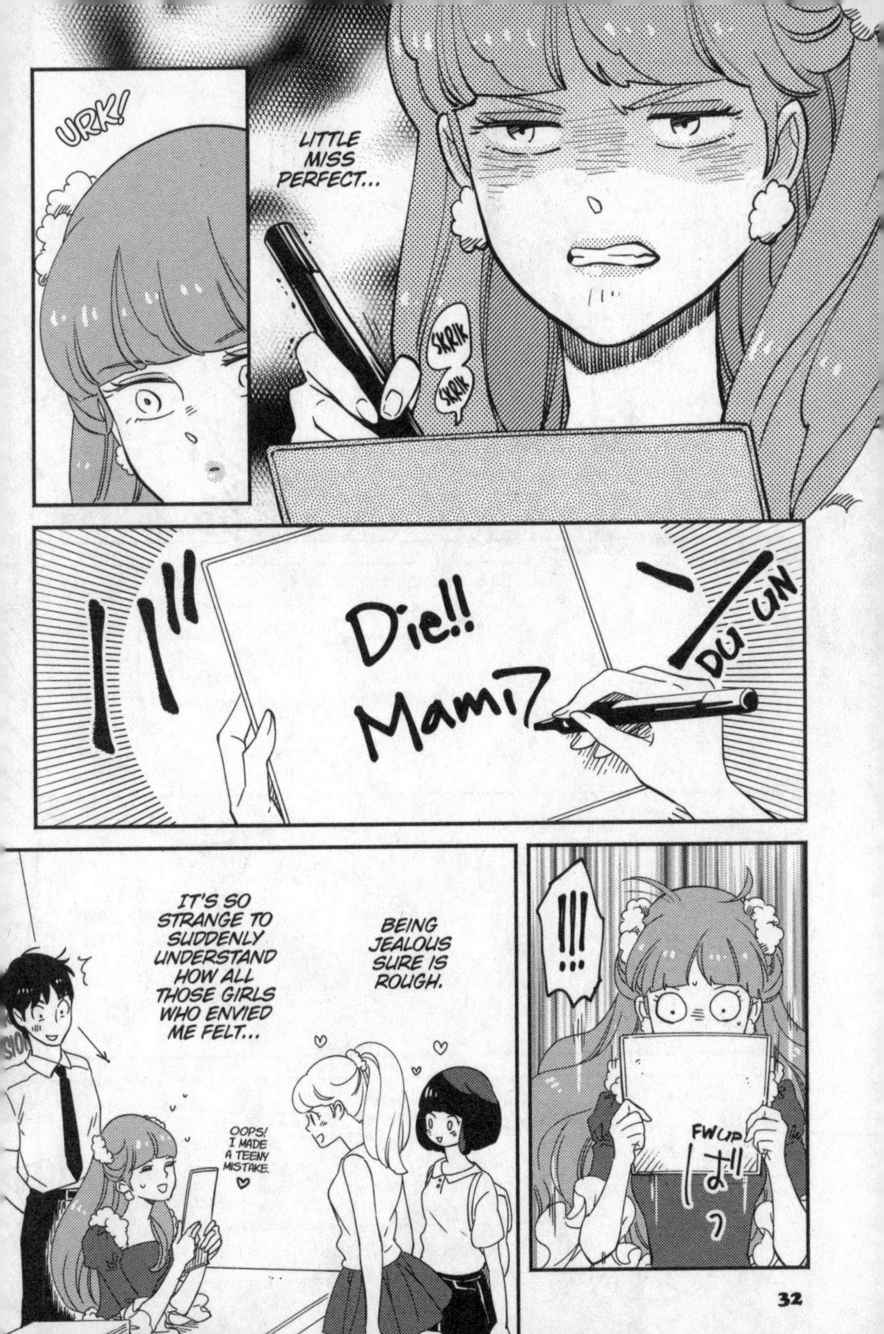
LITTLE MISS PERFECT...
SKRIK SKRIK
URK!
DU UN
Die!!
Mami7
!!!
FWUP
ぱっ
IT'S SO STRANGE TO SUDDENLY UNDERSTAND HOW ALL THOSE GIRLS WHO ENVIED ME FELT...
BEING JEALOUS SURE IS ROUGH.
OOPS! I MADE A TEENY MISTAKE.

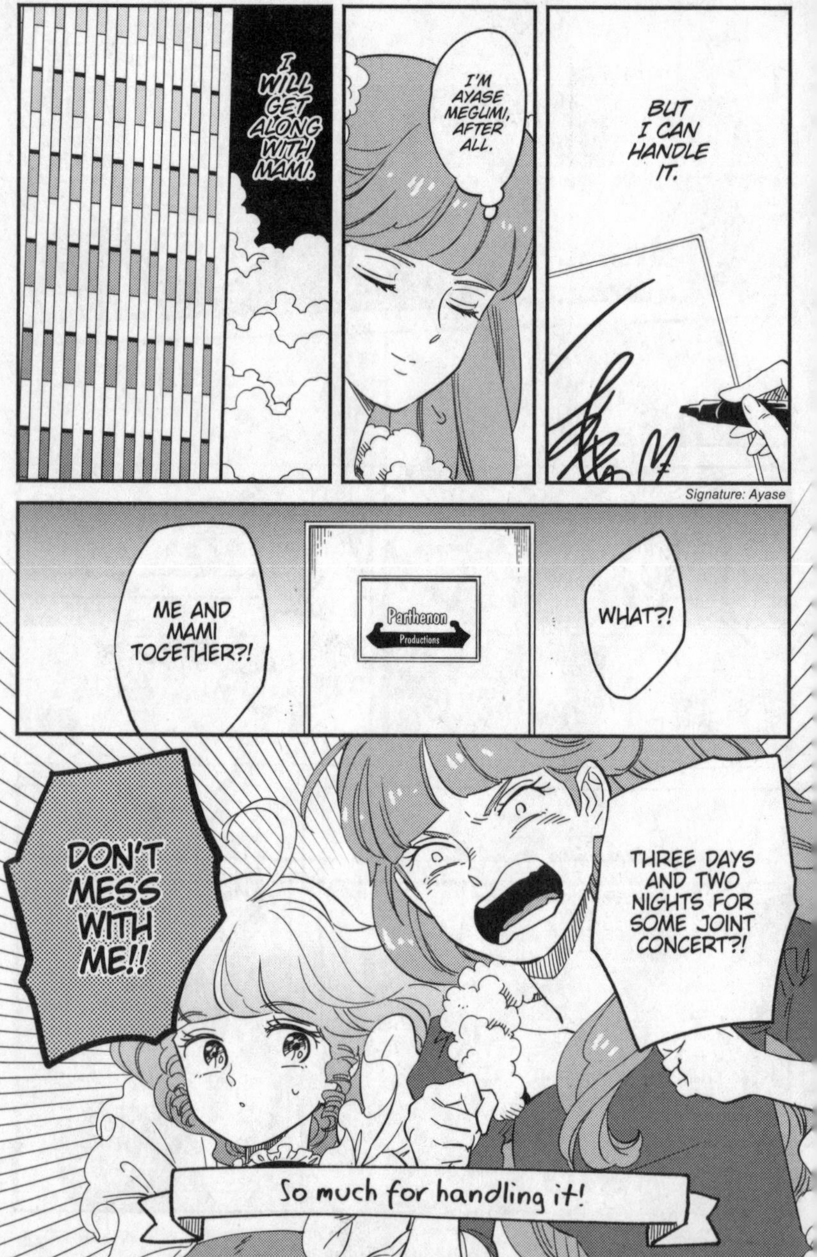
BUT I CAN HANDLE IT.
Signature: Ayase
I'M AYASE MEGUMI, AFTER ALL.
I WILL GET ALONG WITH MAMI.
WHAT?!
Parthenon Productions
ME AND MAMI TOGETHER?!
THREE DAYS AND TWO NIGHTS FOR SOME JOINT CONCERT?!
DON'T MESS WITH ME!!
So much for handling it!

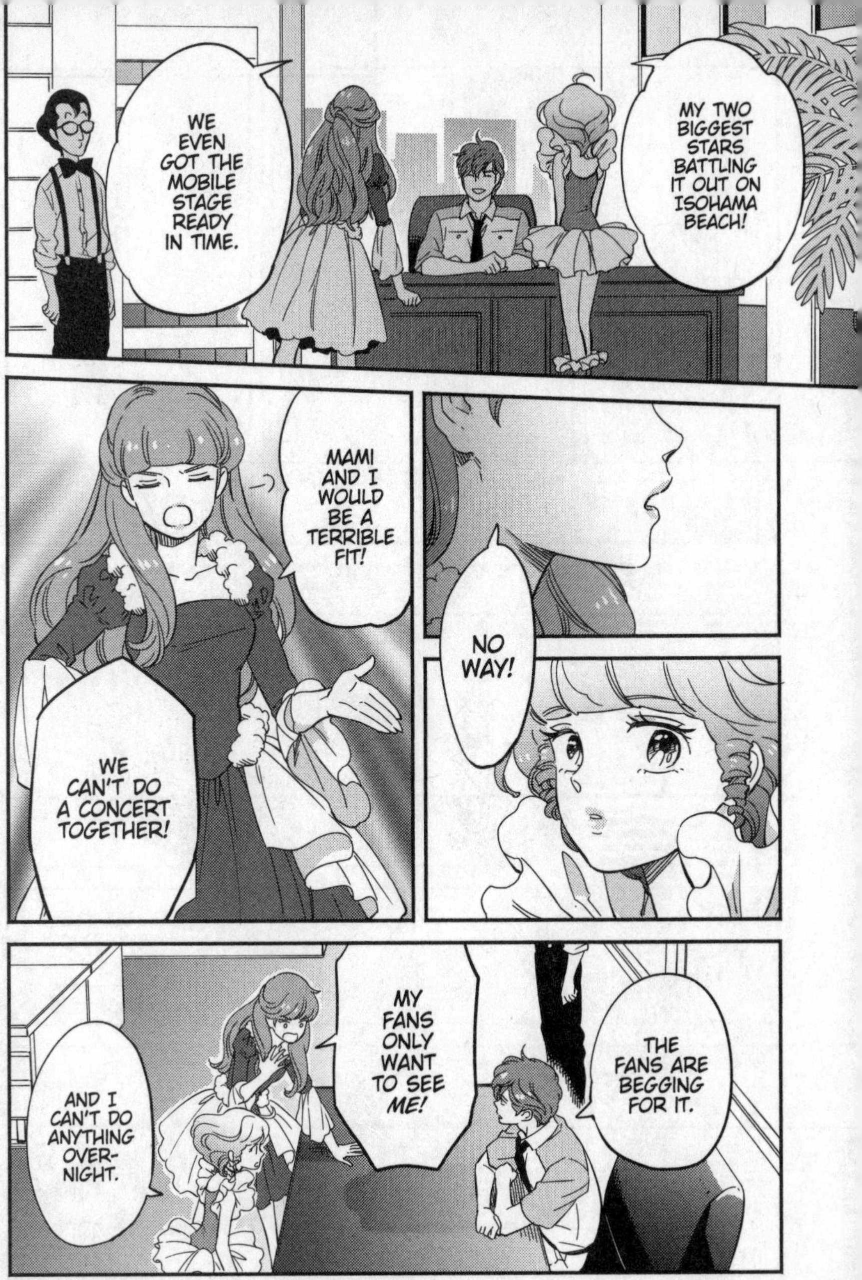
MY TWO BIGGEST STARS BATTLING IT OUT ON ISOHAMA BEACH!
WE EVEN GOT THE MOBILE STAGE READY IN TIME.
NO WAY!
MAMI AND I WOULD BE A TERRIBLE FIT!
WE CAN'T DO A CONCERT TOGETHER!
THE FANS ARE BEGGING FOR IT.
MY FANS ONLY WANT TO SEE *ME!*
AND I CAN'T DO ANYTHING OVER-NIGHT.

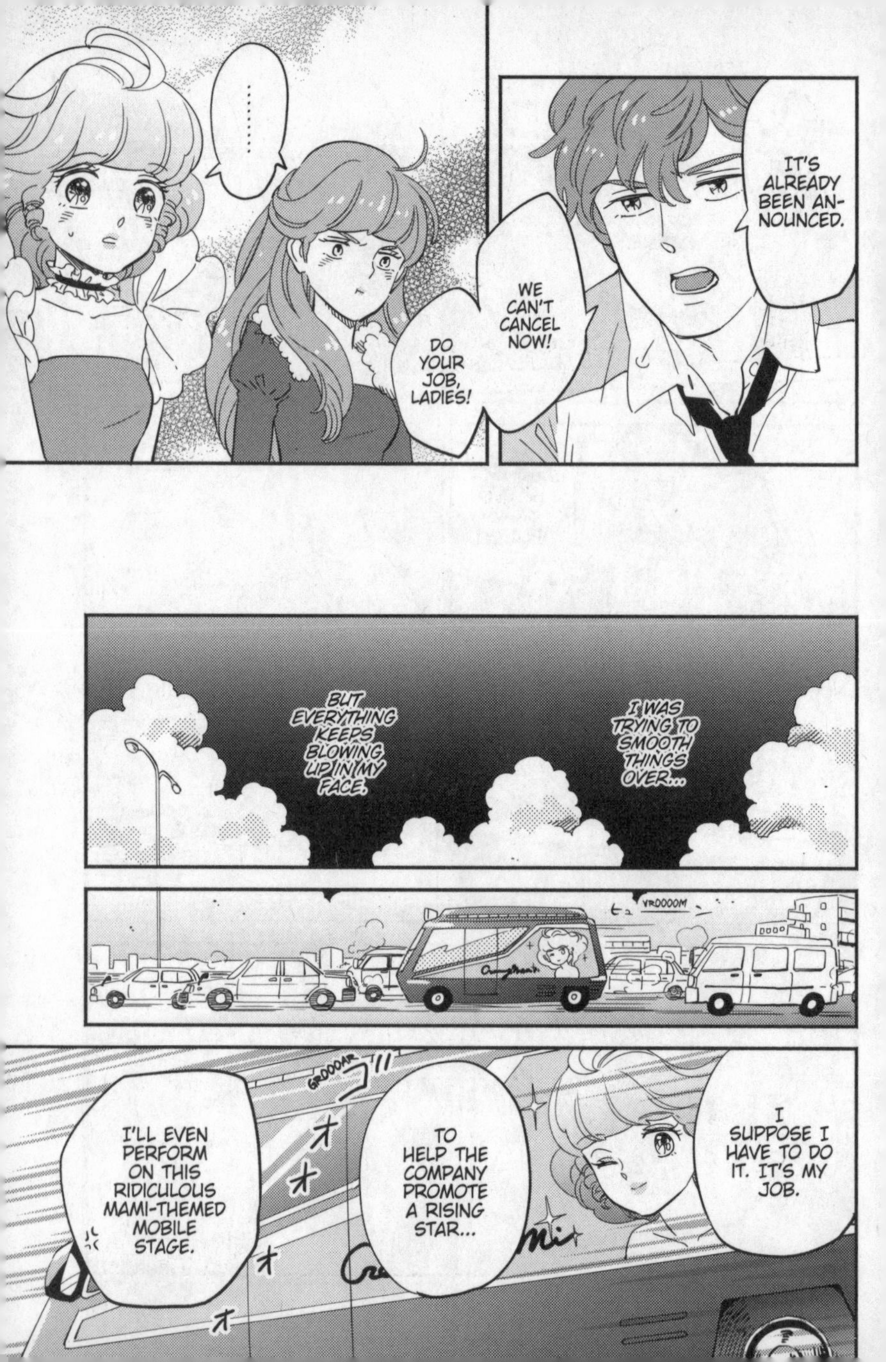
IT'S ALREADY BEEN AN-NOUNCED.
WE CAN'T CANCEL NOW!
DO YOUR JOB, LADIES!
......
I WAS TRYING TO SMOOTH THINGS OVER...
BUT EVERYTHING KEEPS BLOWING UP IN MY FACE.
VROOOOM
GROOOAR
I SUPPOSE I HAVE TO DO IT. IT'S MY JOB.
TO HELP THE COMPANY PROMOTE A RISING STAR...
I'LL EVEN PERFORM ON THIS RIDICULOUS MAMI-THEMED MOBILE STAGE.

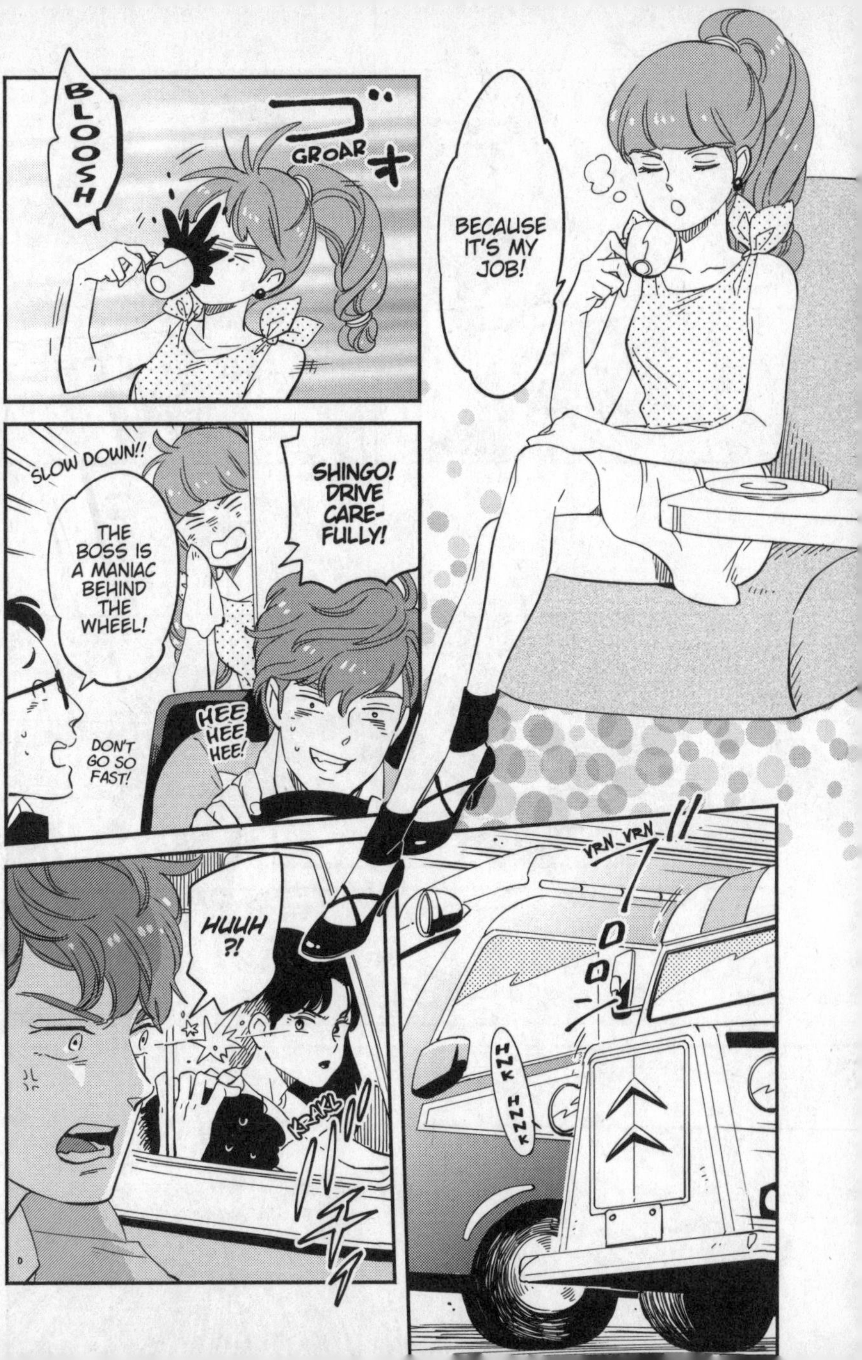
BECAUSE IT'S MY JOB!
BLOOSH
GROAR
SHINGO! DRIVE CARE-FULLY!
SLOW DOWN!!
THE BOSS IS A MANIAC BEHIND THE WHEEL!
HEE HEE HEE!
DON'T GO SO FAST!
VRN VRN
HNK HNNK
HUUH?!
KRAKL

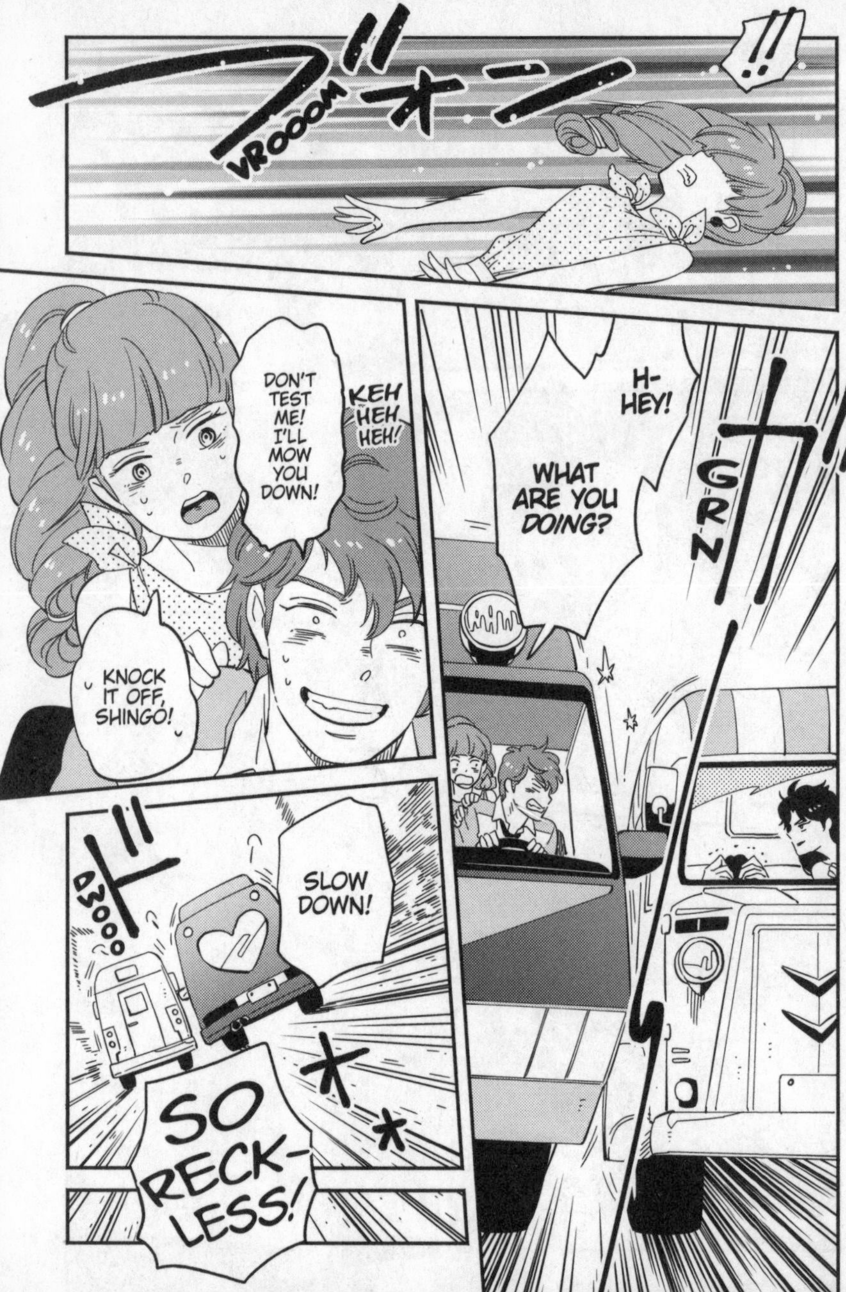
VROOOM
!!
H- HEY!
WHAT ARE YOU DOING?
GRN
DON'T TEST ME! I'LL MOW YOU DOWN!
KEH HEH HEH!
KNOCK IT OFF, SHINGO!
SLOW DOWN!
DWOOO
SO RECKLESS!

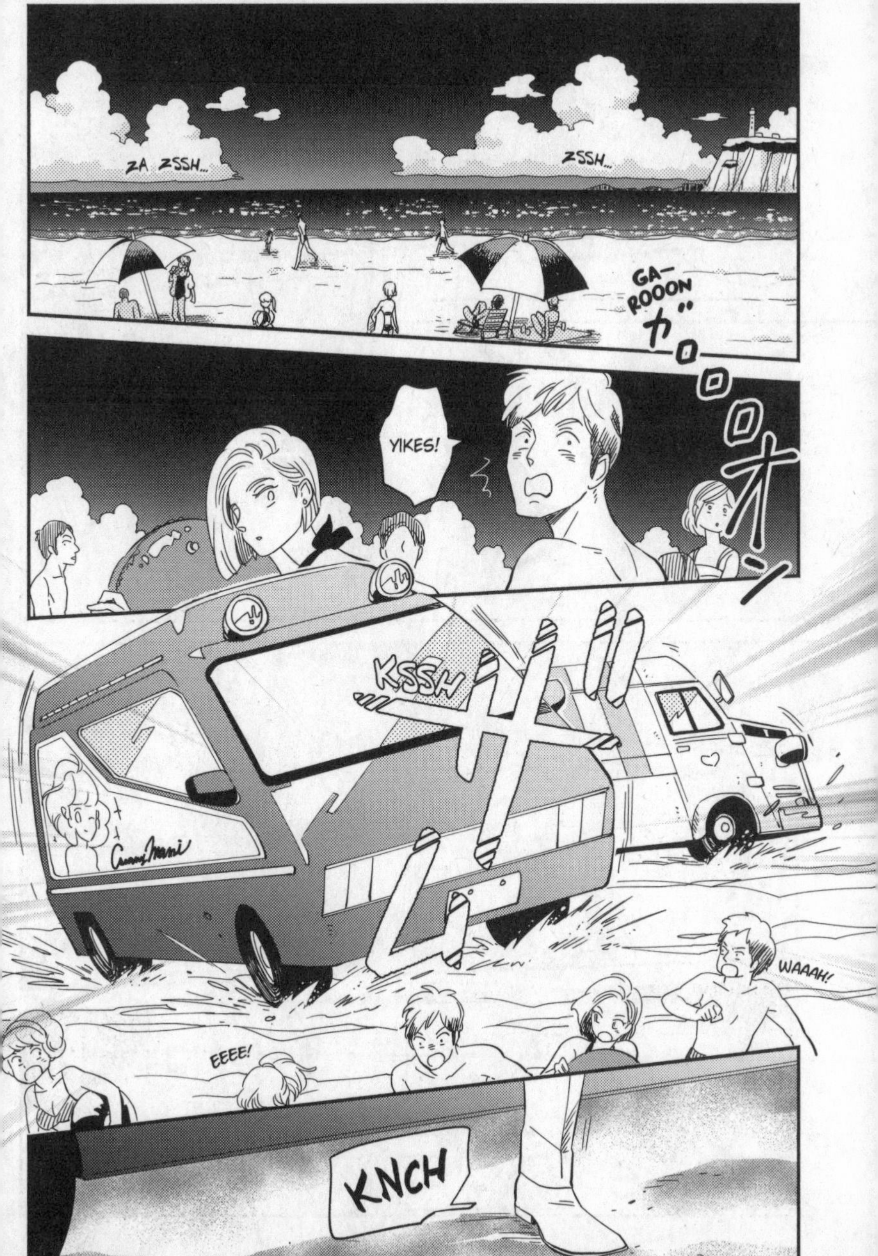

ZSSH...
ZA ZSSH...
GA-ROOON
ガロロロオー
YIKES!
KSSH
WAAAH!
EEEE!
KNCH

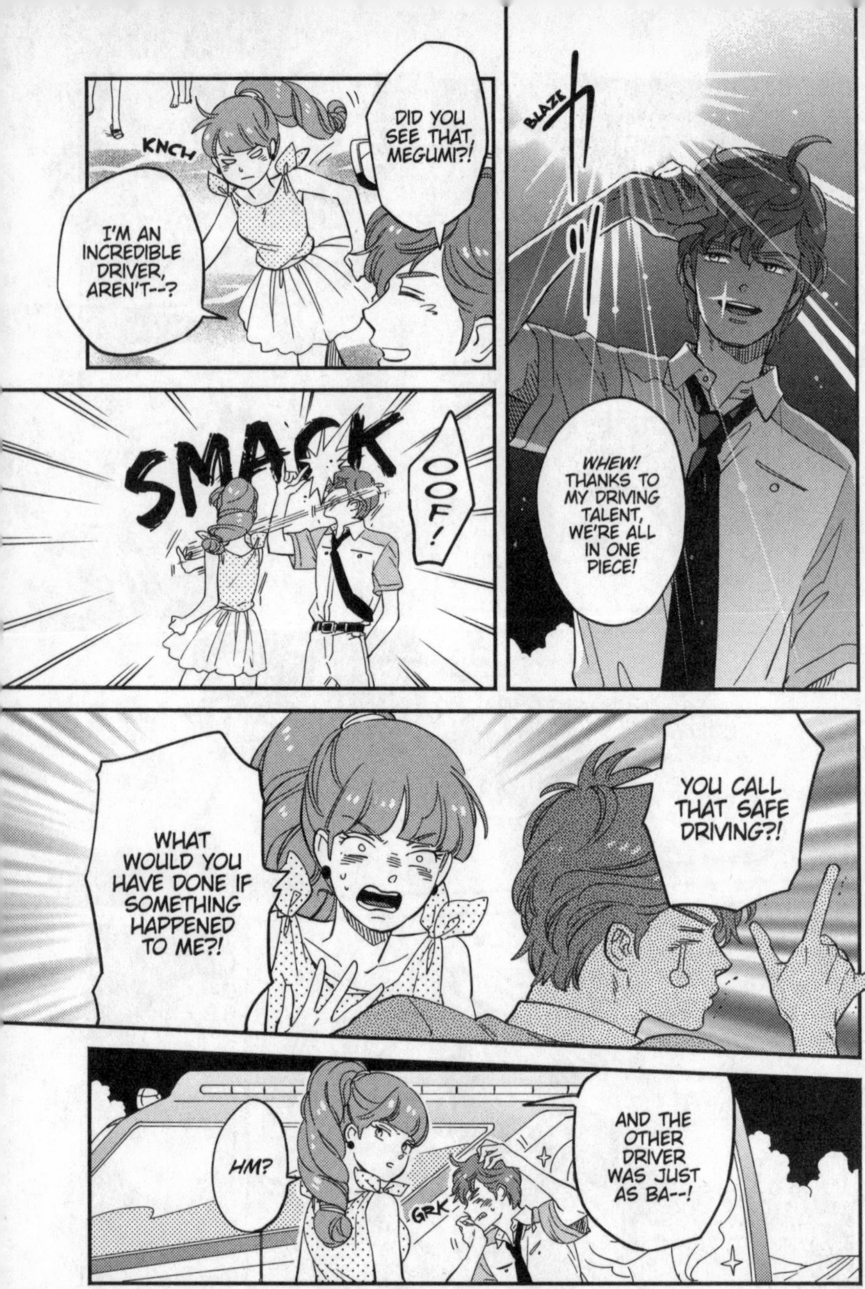
BLAZE
WHEW! THANKS TO MY DRIVING TALENT, WE'RE ALL IN ONE PIECE!
DID YOU SEE THAT, MEGUMI?!
KNCH
I'M AN INCREDIBLE DRIVER, AREN'T--?
OOF!
SMACK
YOU CALL THAT SAFE DRIVING?!
WHAT WOULD YOU HAVE DONE IF SOMETHING HAPPENED TO ME?!
AND THE OTHER DRIVER WAS JUST AS BA--!
GRK
HM?

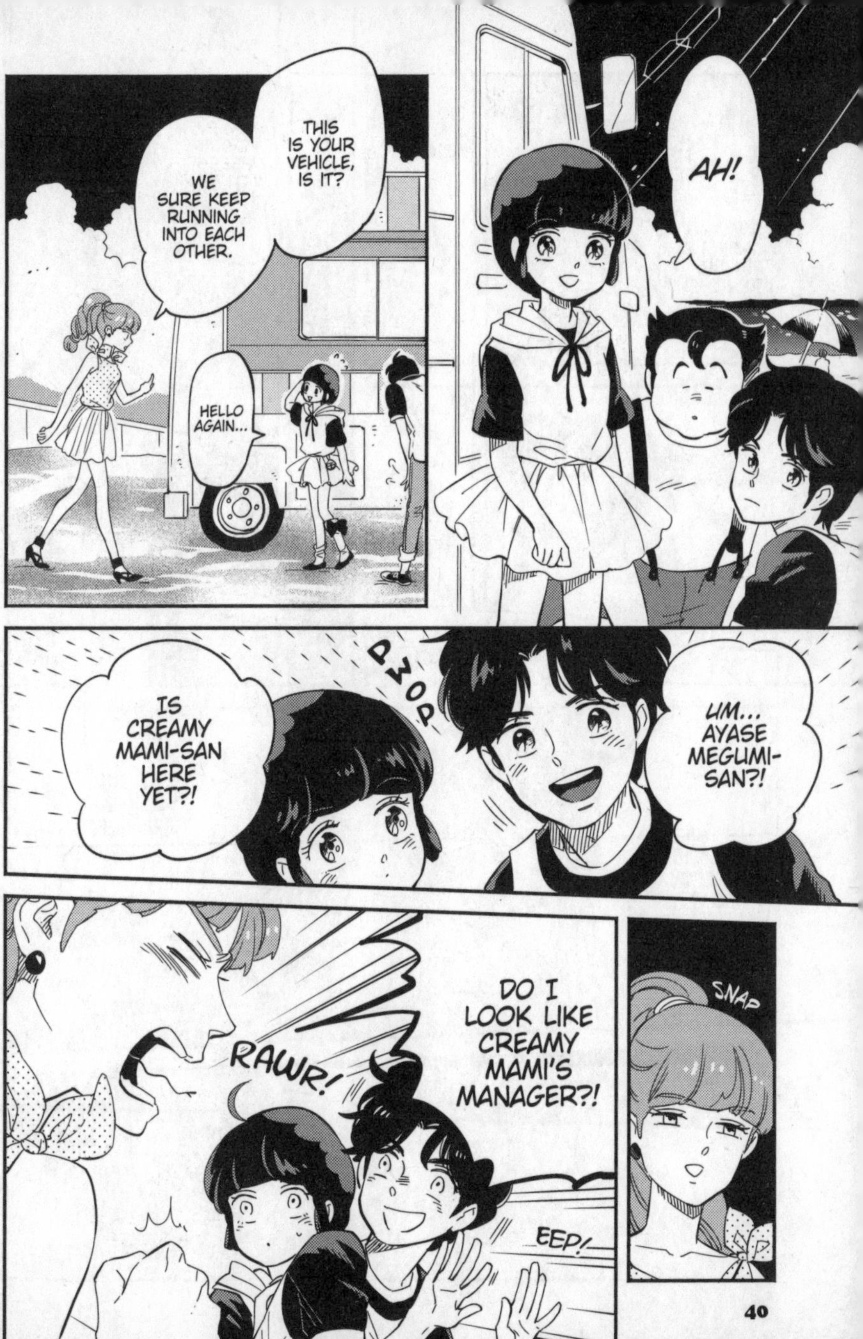
AH!
THIS IS YOUR VEHICLE, IS IT?
WE SURE KEEP RUNNING INTO EACH OTHER.
HELLO AGAIN...
UM... AYASE MEGUMI-SAN?!
IS CREAMY MAMI-SAN HERE YET?!
SNAP
DO I LOOK LIKE CREAMY MAMI'S MANAGER?!
RAWR!
EEP!

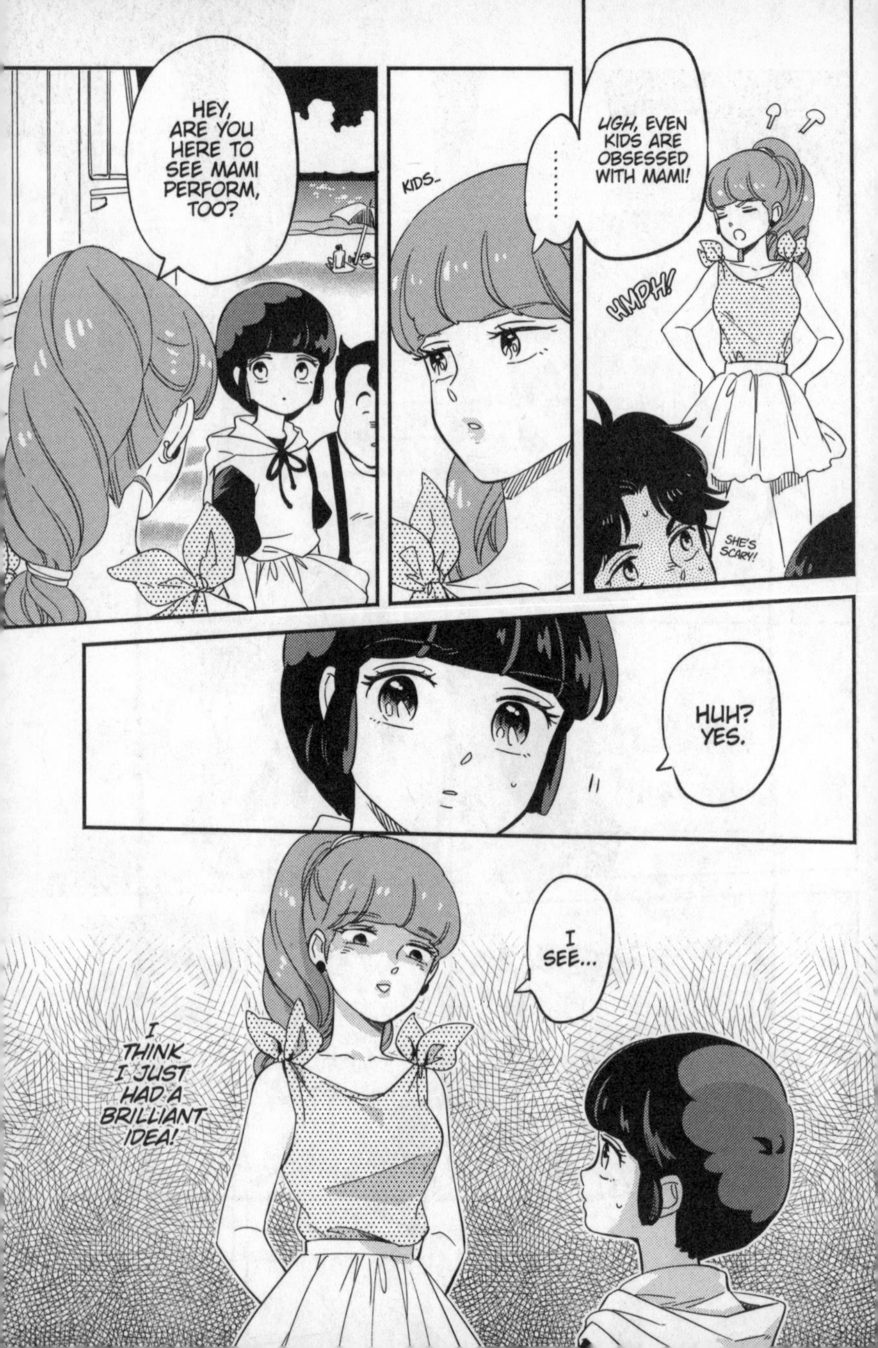
UGH, EVEN KIDS ARE OBSESSED WITH MAMI!
HMPH!
SHE'S SCARY!
......
KIDS...
HEY, ARE YOU HERE TO SEE MAMI PERFORM, TOO?
HUH? YES.
I SEE...
I THINK I JUST HAD A BRILLIANT IDEA!

People of the '80s

YOU COULD ALWAYS FIND ME AT THE ADVANCED-SKATE TIMES AT ROLLER RINKS.
SHWOO—
SINCE I CAN SKATE BACK-WARDS.
SKRII
WE'VE BEEN WAITING FOR YOU, TACHIBANA-SAAAN!!!
EEEE!
EEEE!
HA HA HA HA HA!!
EEEE!
EEEEE!
SWAP
PWAP
PWAP
PWAP—
MAYBE HE SHOULD MAKE HIS OWN PRO DEBUT...
EEEEEE!!
SPIIIN

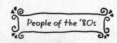

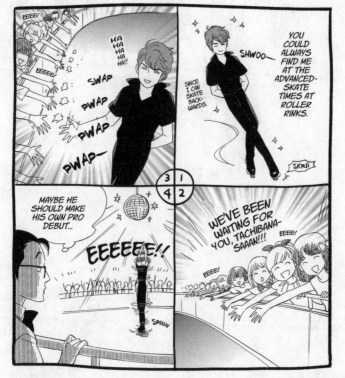

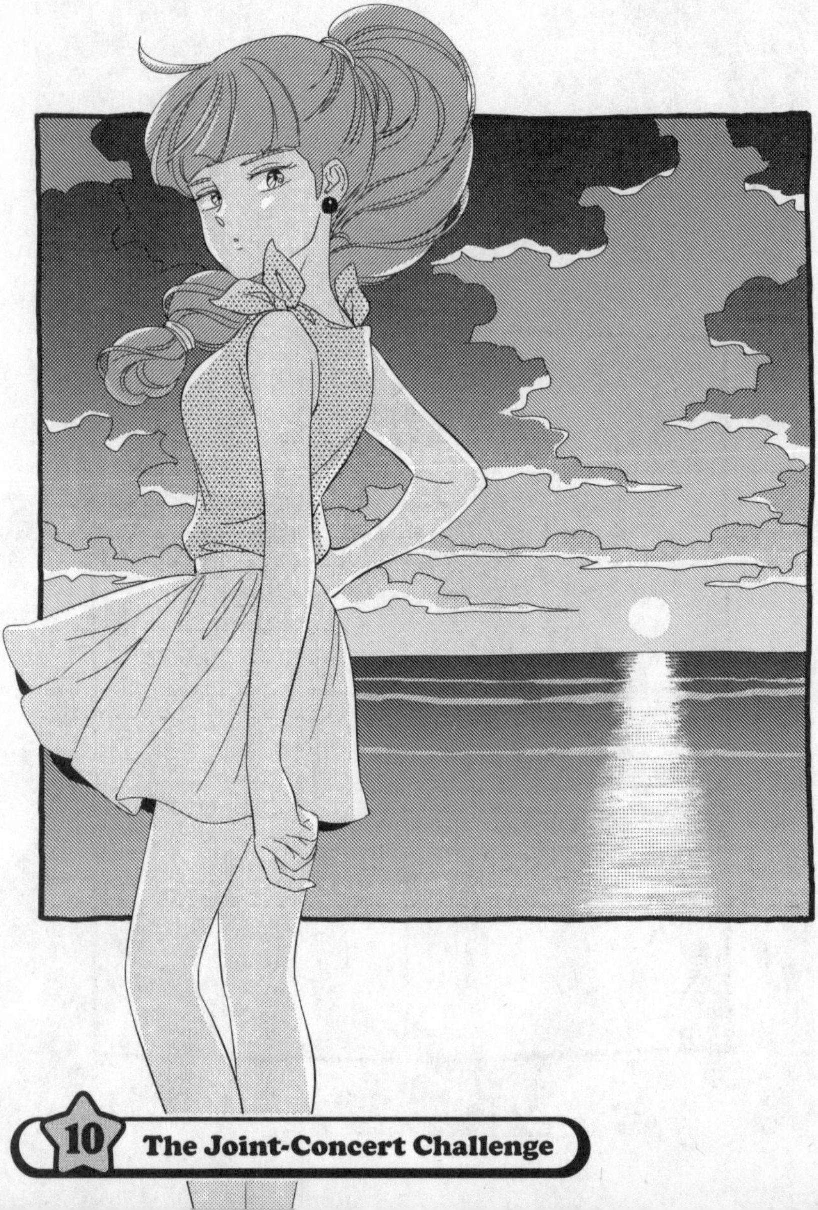

10 The Joint-Concert Challenge

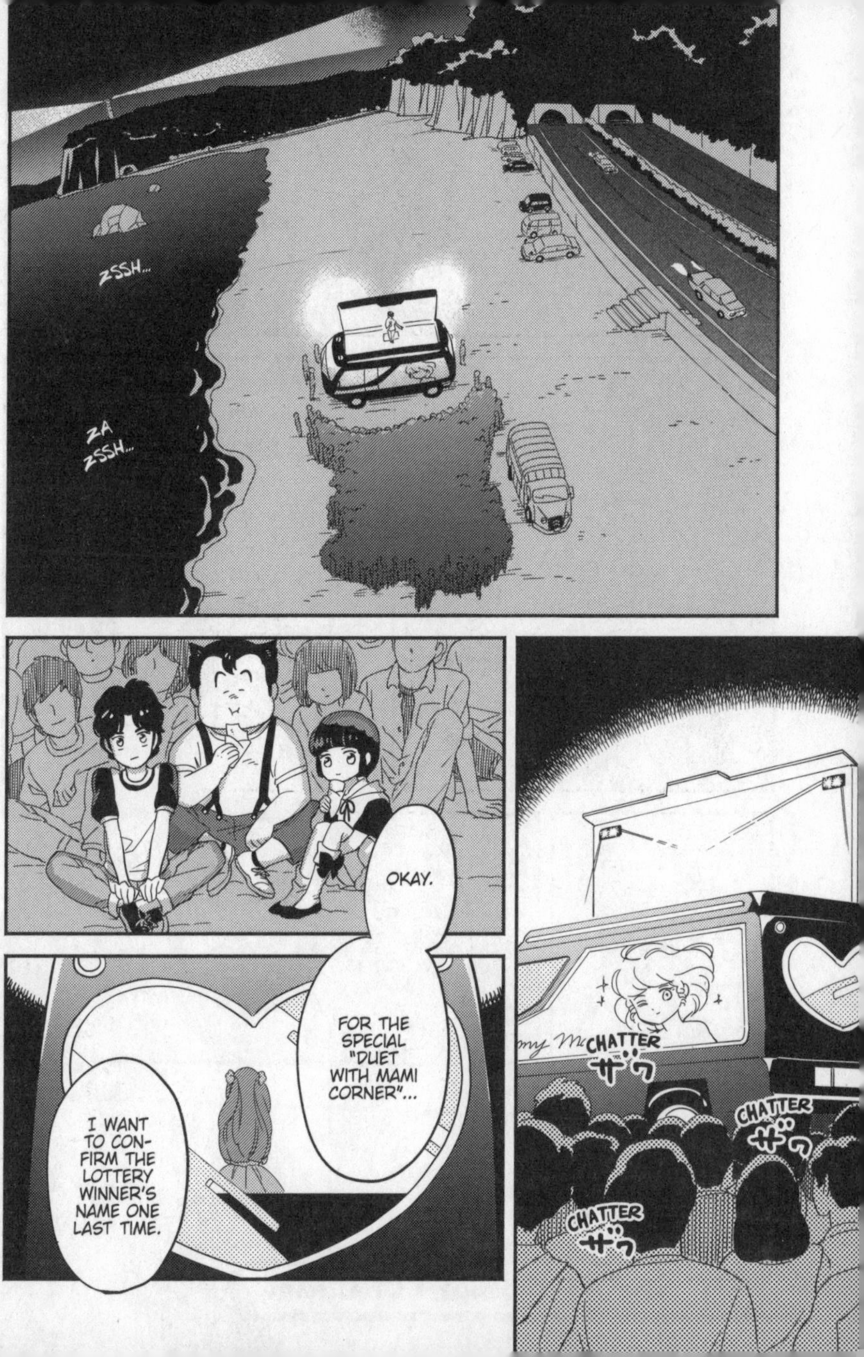
ZSSH...
ZA ZSSH...
CHATTER
CHATTER
CHATTER
OKAY.
FOR THE SPECIAL "DUET WITH MAMI CORNER"...
I WANT TO CONFIRM THE LOTTERY WINNER'S NAME ONE LAST TIME.

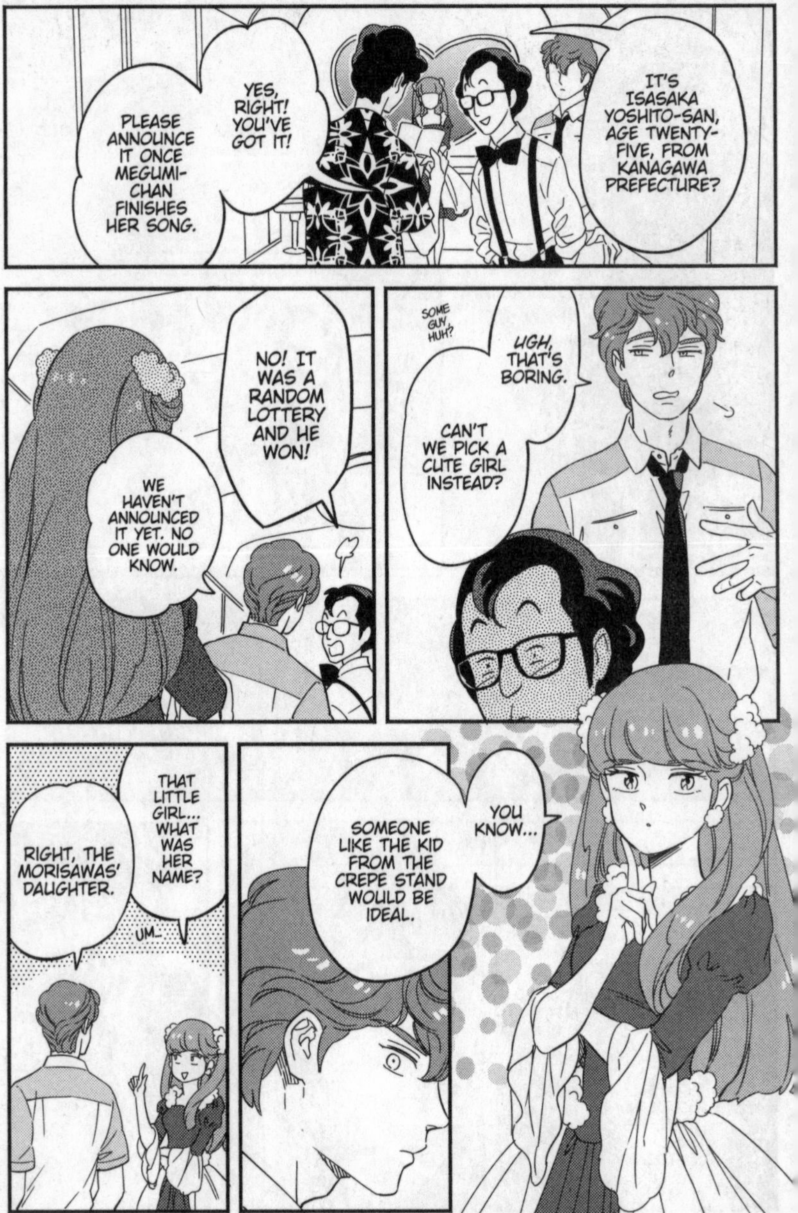
IT'S ISASAKA YOSHITO-SAN, AGE TWENTY-FIVE, FROM KANAGAWA PREFECTURE?
YES, RIGHT! YOU'VE GOT IT!
PLEASE ANNOUNCE IT ONCE MEGUMI-CHAN FINISHES HER SONG.
UGH, THAT'S BORING.
SOME GUY, HUH?
CAN'T WE PICK A CUTE GIRL INSTEAD?
NO! IT WAS A RANDOM LOTTERY AND HE WON!
WE HAVEN'T ANNOUNCED IT YET. NO ONE WOULD KNOW.
YOU KNOW...
SOMEONE LIKE THE KID FROM THE CREPE STAND WOULD BE IDEAL.
THAT LITTLE GIRL... WHAT WAS HER NAME?
UM...
RIGHT, THE MORISAWAS' DAUGHTER.

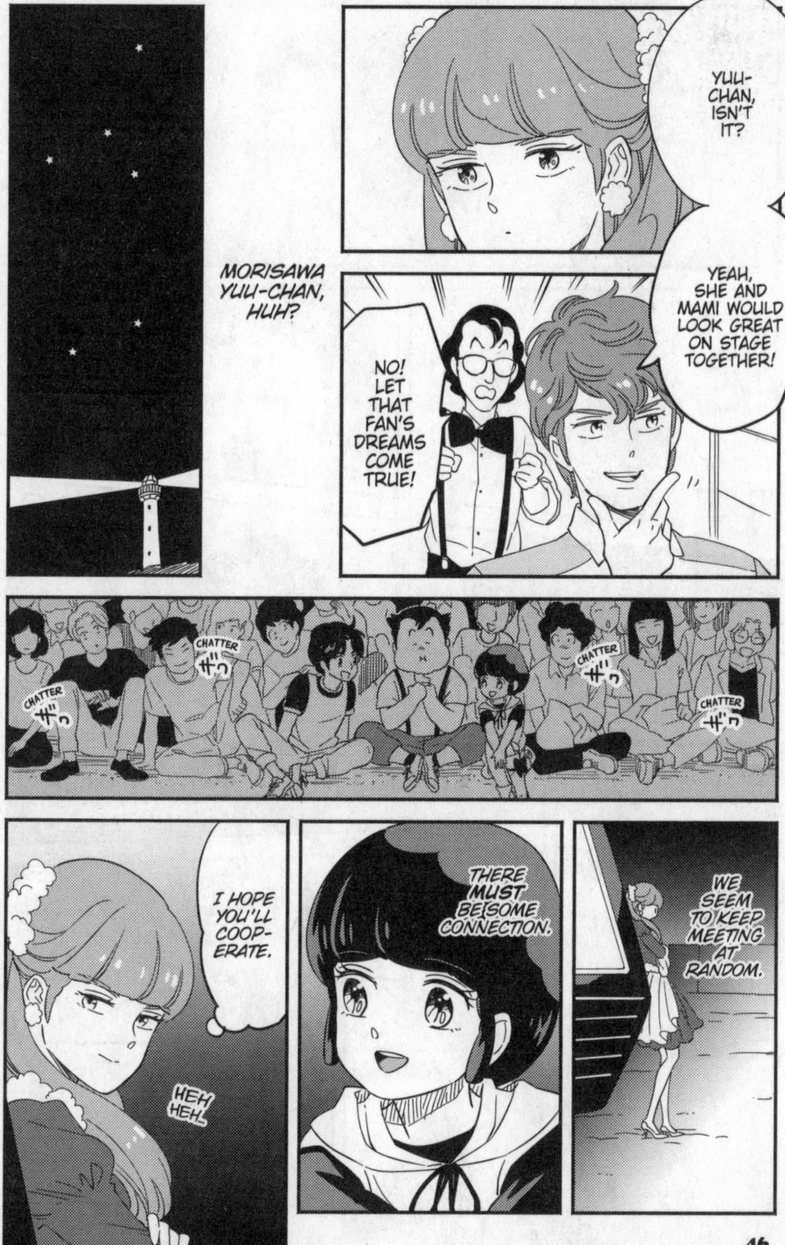
YUU-CHAN, ISN'T IT?
YEAH, SHE AND MAMI WOULD LOOK GREAT ON STAGE TOGETHER!
NO! LET THAT FAN'S DREAMS COME TRUE!
MORISAWA YUU-CHAN, HUH?
CHATTER
CHATTER
CHATTER
CHATTER
WE SEEM TO KEEP MEETING AT RANDOM.
THERE MUST BE SOME CONNECTION.
I HOPE YOU'LL COOP-ERATE.
HEH HEH.

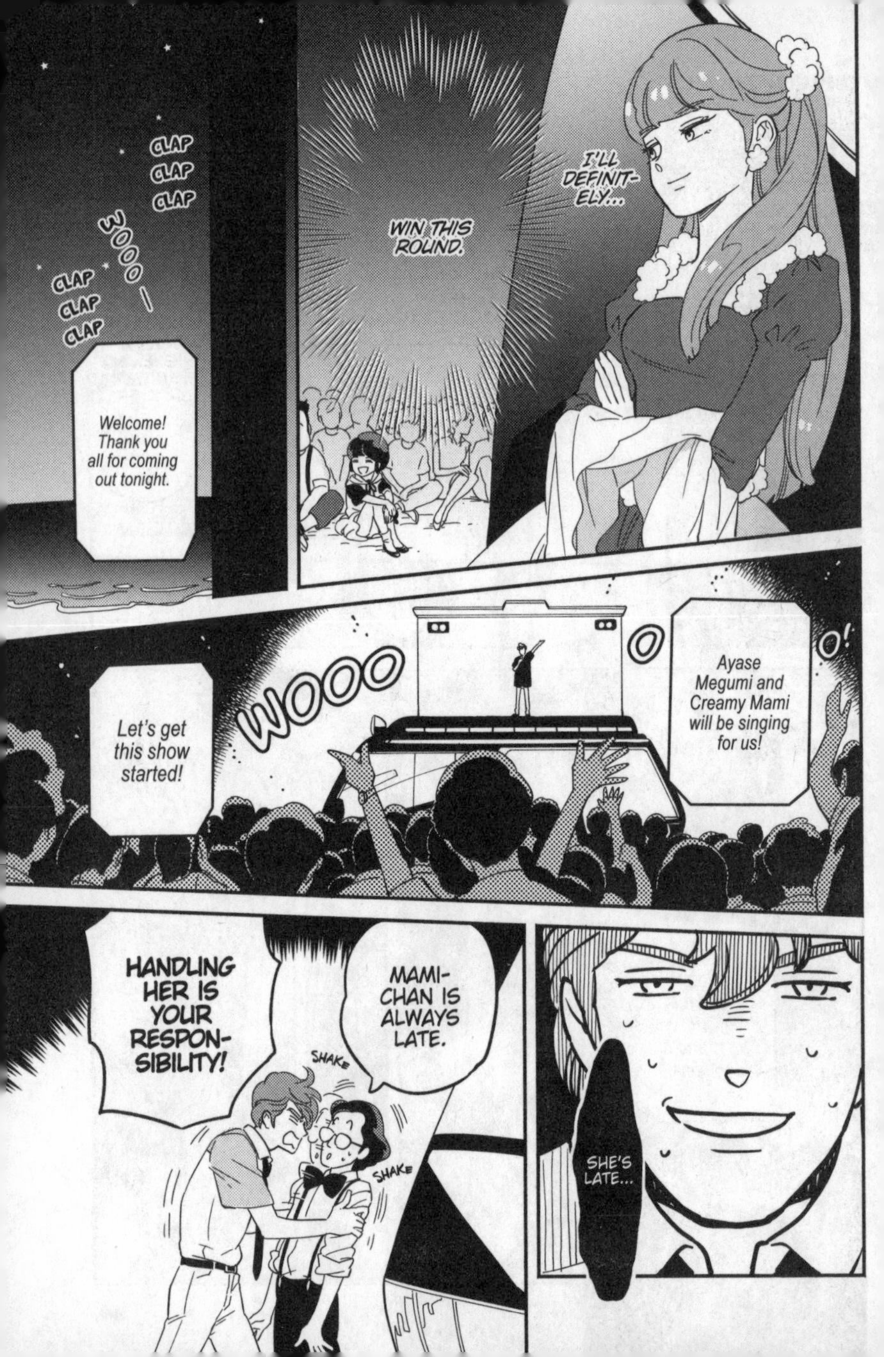

I'LL DEFINITELY...
WIN THIS ROUND.
CLAP CLAP CLAP
WOOO—
CLAP CLAP CLAP
Welcome! Thank you all for coming out tonight.
Ayase Megumi and Creamy Mami will be singing for us!
WOOOOO!
Let's get this show started!
SHE'S LATE...
MAMI-CHAN IS ALWAYS LATE.
SHAKE
SHAKE
HANDLING HER IS YOUR RESPONSIBILITY!

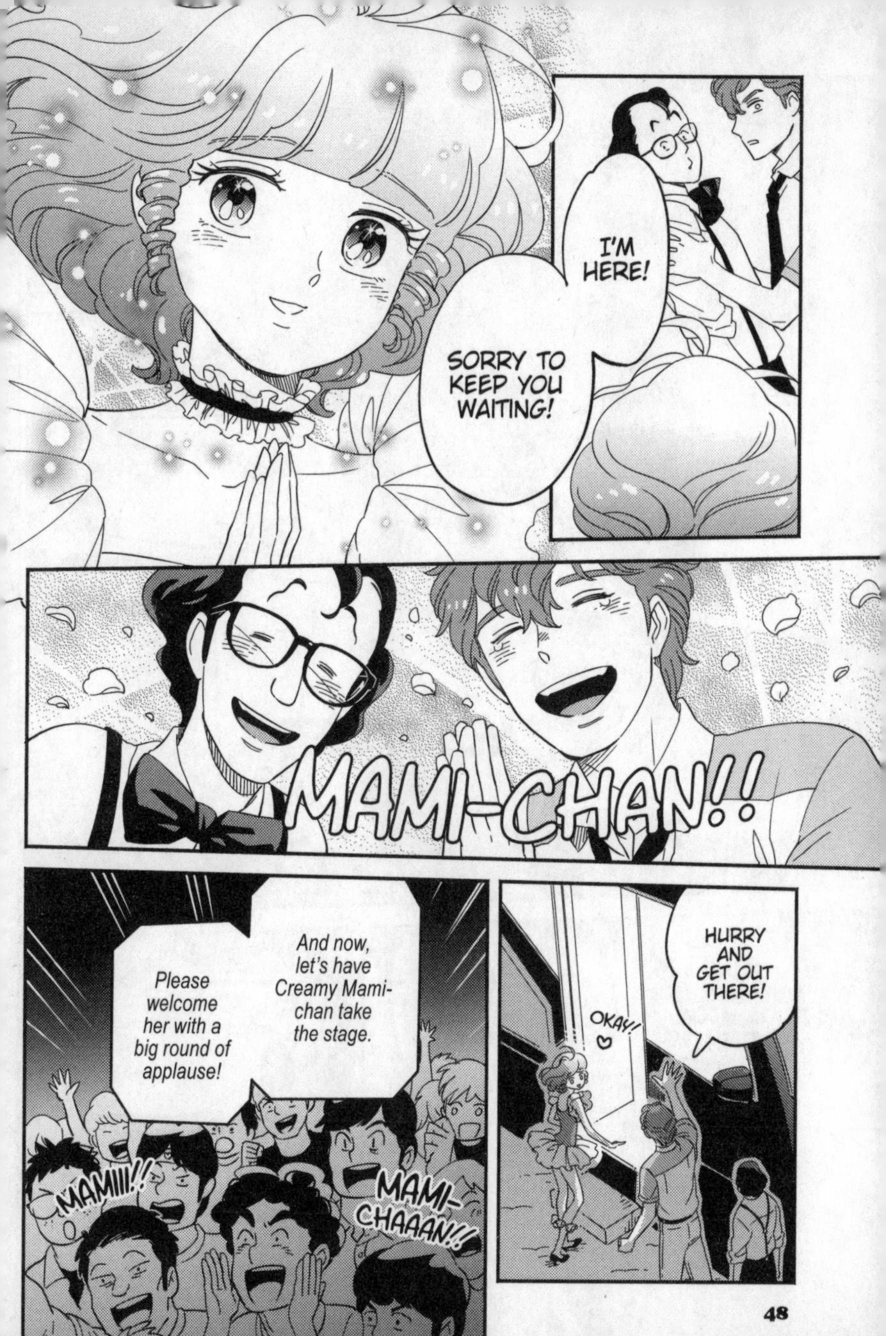
I'M HERE!
SORRY TO KEEP YOU WAITING!
MAMI-CHAN!!
HURRY AND GET OUT THERE!
OKAY! ♡
And now, let's have Creamy Mami-chan take the stage.
Please welcome her with a big round of applause!
MAMI-CHAAAN!!
MAMIII!!

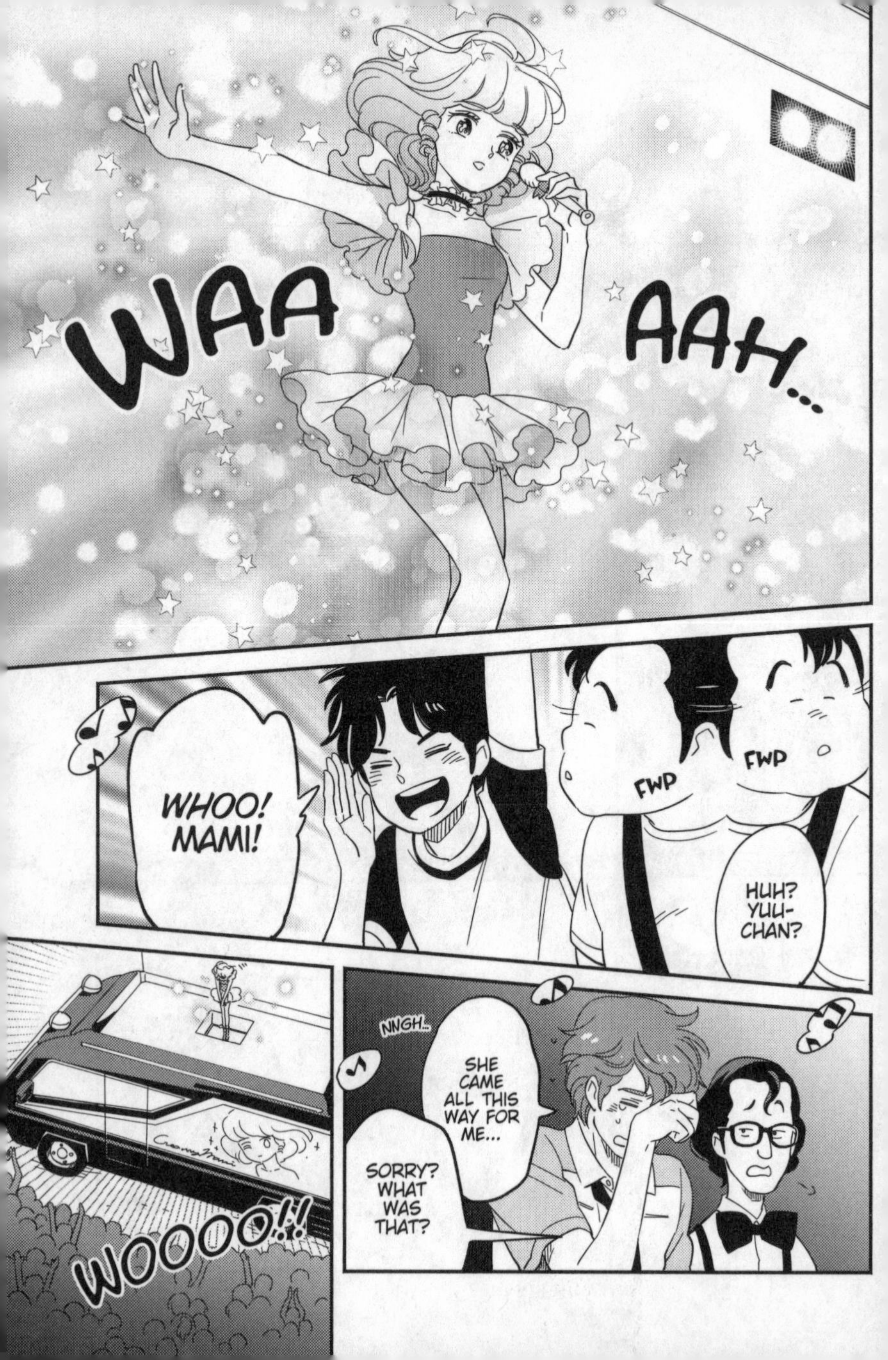
WAA AAH...
FWP
FWP
WHOO! MAMI!
HUH? YUU-CHAN?
NNGH..
SHE CAME ALL THIS WAY FOR ME...
SORRY? WHAT WAS THAT?
WOOOO!!

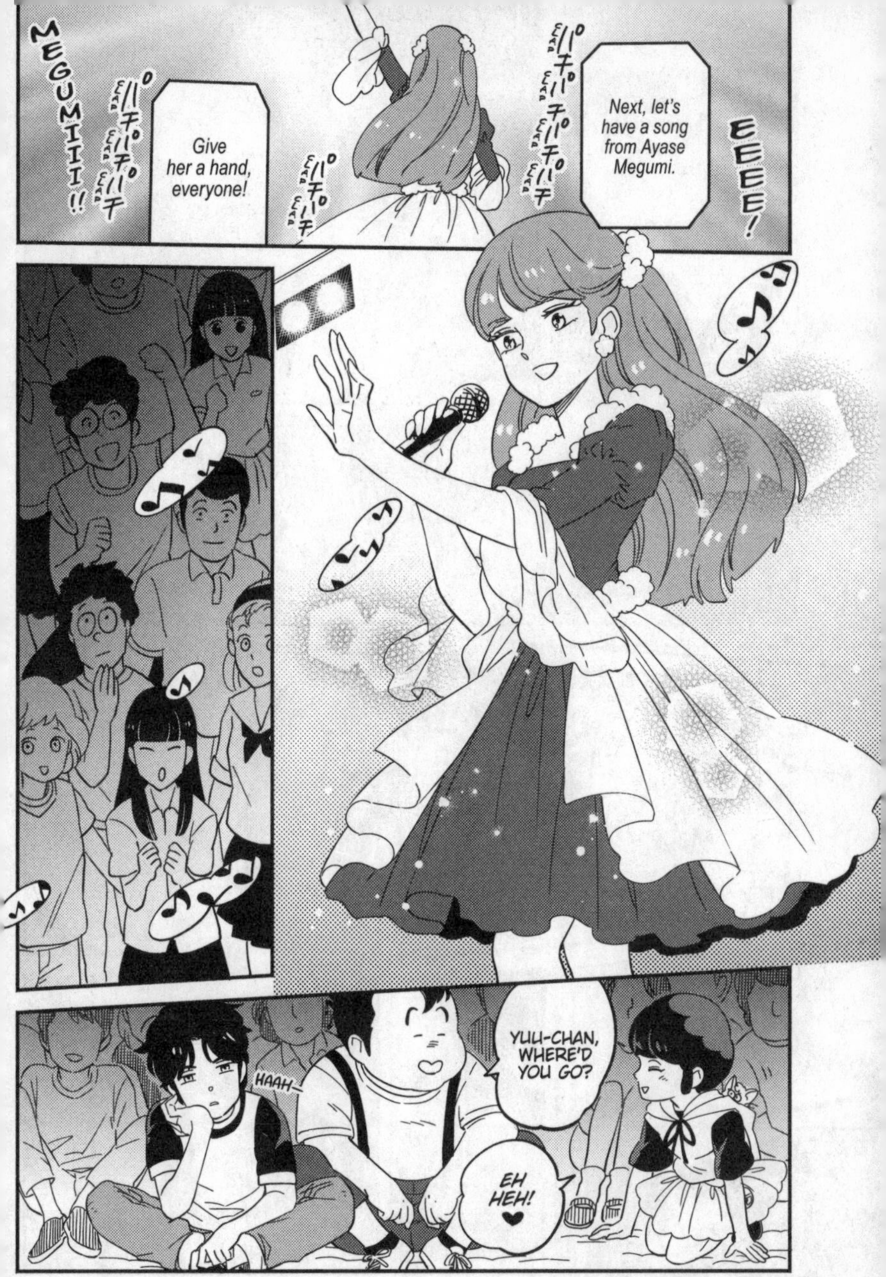
EEEE!
Next, let's have a song from Ayase Megumi.
Give her a hand, everyone!
MEGUMIII!!
YUU-CHAN, WHERE'D YOU GO?
EH HEH! ♥
HAAH—

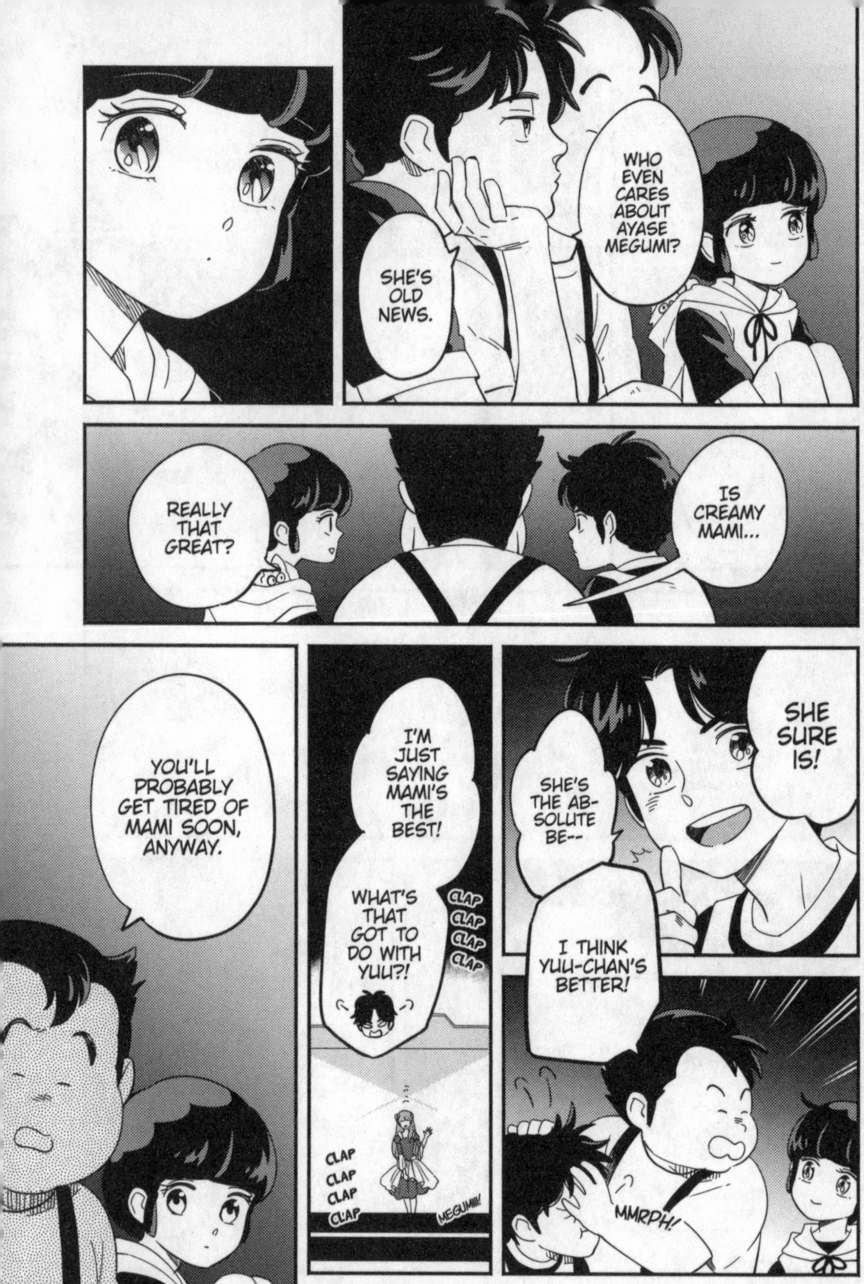
WHO EVEN CARES ABOUT AYASE MEGUMI?
SHE'S OLD NEWS.
IS CREAMY MAMI...
REALLY THAT GREAT?
SHE SURE IS!
SHE'S THE AB- SOLUTE BE--
I THINK YUU-CHAN'S BETTER!
MMRPH!
I'M JUST SAYING MAMI'S THE BEST!
WHAT'S THAT GOT TO DO WITH YUU?!
CLAP CLAP CLAP CLAP
CLAP CLAP CLAP CLAP
MEGUMI!!
YOU'LL PROBABLY GET TIRED OF MAMI SOON, ANYWAY.

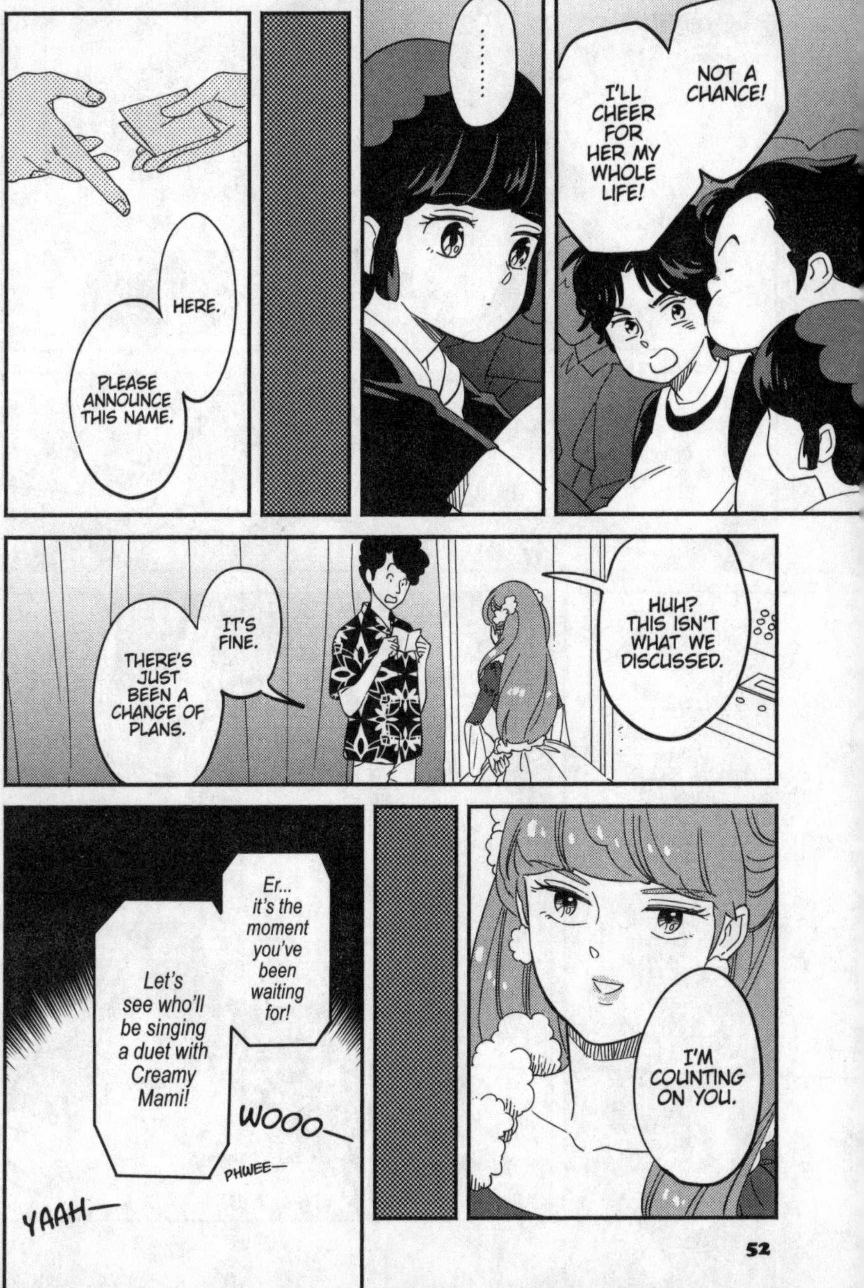
NOT A CHANCE!
I'LL CHEER FOR HER MY WHOLE LIFE!
……
HERE.
PLEASE ANNOUNCE THIS NAME.
HUH? THIS ISN'T WHAT WE DISCUSSED.
IT'S FINE.
THERE'S JUST BEEN A CHANGE OF PLANS.
I'M COUNTING ON YOU.
Er... it's the moment you've been waiting for!
Let's see who'll be singing a duet with Creamy Mami!
WOOO—
PHWEE—
YAAH—

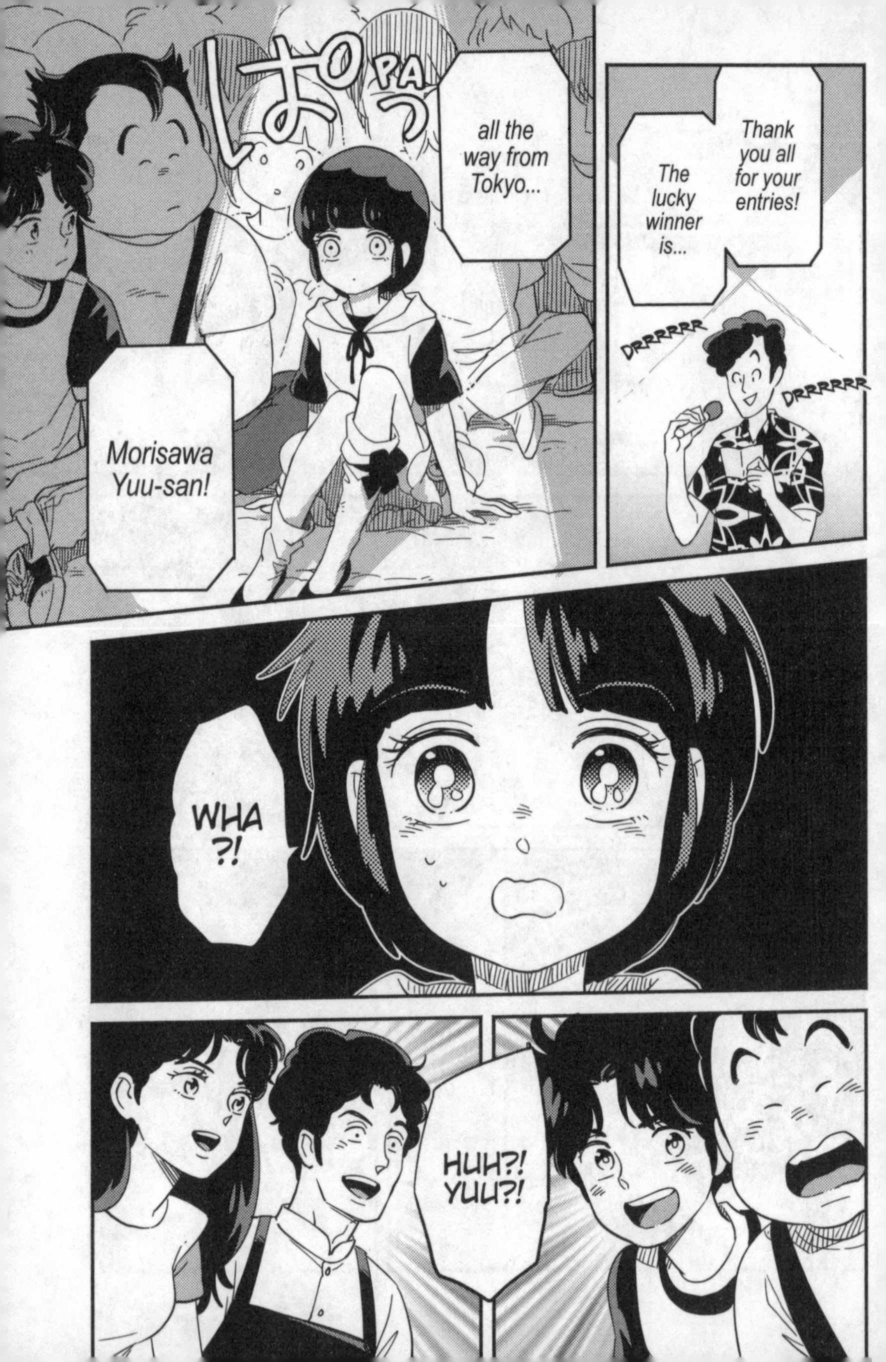
Thank you all for your entries!
The lucky winner is...
DRRRRRR
DRRRRRR
PA
all the way from Tokyo...
Morisawa Yuu-san!
WHA?!
HUH?! YUU?!

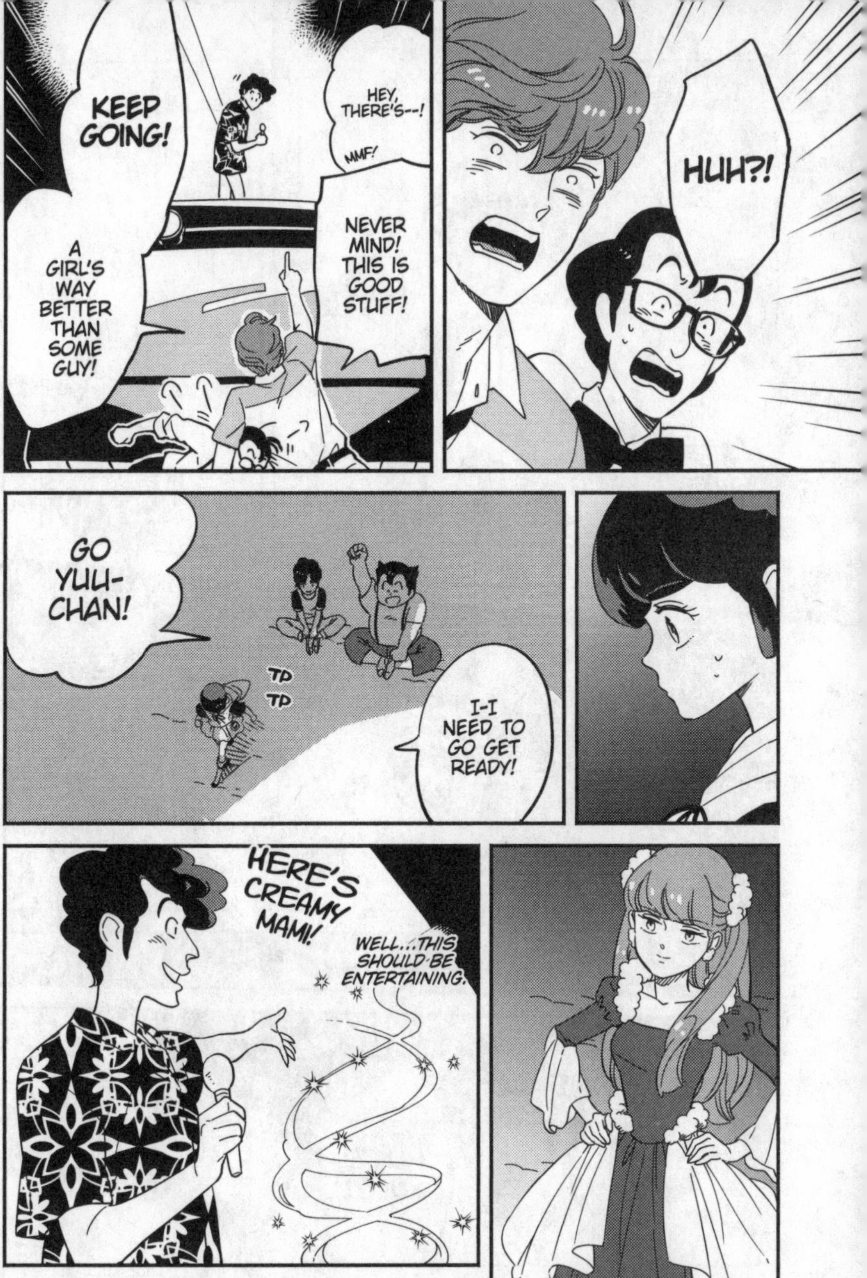
HUH?!
HEY, THERE'S--!
MMF!
NEVER MIND! THIS IS GOOD STUFF!
KEEP GOING!
A GIRL'S WAY BETTER THAN SOME GUY!
I-I NEED TO GO GET READY!
TP TP
GO YUU-CHAN!
HERE'S CREAMY MAMI!
WELL...THIS SHOULD BE ENTERTAINING.

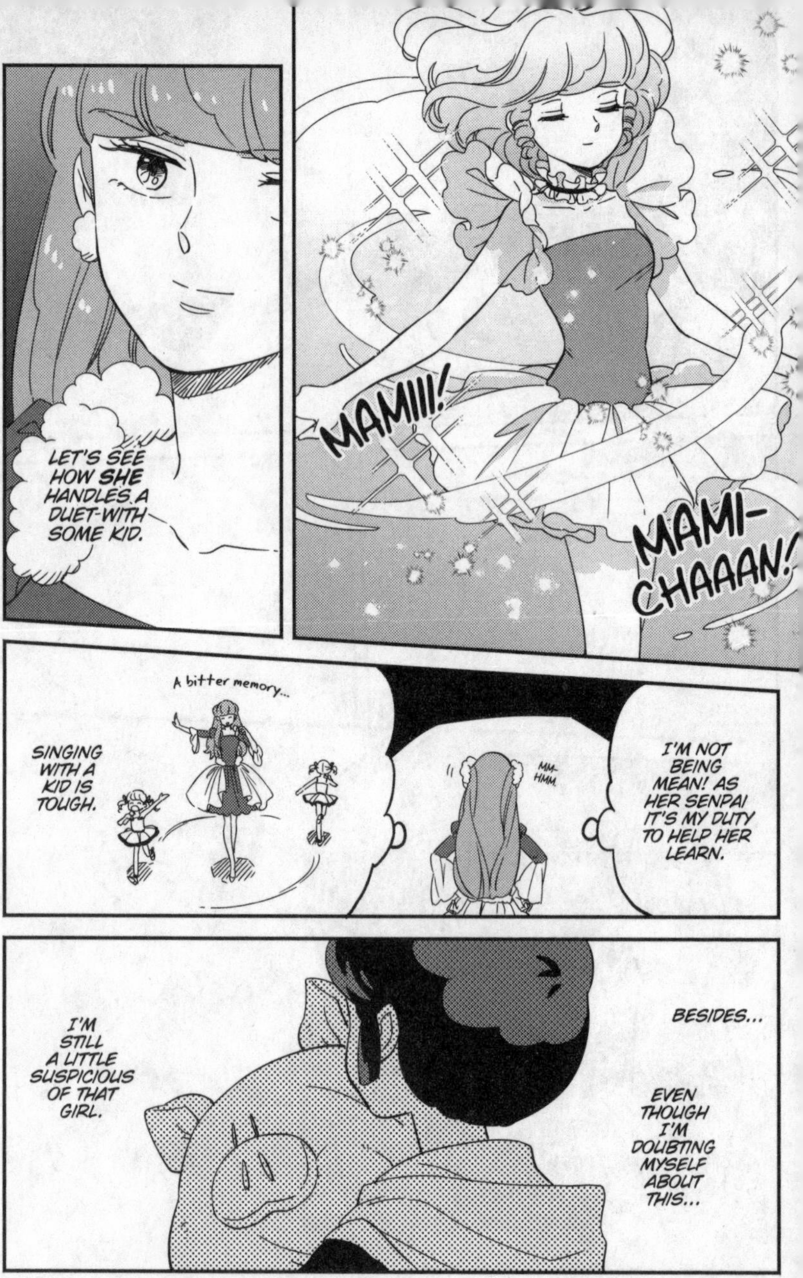
MAMIII!
MAMI-CHAAAN!
LET'S SEE HOW SHE HANDLES A DUET WITH SOME KID.
I'M NOT BEING MEAN! AS HER SENPAI IT'S MY DUTY TO HELP HER LEARN.
MM-HMM.
A bitter memory...
SINGING WITH A KID IS TOUGH.
BESIDES...
EVEN THOUGH I'M DOUBTING MYSELF ABOUT THIS...
I'M STILL A LITTLE SUSPICIOUS OF THAT GIRL.

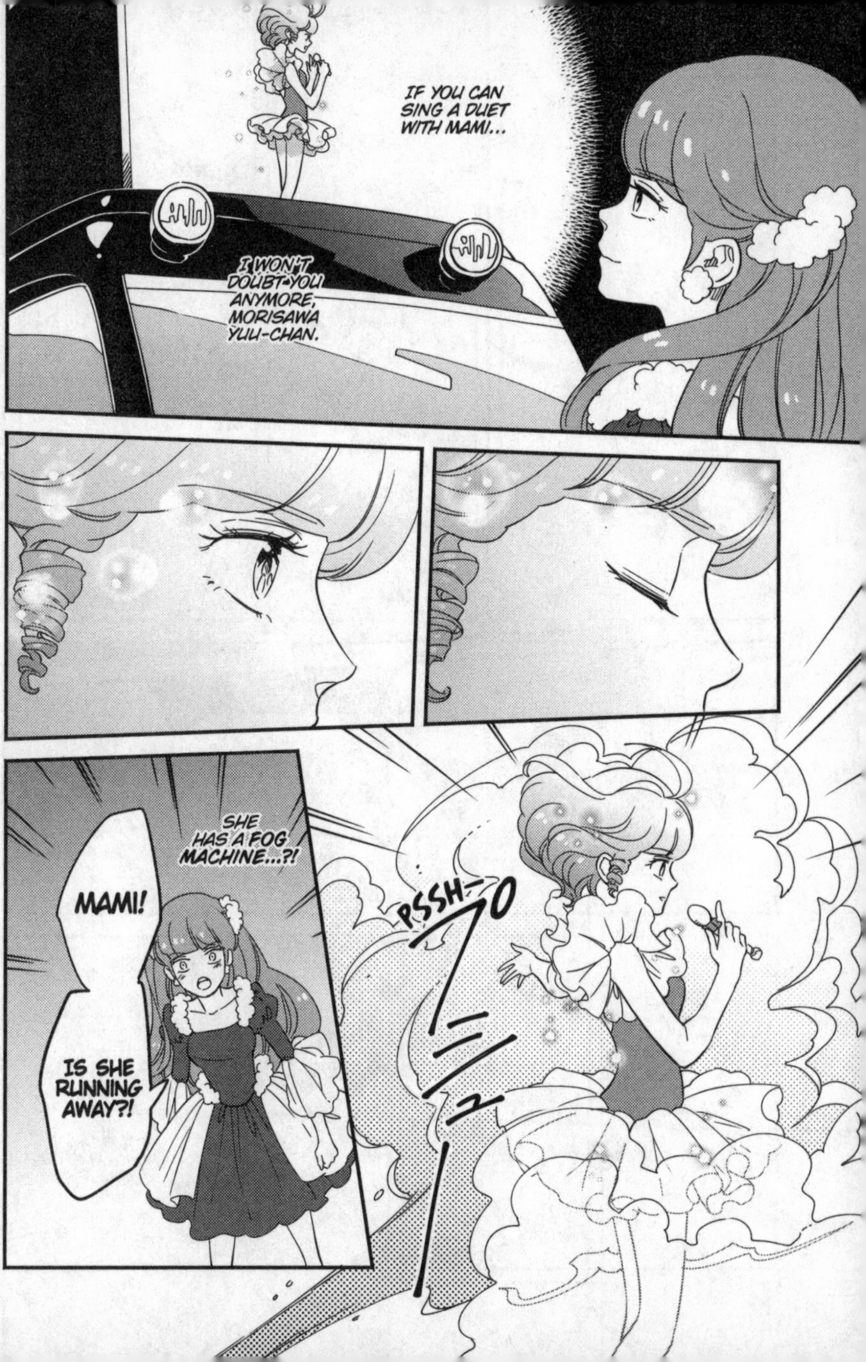
IF YOU CAN SING A DUET WITH MAMI...
I WON'T DOUBT YOU ANYMORE, MORISAWA YUU-CHAN.
PSSH
SHE HAS A FOG MACHINE...?!
MAMI!
IS SHE RUNNING AWAY?!

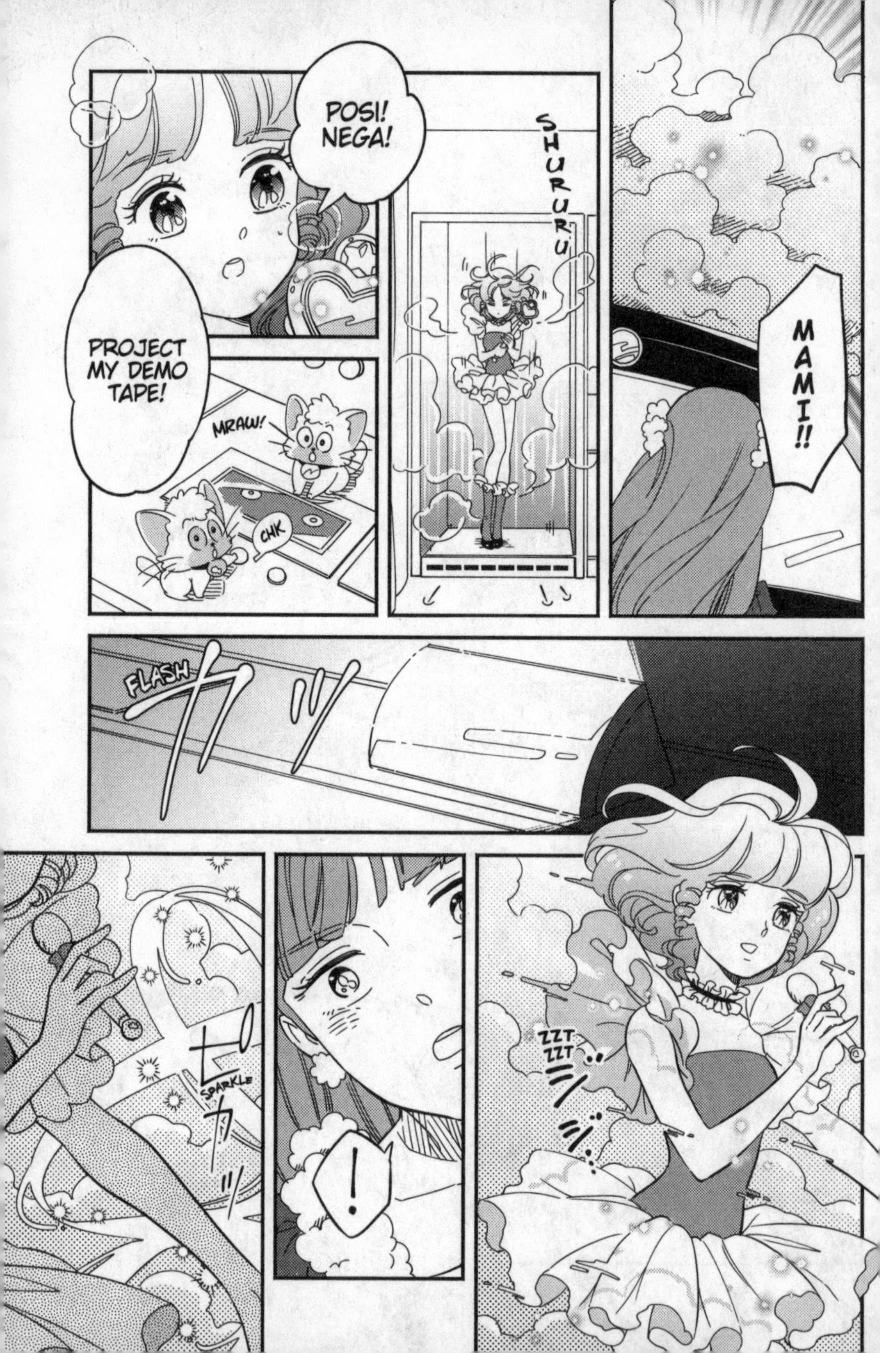
MAMI!!
SHURURU
POSI! NEGA!
PROJECT MY DEMO TAPE!
MRAW!
CHK
FLASH
ZZT ZZT
!
SPARKLE

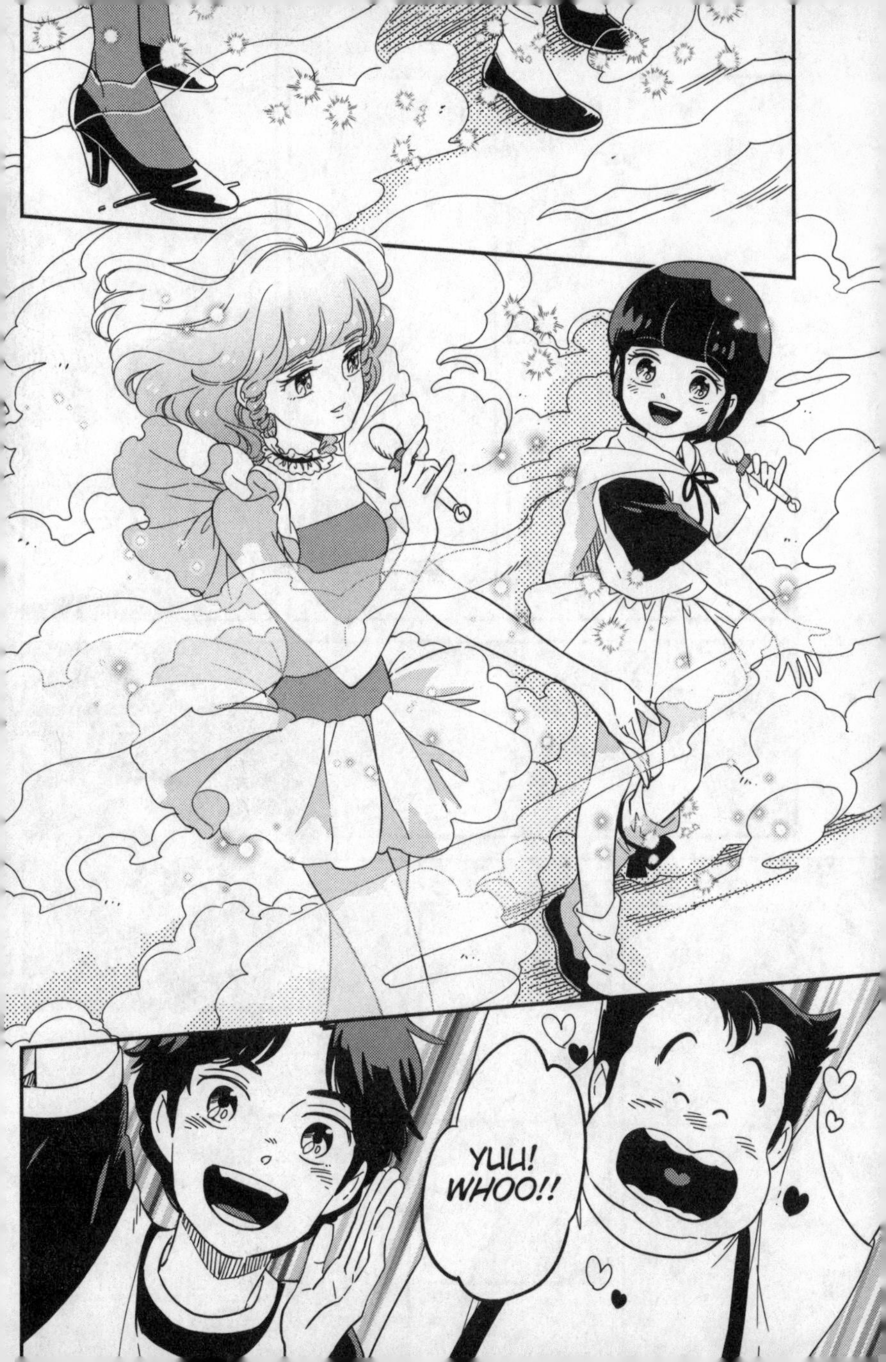
YUU!
WHOO!!

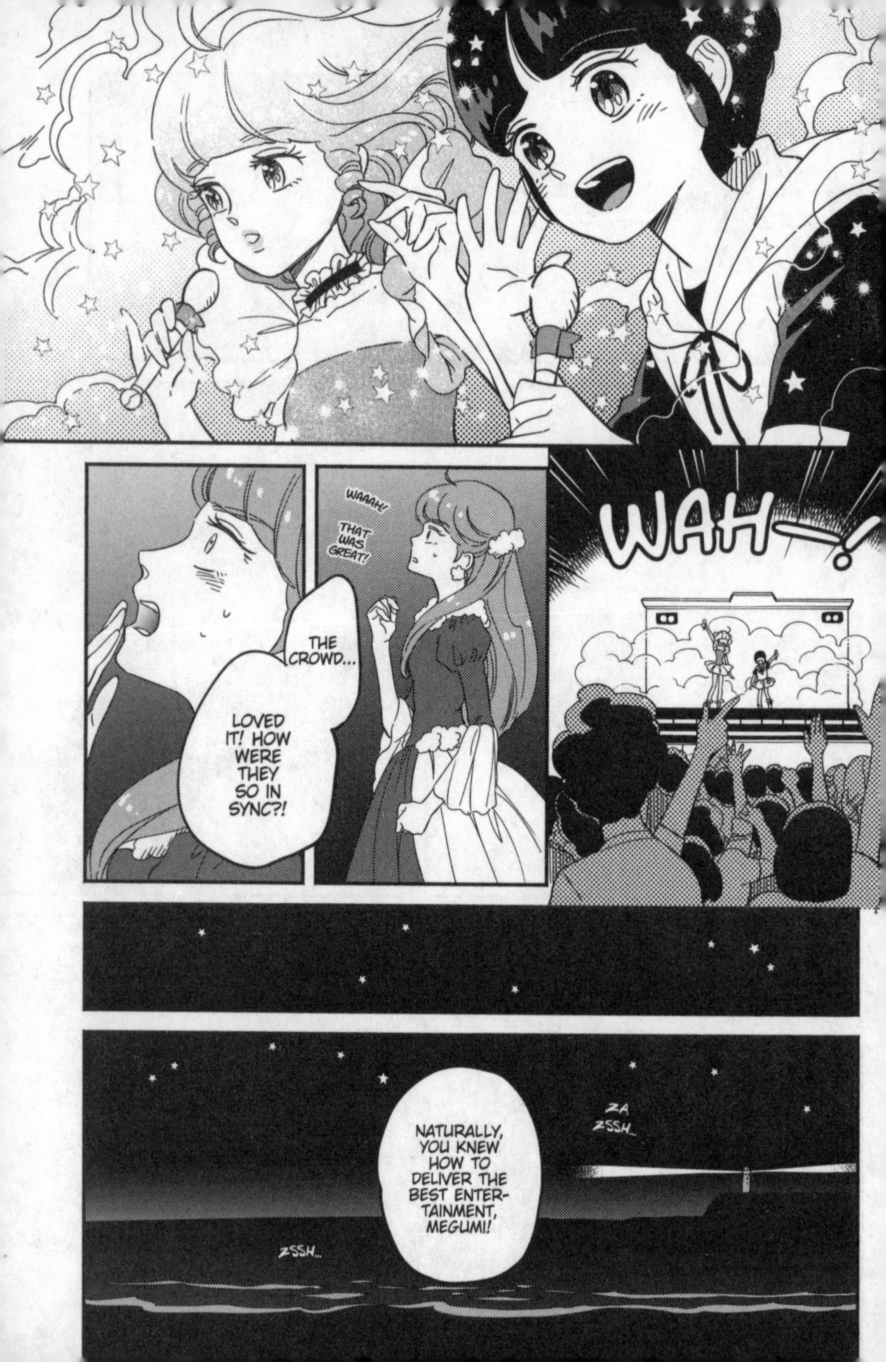
WAH—!
WAAAH!
THAT WAS GREAT!
THE CROWD...
LOVED IT! HOW WERE THEY SO IN SYNC?!
ZA ZSSH...
NATURALLY, YOU KNEW HOW TO DELIVER THE BEST ENTERTAINMENT, MEGUMI!
ZSSH...

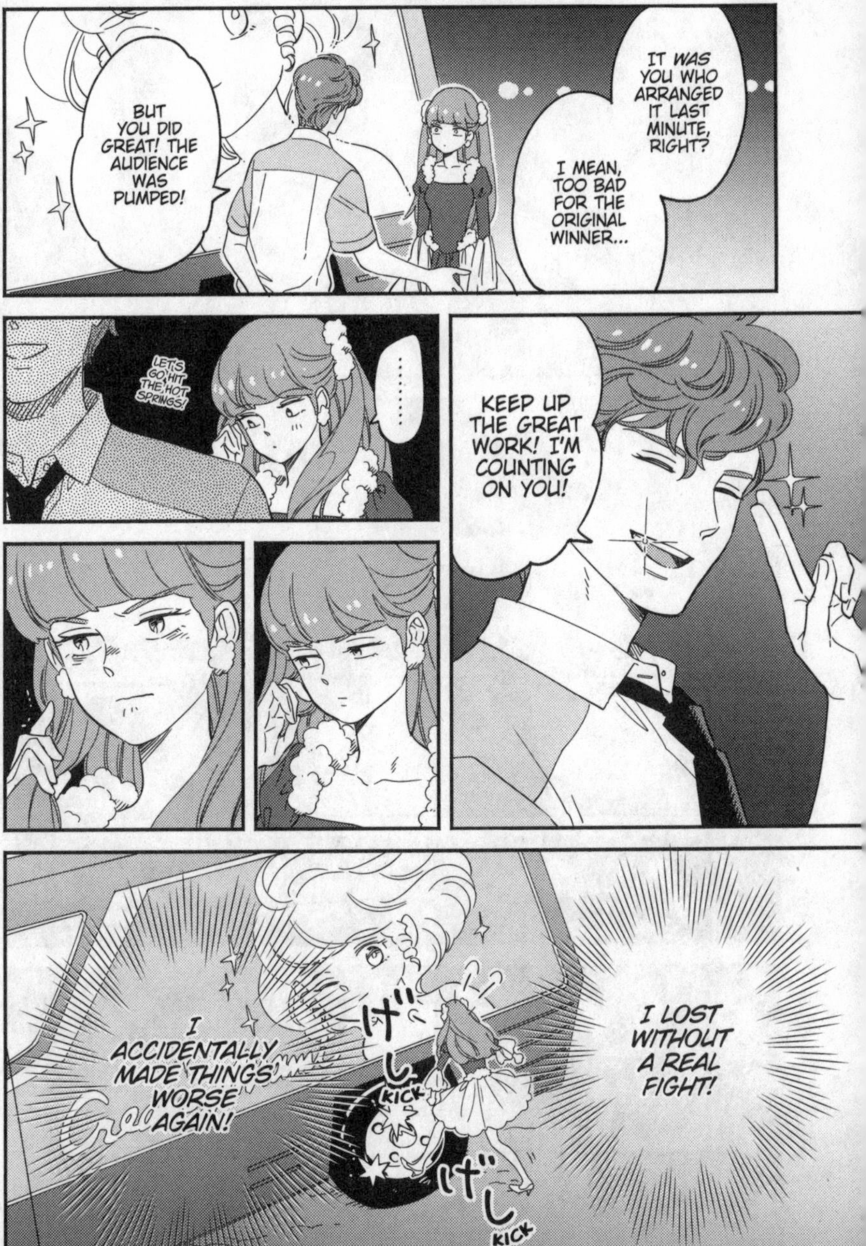
IT WAS YOU WHO ARRANGED IT LAST MINUTE, RIGHT?
I MEAN, TOO BAD FOR THE ORIGINAL WINNER...
BUT YOU DID GREAT! THE AUDIENCE WAS PUMPED!
KEEP UP THE GREAT WORK! I'M COUNTING ON YOU!
......
LET'S GO HIT THE HOT SPRINGS!
I LOST WITHOUT A REAL FIGHT!
げし
KICK
げし
KICK
I ACCIDENTALLY MADE THINGS WORSE AGAIN!

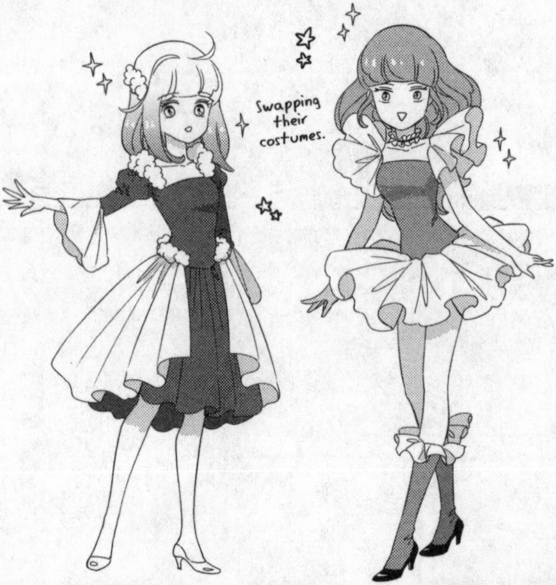
Swapping their costumes.

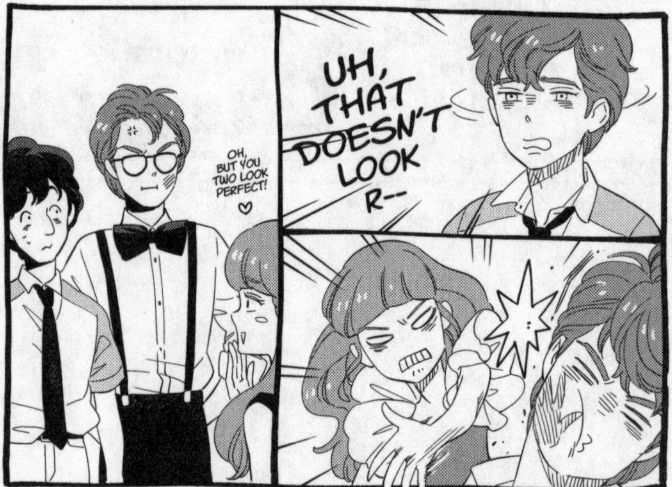
UH, THAT DOESN'T LOOK R--
OH, BUT YOU TWO LOOK PERFECT! ♡

Magical Angel

Creamy Mami

and the
Spoiled Princess

11 Studio Blackout: Part 1

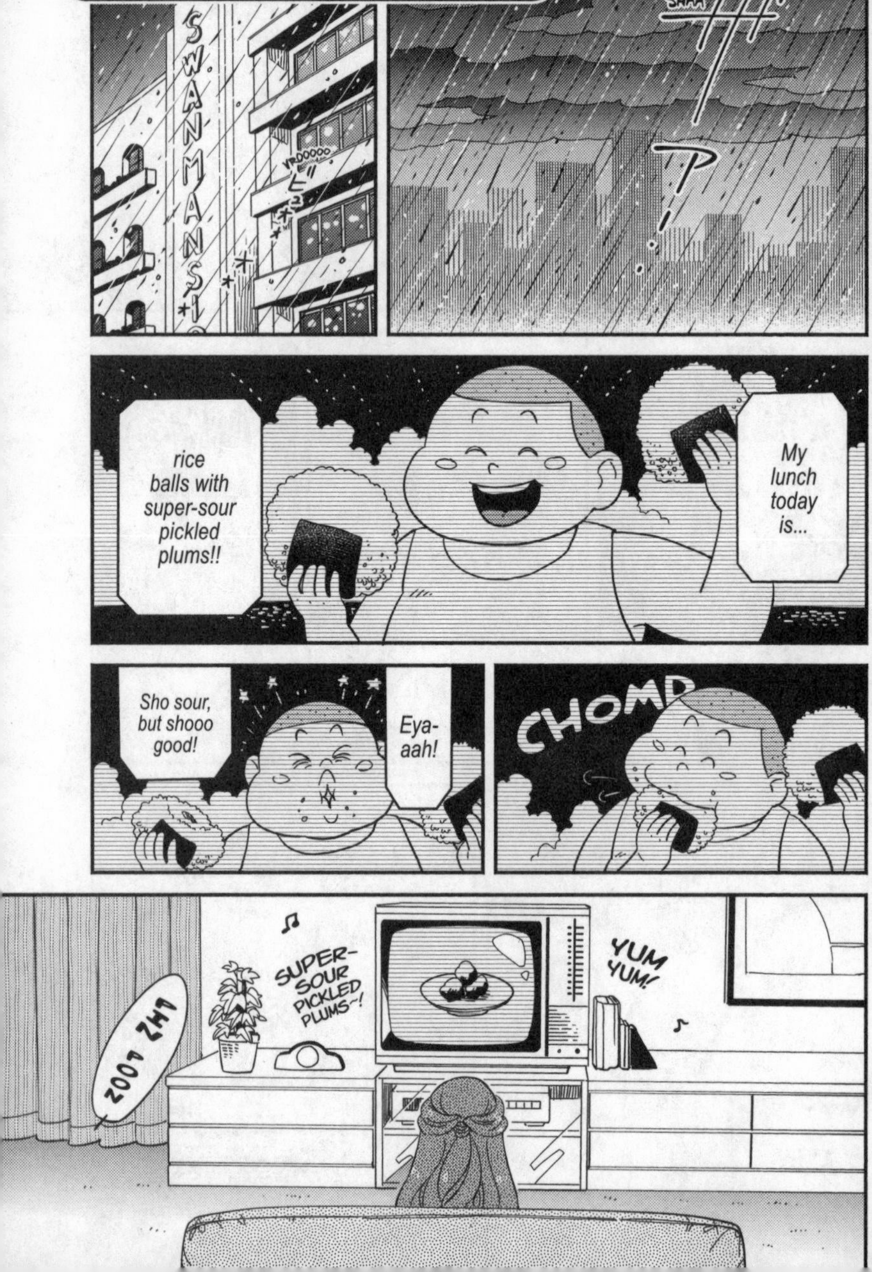
SHAA
VRDOOOO
My lunch today is...
rice balls with super-sour pickled plums!!
CHOMP
Eya-aah!
Sho sour, but shooo good!
YUM YUM!
SUPER-SOUR PICKLED PLUMS~!

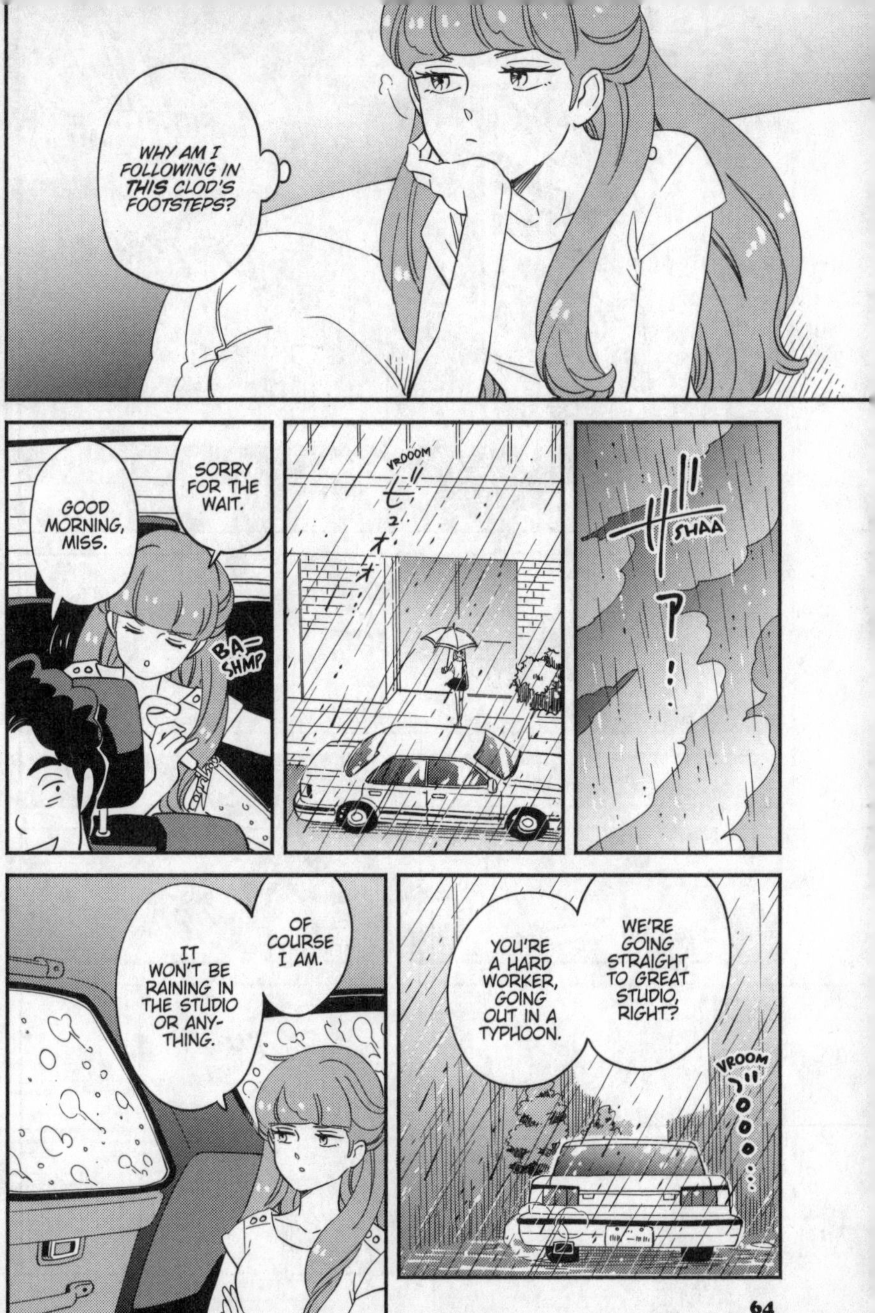
WHY AM I FOLLOWING IN THIS CLOD'S FOOTSTEPS?
SHAA
VROOM
SORRY FOR THE WAIT.
GOOD MORNING, MISS.
BA-SHMP
WE'RE GOING STRAIGHT TO GREAT STUDIO, RIGHT?
YOU'RE A HARD WORKER, GOING OUT IN A TYPHOON.
VROOM
OF COURSE I AM.
IT WON'T BE RAINING IN THE STUDIO OR ANYTHING.

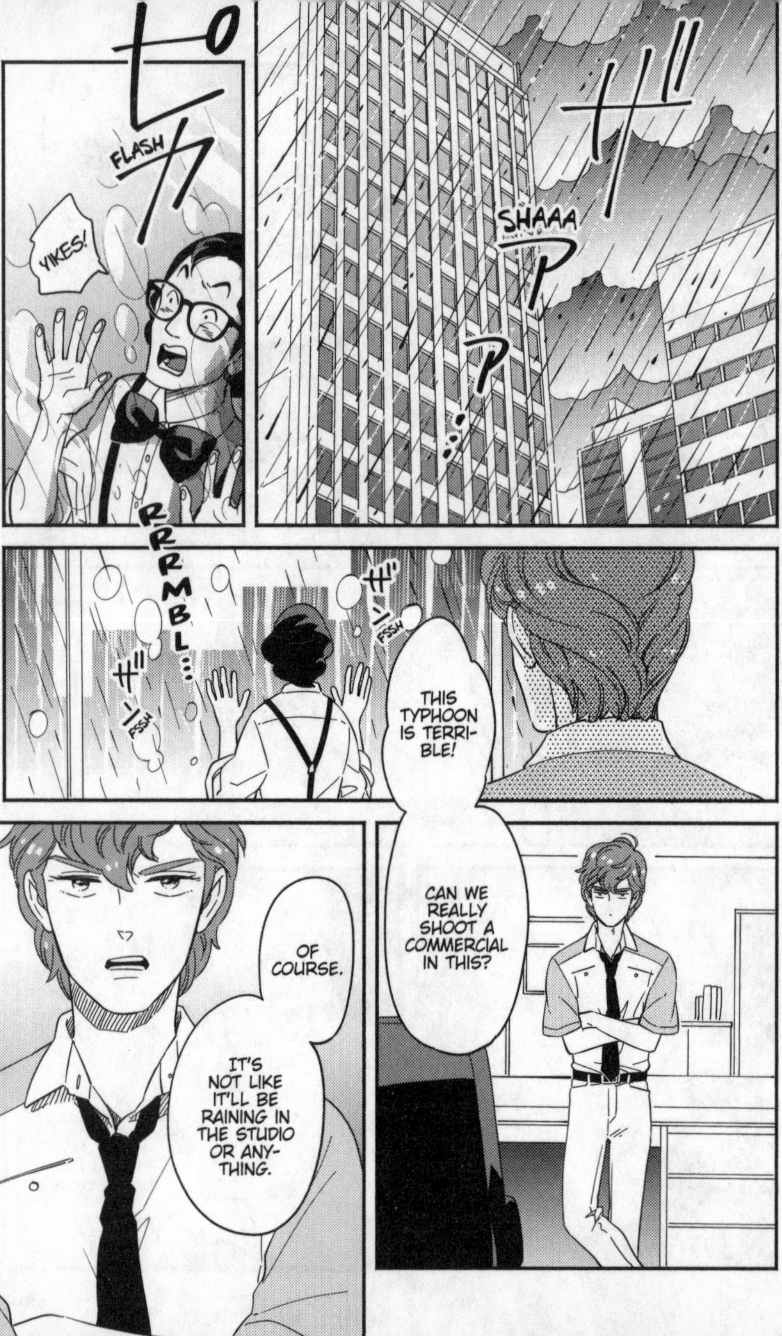
SHAAA
FLASH
YIKES!
RRRMBL...
FSSH
FSSH
THIS TYPHOON IS TERRIBLE!
CAN WE REALLY SHOOT A COMMERCIAL IN THIS?
OF COURSE.
IT'S NOT LIKE IT'LL BE RAINING IN THE STUDIO OR ANYTHING.

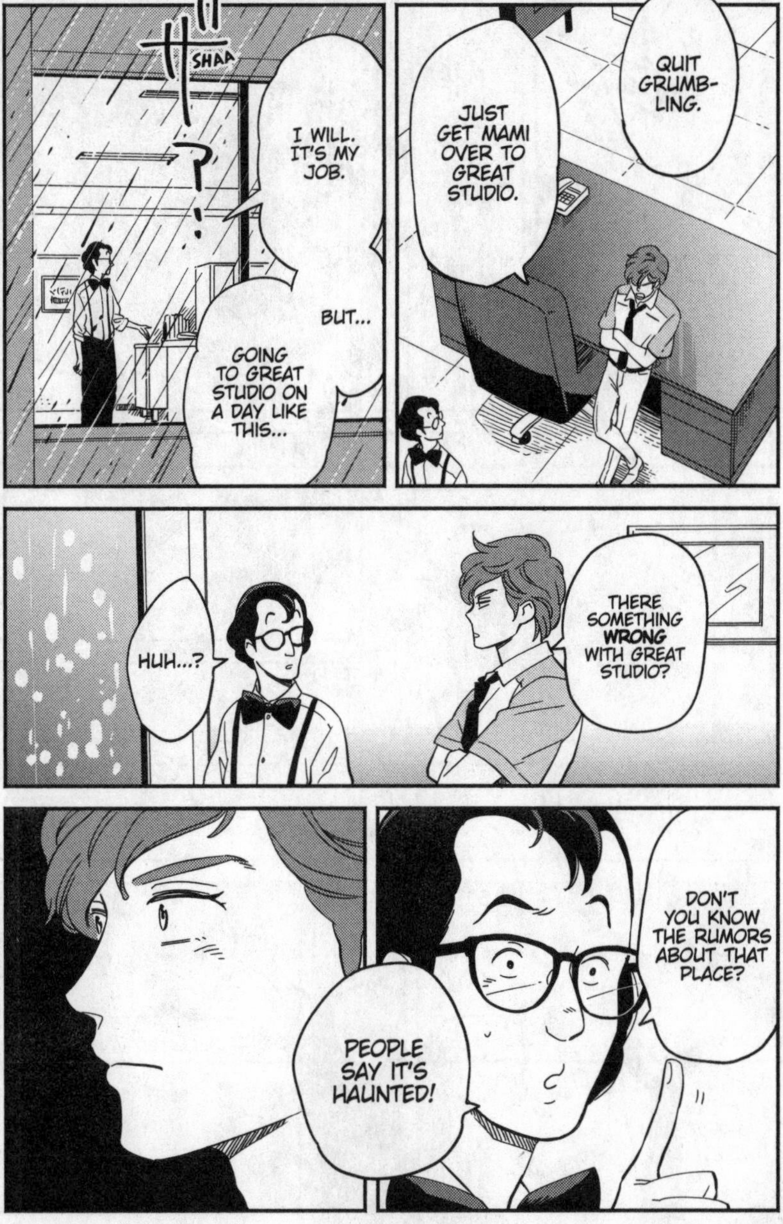
QUIT GRUMBLING.
JUST GET MAMI OVER TO GREAT STUDIO.
SHAA
I WILL. IT'S MY JOB.
BUT...
GOING TO GREAT STUDIO ON A DAY LIKE THIS...
THERE SOMETHING **WRONG** WITH GREAT STUDIO?
HUH...?
DON'T YOU KNOW THE RUMORS ABOUT THAT PLACE?
PEOPLE SAY IT'S HAUNTED!

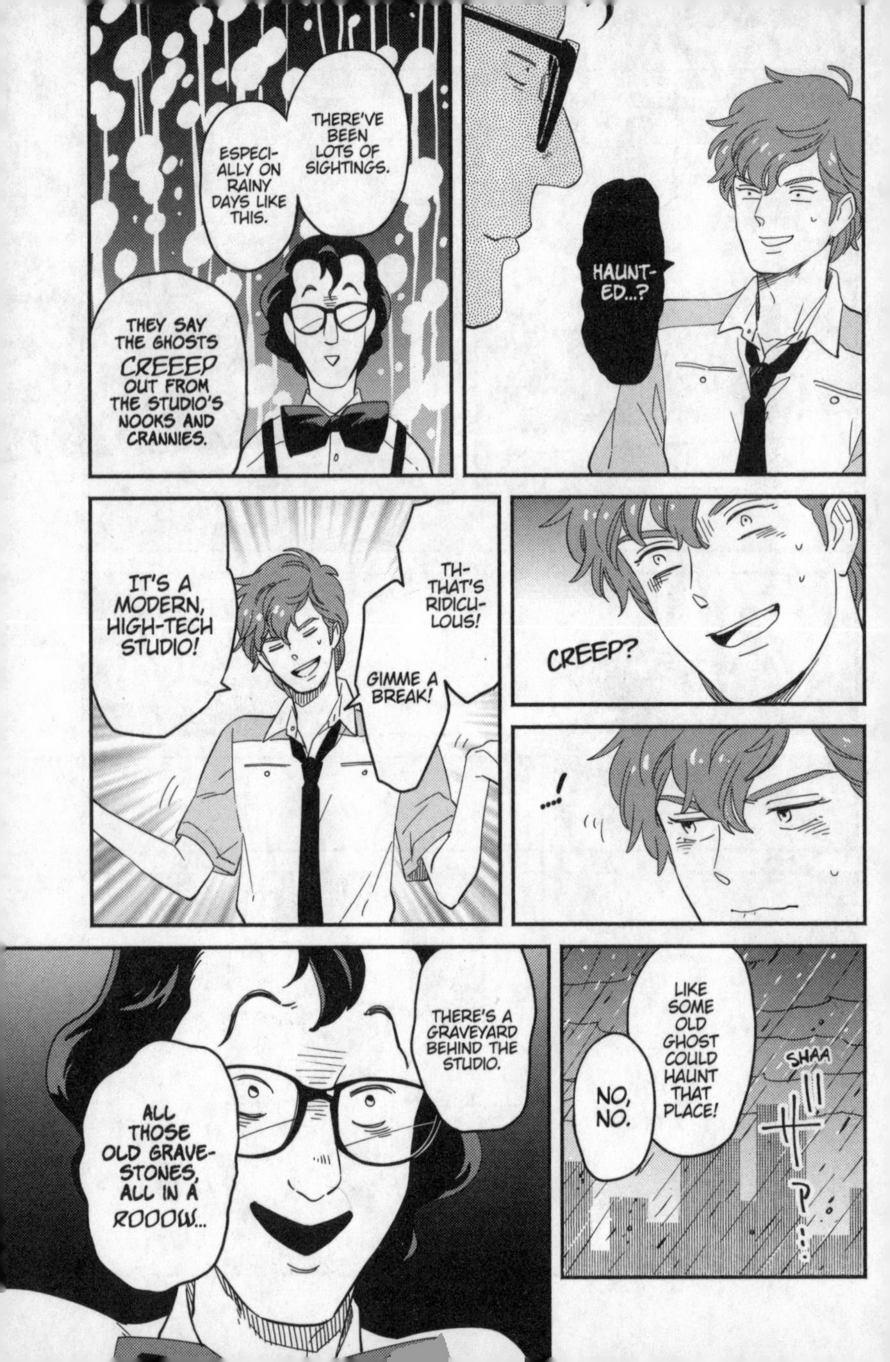
HAUNTED...?
THERE'VE BEEN LOTS OF SIGHTINGS.
ESPECIALLY ON RAINY DAYS LIKE THIS.
THEY SAY THE GHOSTS CREEEP OUT FROM THE STUDIO'S NOOKS AND CRANNIES.
CREEP?
...!
TH-THAT'S RIDICULOUS!
GIMME A BREAK!
IT'S A MODERN, HIGH-TECH STUDIO!
LIKE SOME OLD GHOST COULD HAUNT THAT PLACE!
NO, NO.
SHAA
THERE'S A GRAVEYARD BEHIND THE STUDIO.
ALL THOSE OLD GRAVESTONES, ALL IN A ROOOW...

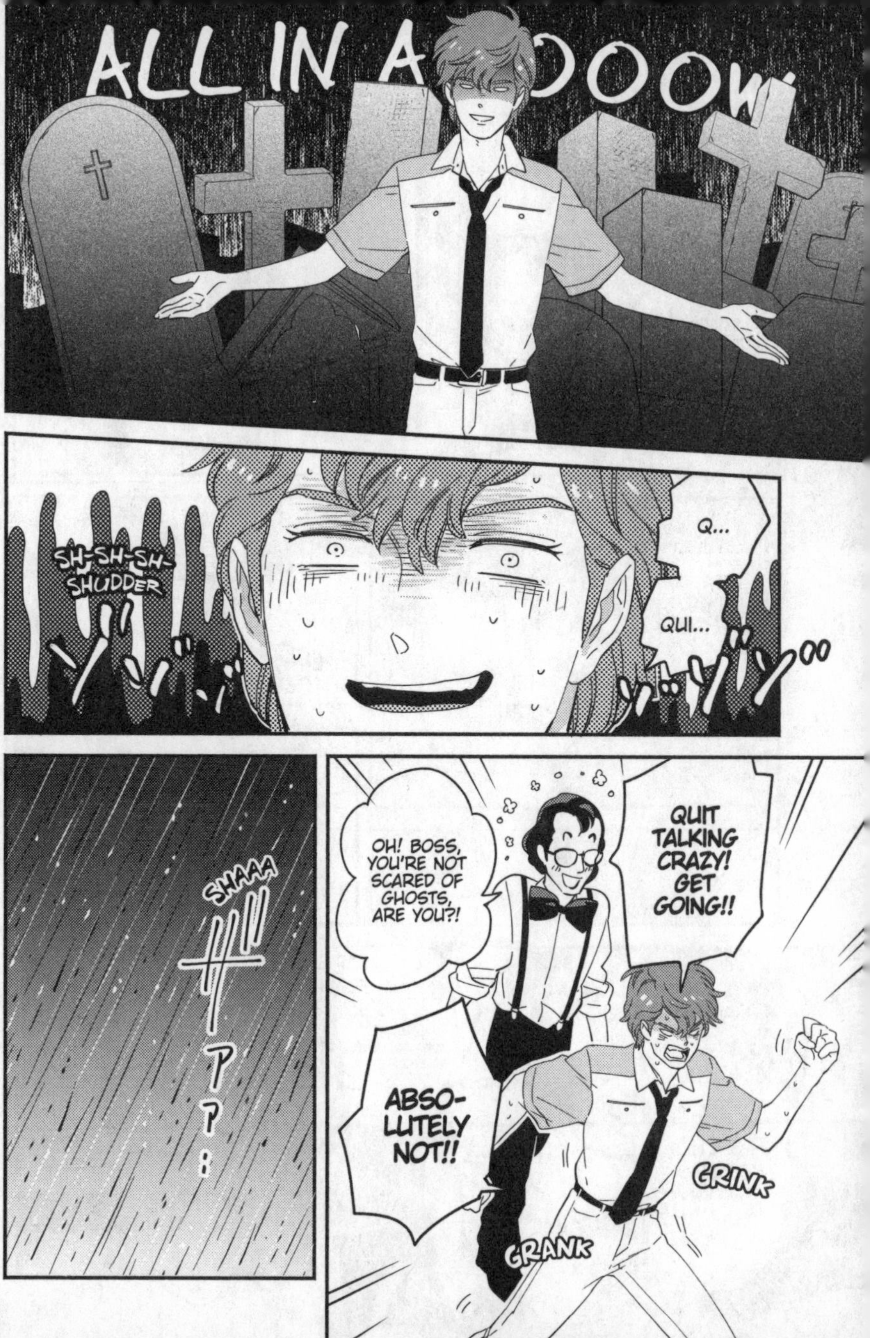
ALL IN A
OOOW
Q...
QUI...
SH-SH-SH-SHUDDER
QUIT TALKING CRAZY! GET GOING!!
OH! BOSS, YOU'RE NOT SCARED OF GHOSTS, ARE YOU?!
ABSO-LUTELY NOT!!
GRINK
GRANK
SHAAA

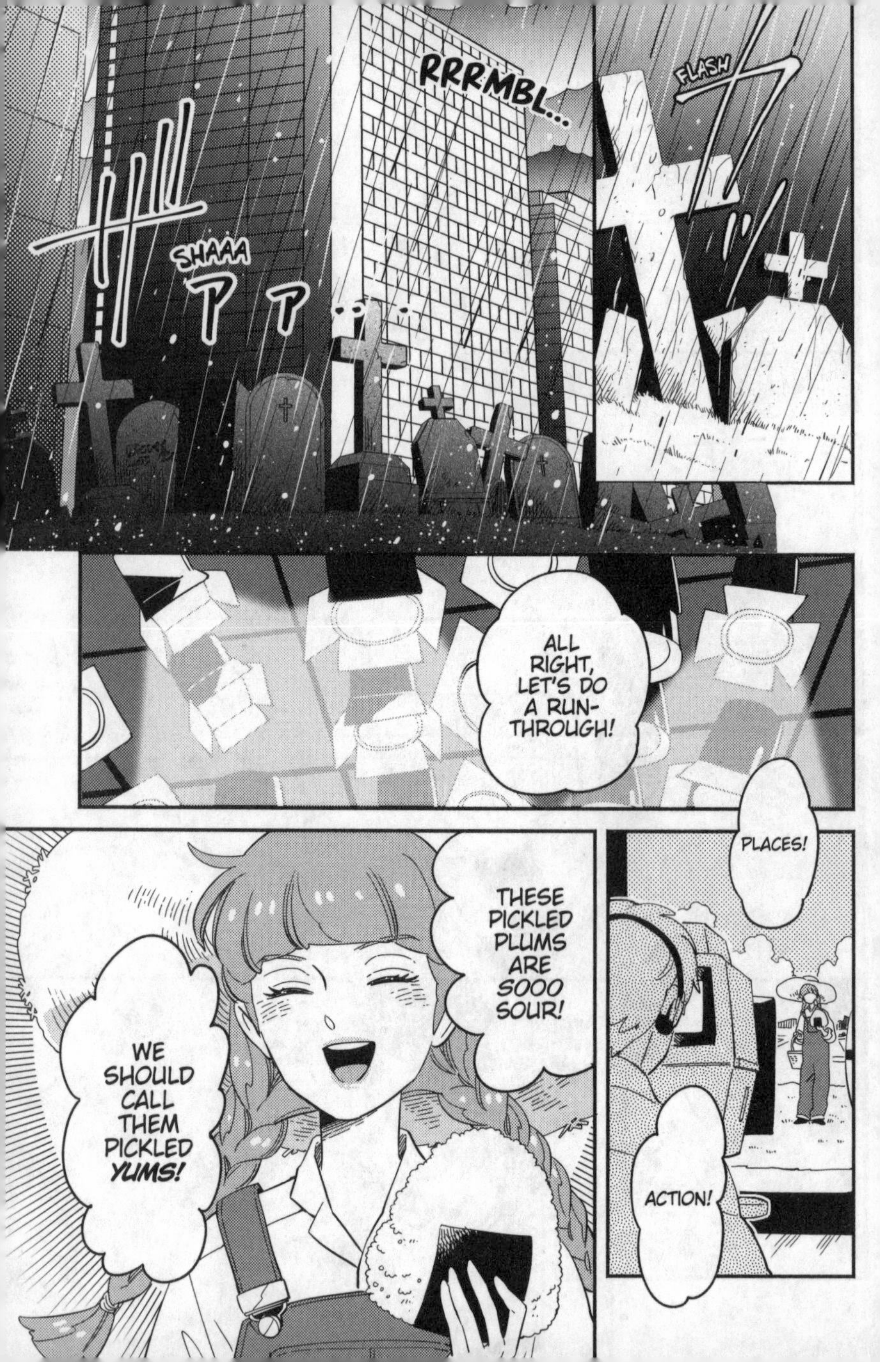
FLASH
RRRMBL...
SHAAA
ALL RIGHT, LET'S DO A RUN-THROUGH!
PLACES!
ACTION!
THESE PICKLED PLUMS ARE SOOO SOUR!
WE SHOULD CALL THEM PICKLED YUMS!

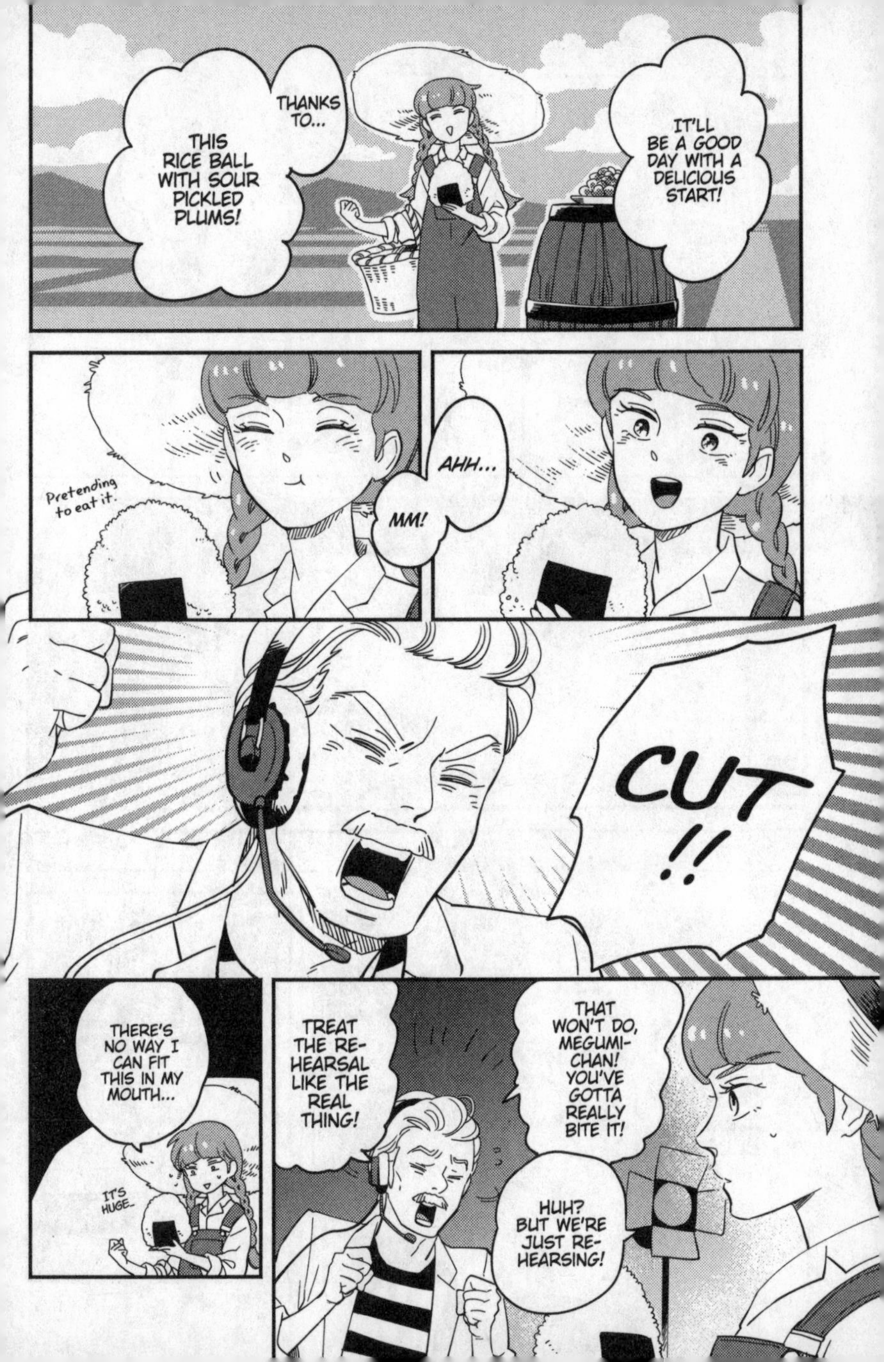
IT'LL BE A GOOD DAY WITH A DELICIOUS START!
THANKS TO...
THIS RICE BALL WITH SOUR PICKLED PLUMS!
AHH...
MM!
Pretending to eat it.
CUT!!
THAT WON'T DO, MEGUMI-CHAN! YOU'VE GOTTA REALLY BITE IT!
HUH? BUT WE'RE JUST RE-HEARSING!
TREAT THE RE-HEARSAL LIKE THE REAL THING!
THERE'S NO WAY I CAN FIT THIS IN MY MOUTH...
IT'S HUGE...

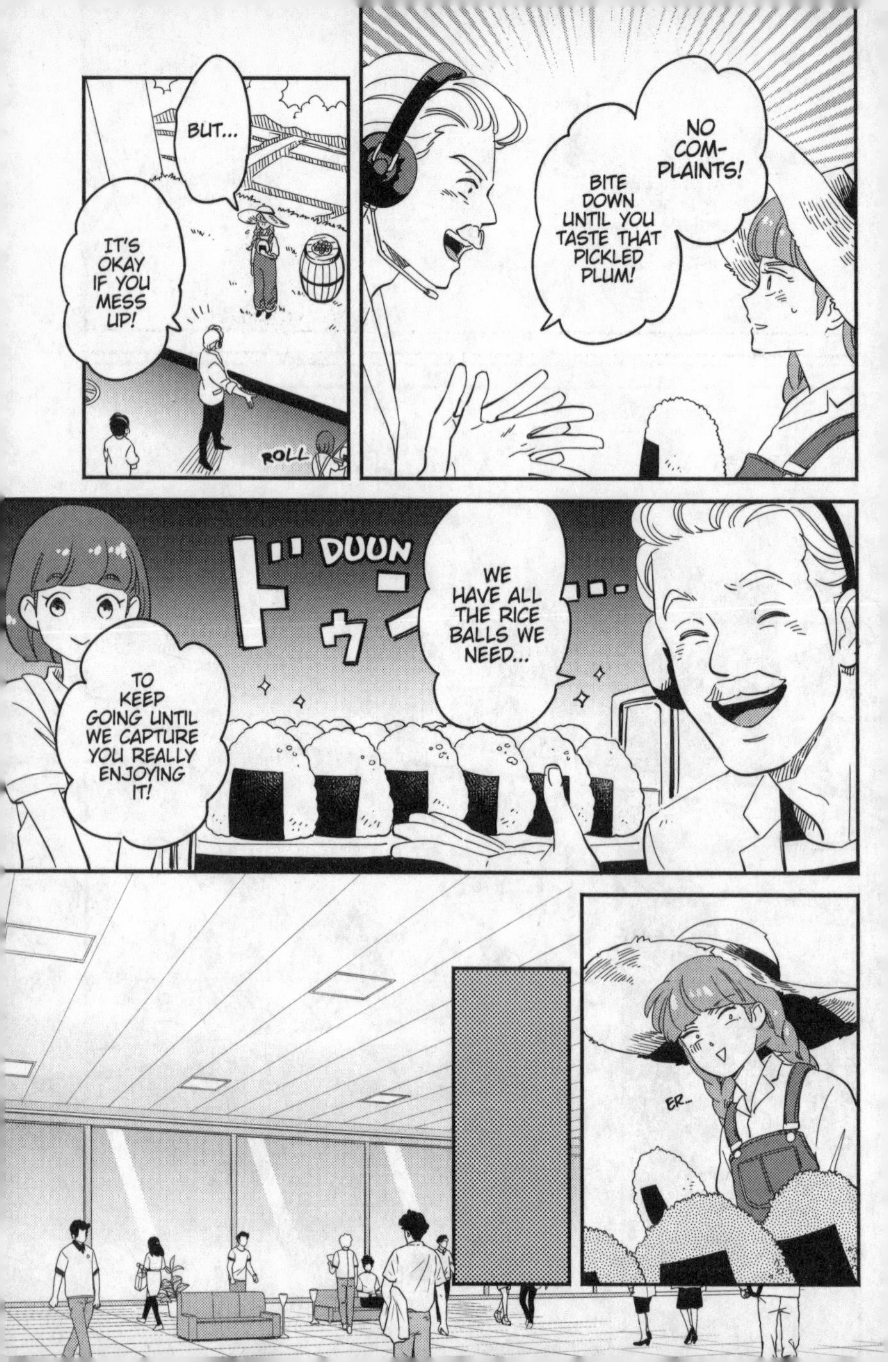
NO COM-PLAINTS!
BITE DOWN UNTIL YOU TASTE THAT PICKLED PLUM!
BUT...
IT'S OKAY IF YOU MESS UP!
ROLL
WE HAVE ALL THE RICE BALLS WE NEED...
DUUN
TO KEEP GOING UNTIL WE CAPTURE YOU REALLY ENJOYING IT!
ER..

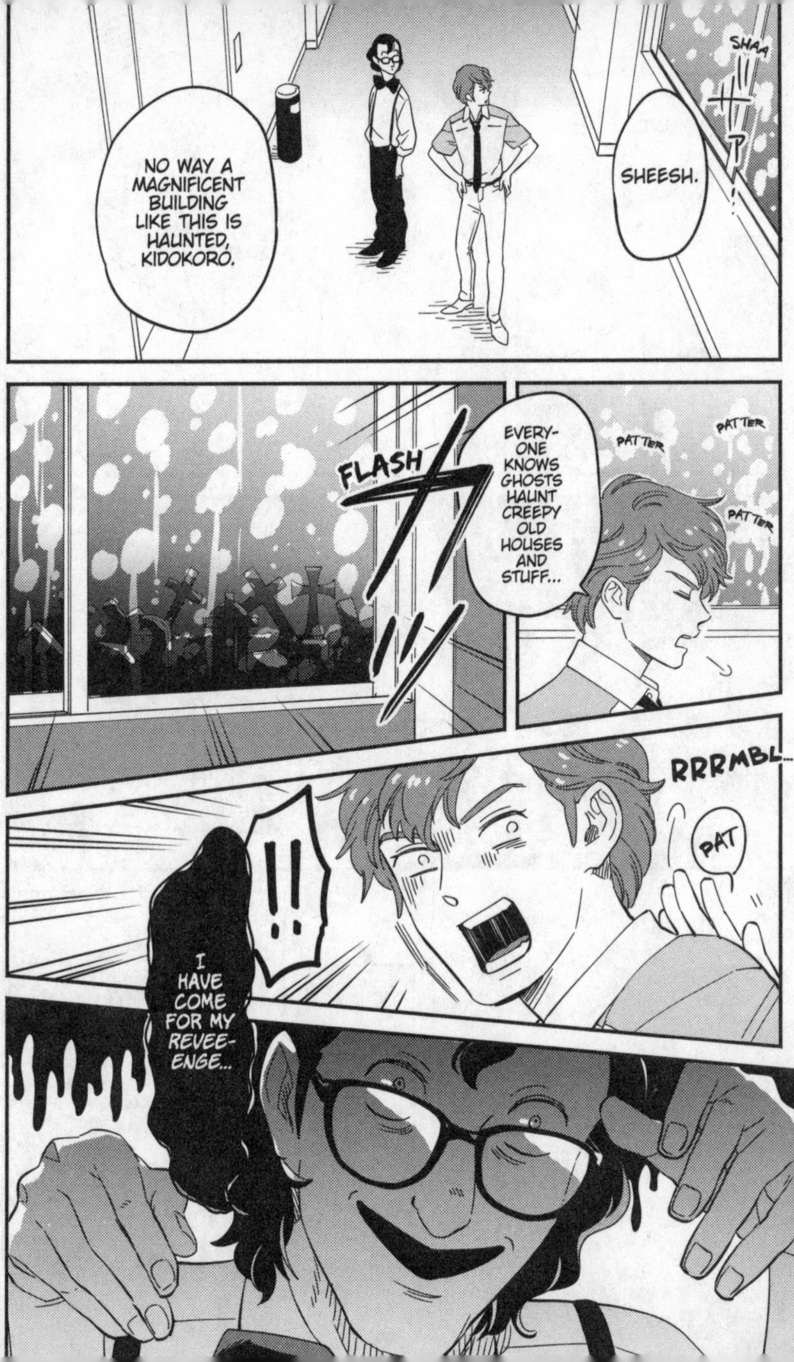
SHAA
SHEESH.
NO WAY A MAGNIFICENT BUILDING LIKE THIS IS HAUNTED, KIDOKORO.
PATTER
PATTER
PATTER
EVERY-ONE KNOWS GHOSTS HAUNT CREEPY OLD HOUSES AND STUFF...
FLASH
RRRMBL...
PAT
!!
I HAVE COME FOR MY REVEEE-ENGE...

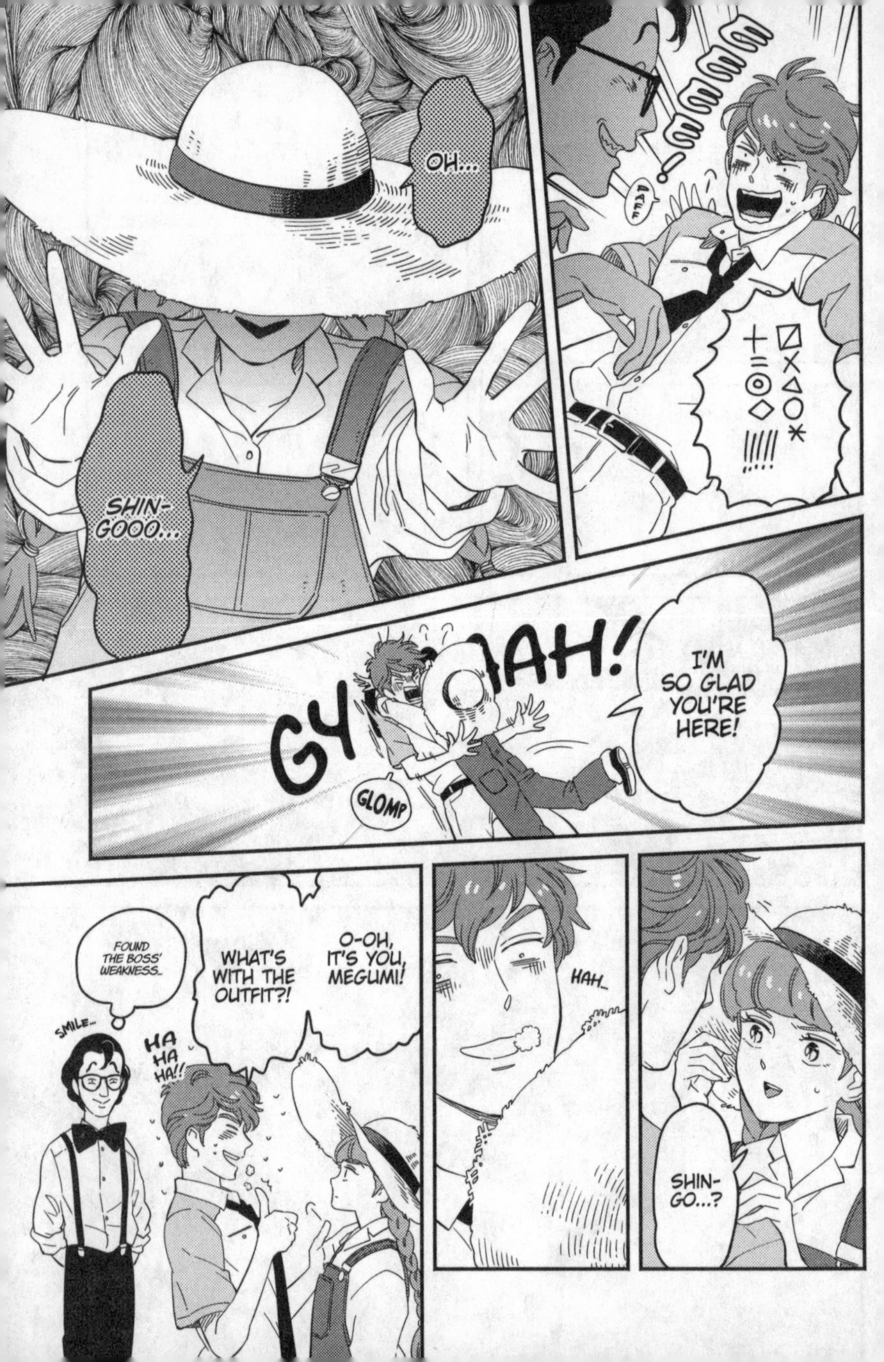

EEEEEE!
PAFF
!!!!!
OH...
SHIN-GOOO...
GY AH!
I'M SO GLAD YOU'RE HERE!
GLOMP
SHIN-GO...?
HAH...
O-OH, IT'S YOU, MEGUMI!
WHAT'S WITH THE OUTFIT?!
HA HA HA!!
FOUND THE BOSS' WEAKNESS...
SMILE...

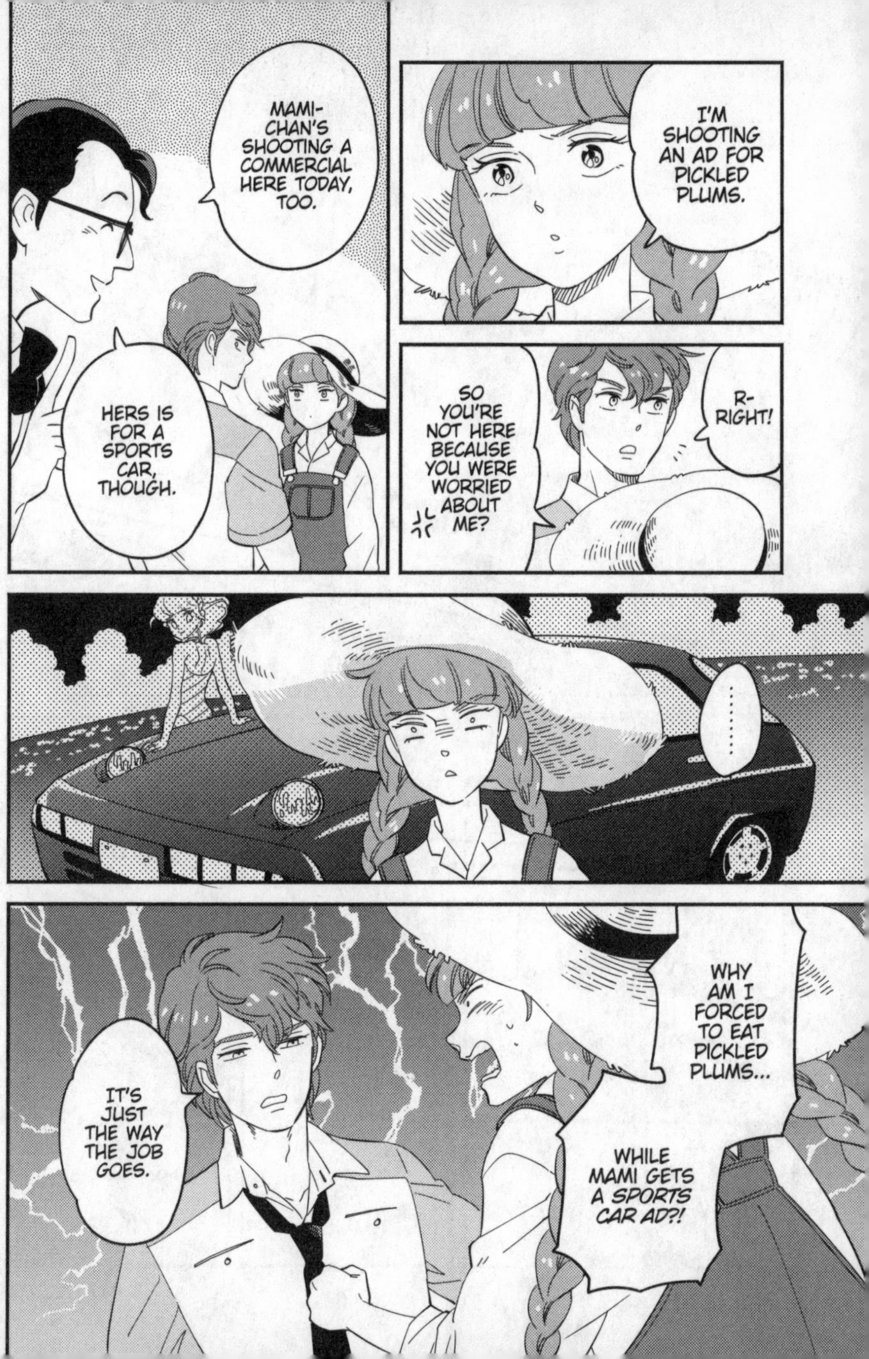
I'M SHOOTING AN AD FOR PICKLED PLUMS.
R-RIGHT!
SO YOU'RE NOT HERE BECAUSE YOU WERE WORRIED ABOUT ME?
MAMI-CHAN'S SHOOTING A COMMERCIAL HERE TODAY, TOO.
HERS IS FOR A SPORTS CAR, THOUGH.
......
WHY AM I FORCED TO EAT PICKLED PLUMS...
WHILE MAMI GETS A *SPORTS CAR AD*?!
IT'S JUST THE WAY THE JOB GOES.

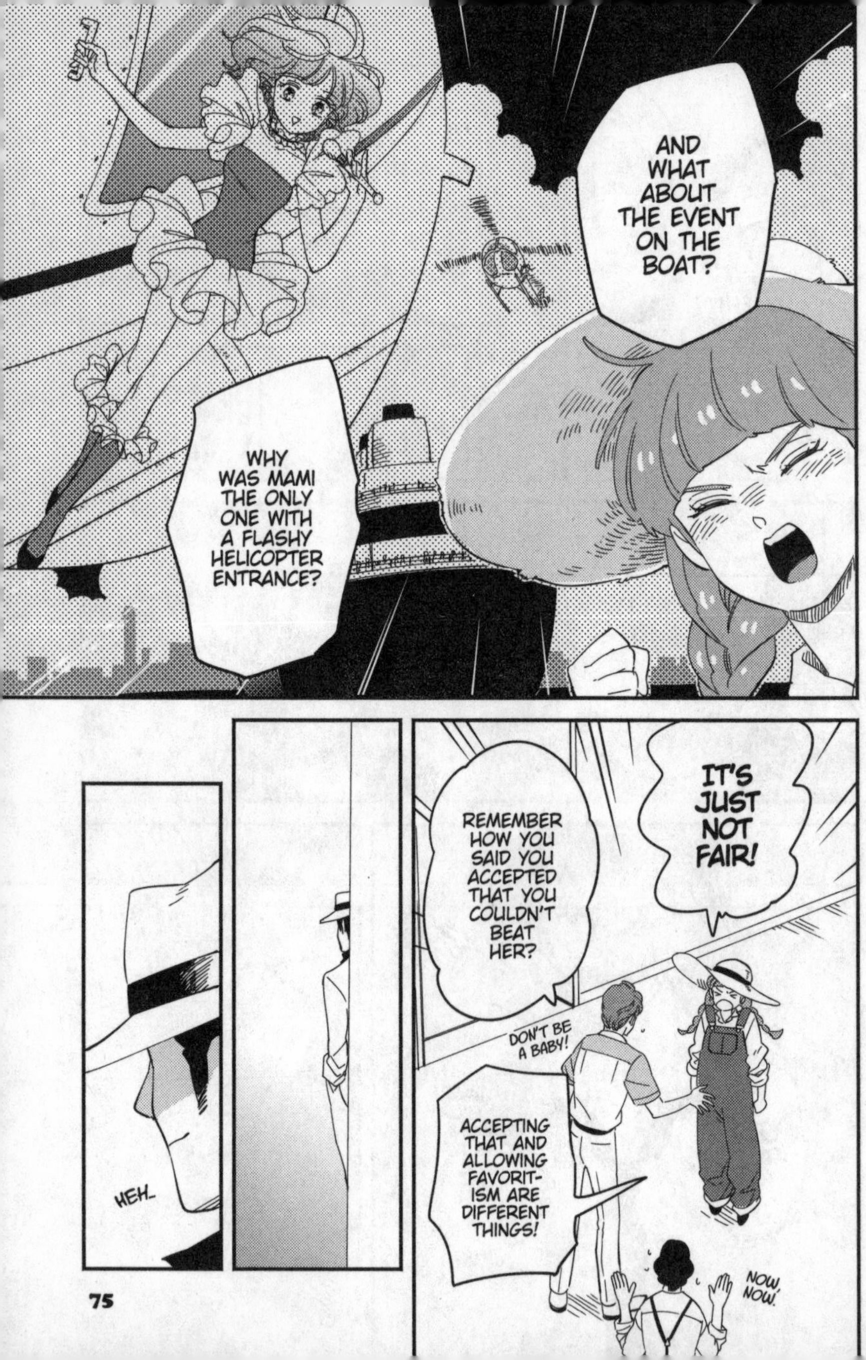
AND WHAT ABOUT THE EVENT ON THE BOAT?
WHY WAS MAMI THE ONLY ONE WITH A FLASHY HELICOPTER ENTRANCE?
IT'S JUST NOT FAIR!
REMEMBER HOW YOU SAID YOU ACCEPTED THAT YOU COULDN'T BEAT HER?
DON'T BE A BABY!
ACCEPTING THAT AND ALLOWING FAVORIT-ISM ARE DIFFERENT THINGS!
NOW, NOW.
HEH...

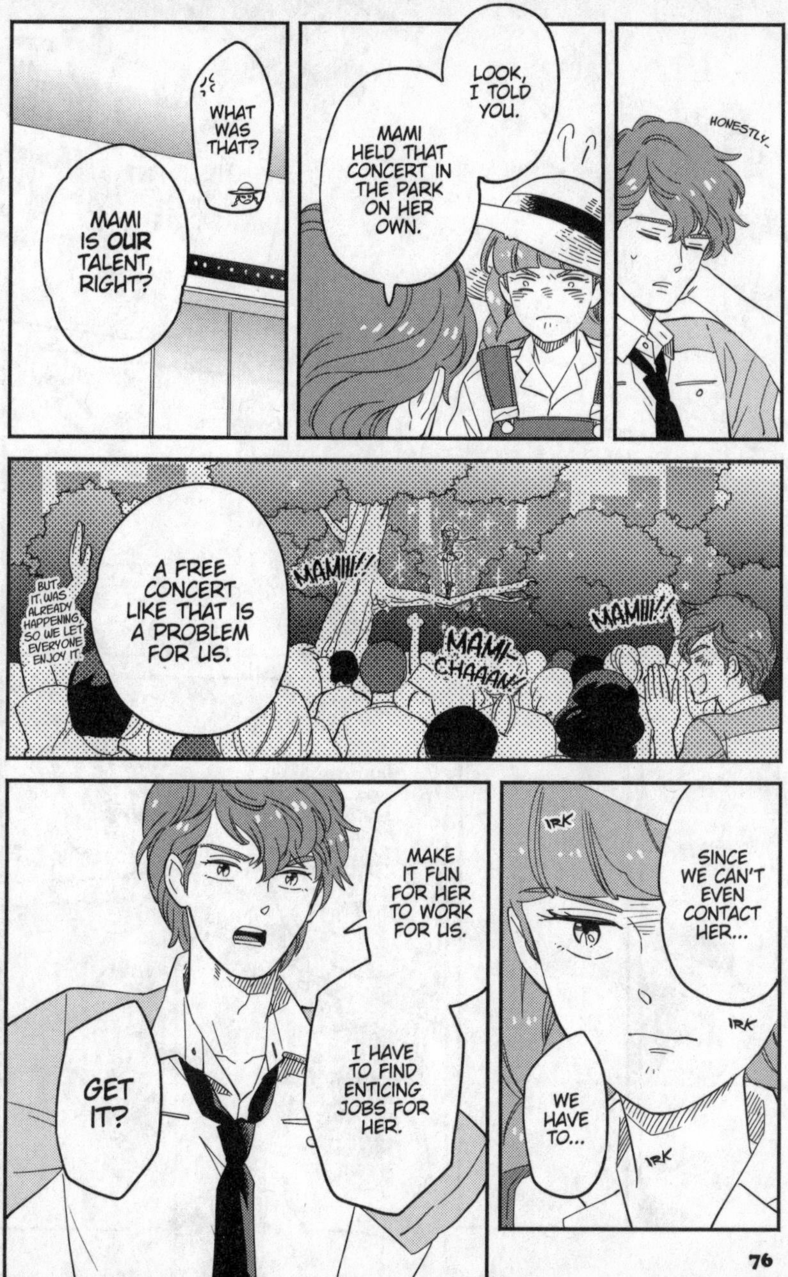
HONESTLY_
LOOK, I TOLD YOU.
MAMI HELD THAT CONCERT IN THE PARK ON HER OWN.
WHAT WAS THAT?
MAMI IS **OUR** TALENT, RIGHT?
MAMIII!!
MAMIII!!
A FREE CONCERT LIKE THAT IS A PROBLEM FOR US.
MAMI-CHAAAN!!
BUT IT WAS ALREADY HAPPENING, SO WE LET EVERYONE ENJOY IT.
IRK
SINCE WE CAN'T EVEN CONTACT HER...
IRK
WE HAVE TO...
IRK
MAKE IT FUN FOR HER TO WORK FOR US.
I HAVE TO FIND ENTICING JOBS FOR HER.
GET IT?

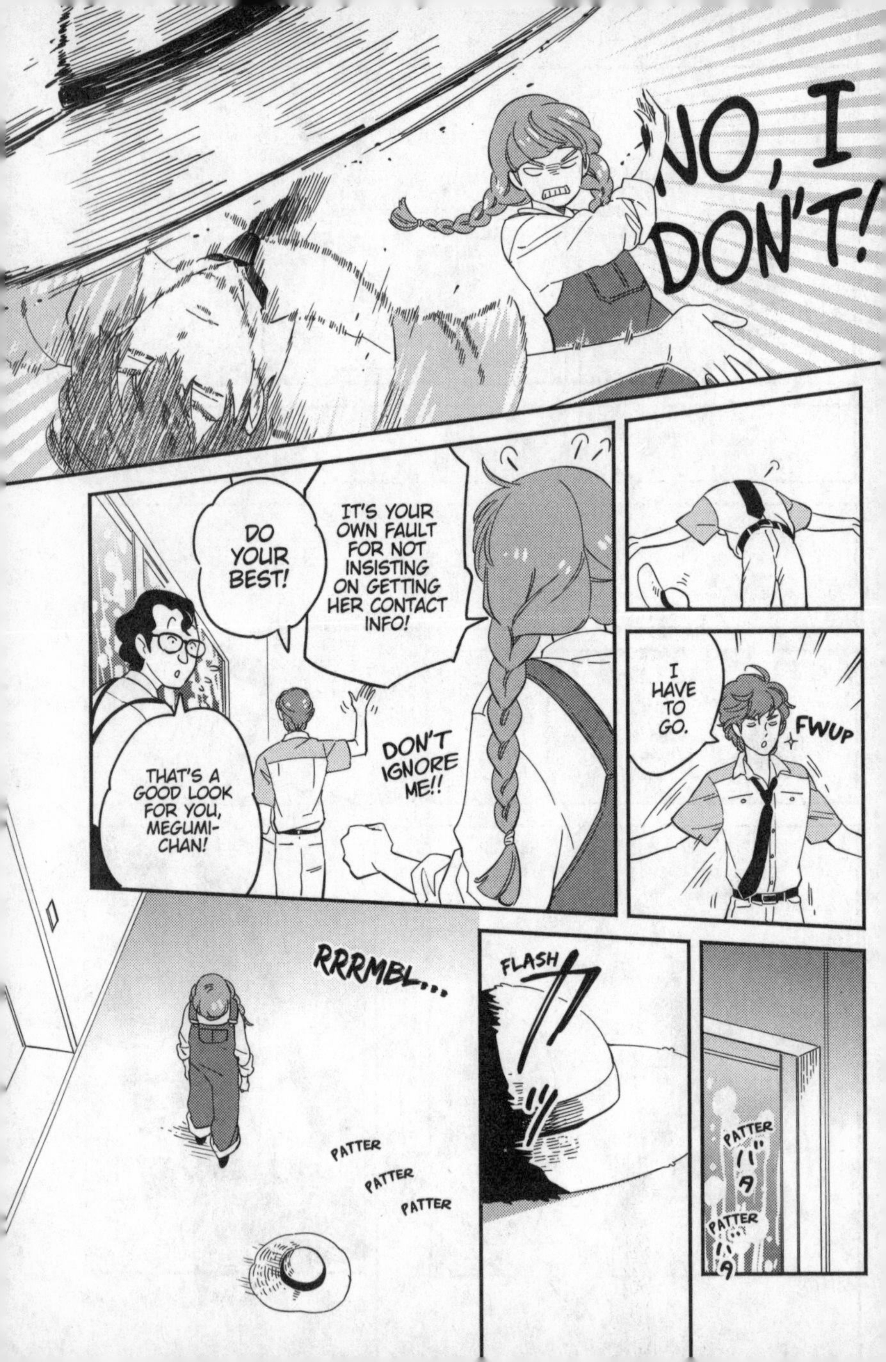
NO, I DON'T!
I HAVE TO GO.
FWUP
IT'S YOUR OWN FAULT FOR NOT INSISTING ON GETTING HER CONTACT INFO!
DO YOUR BEST!
DON'T IGNORE ME!!
THAT'S A GOOD LOOK FOR YOU, MEGUMI-CHAN!
PATTER
パタ
PATTER
パタ
FLASH
RRRMBL...
PATTER
PATTER
PATTER

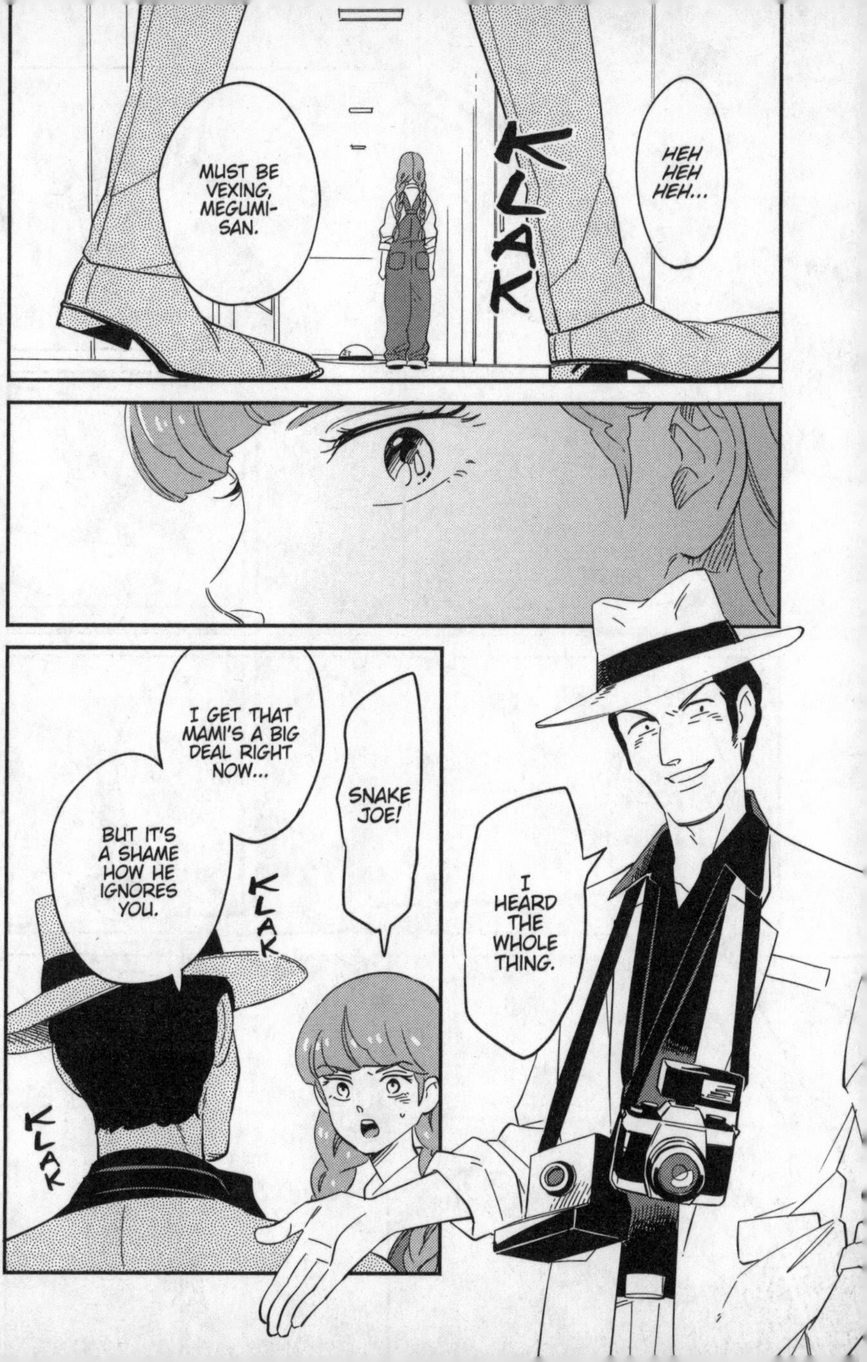

HEH HEH HEH...
KLAK
MUST BE VEXING, MEGUMI-SAN.
I HEARD THE WHOLE THING.
SNAKE JOE!
I GET THAT MAMI'S A BIG DEAL RIGHT NOW...
BUT IT'S A SHAME HOW HE IGNORES YOU.
KLAK
KLAK

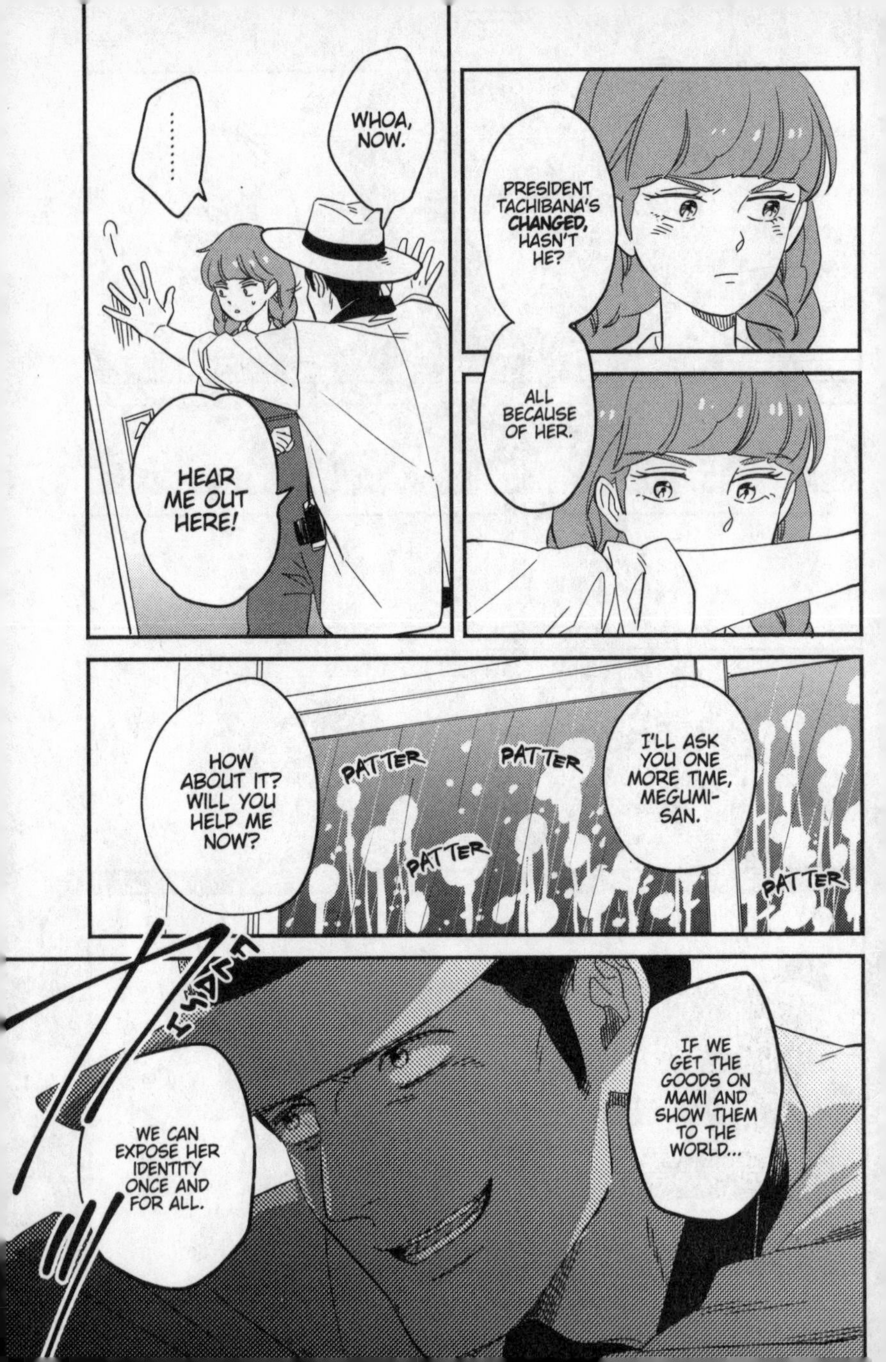
PRESIDENT TACHIBANA'S CHANGED, HASN'T HE?
ALL BECAUSE OF HER.
WHOA, NOW.
......
HEAR ME OUT HERE!
I'LL ASK YOU ONE MORE TIME, MEGUMI-SAN.
PATTER
PATTER
PATTER
PATTER
HOW ABOUT IT? WILL YOU HELP ME NOW?
IF WE GET THE GOODS ON MAMI AND SHOW THEM TO THE WORLD...
WE CAN EXPOSE HER IDENTITY ONCE AND FOR ALL.

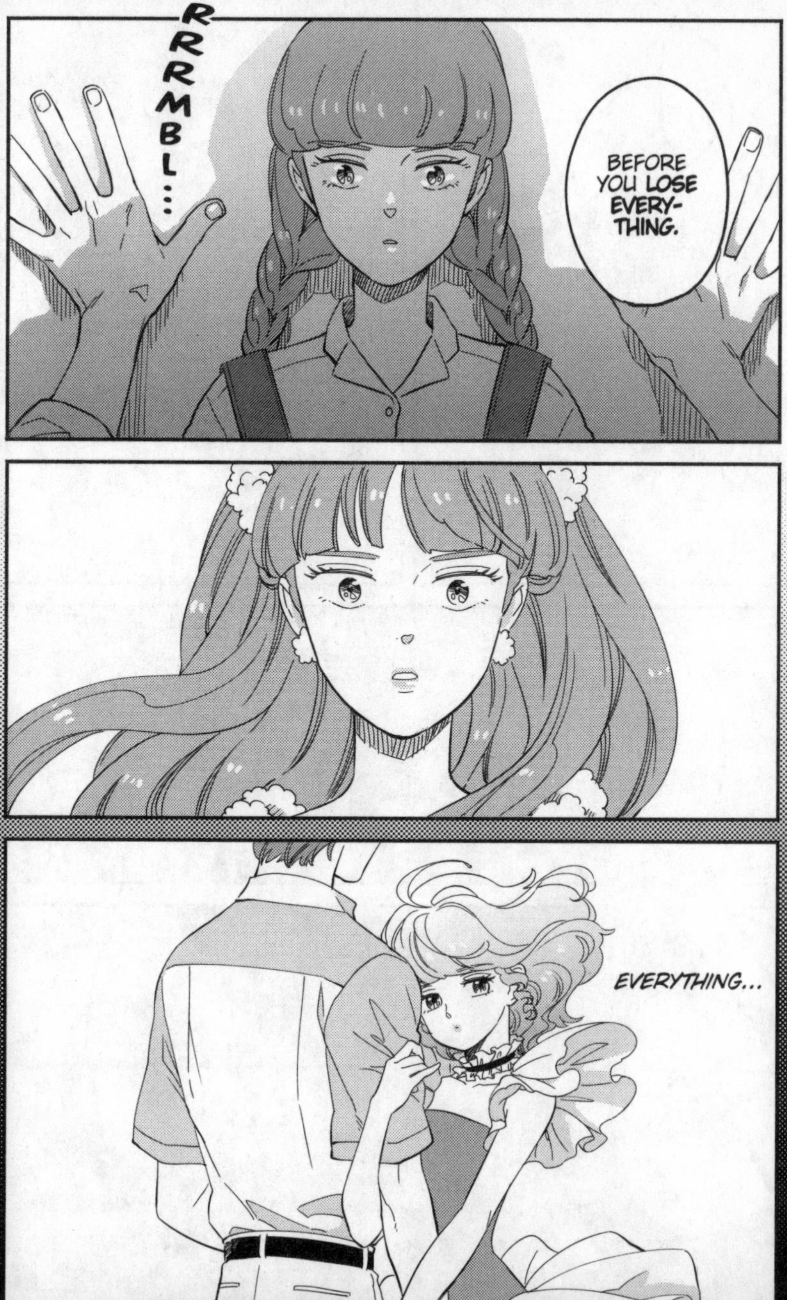
BEFORE YOU LOSE EVERY-THING.
RRRMBL...
EVERYTHING...

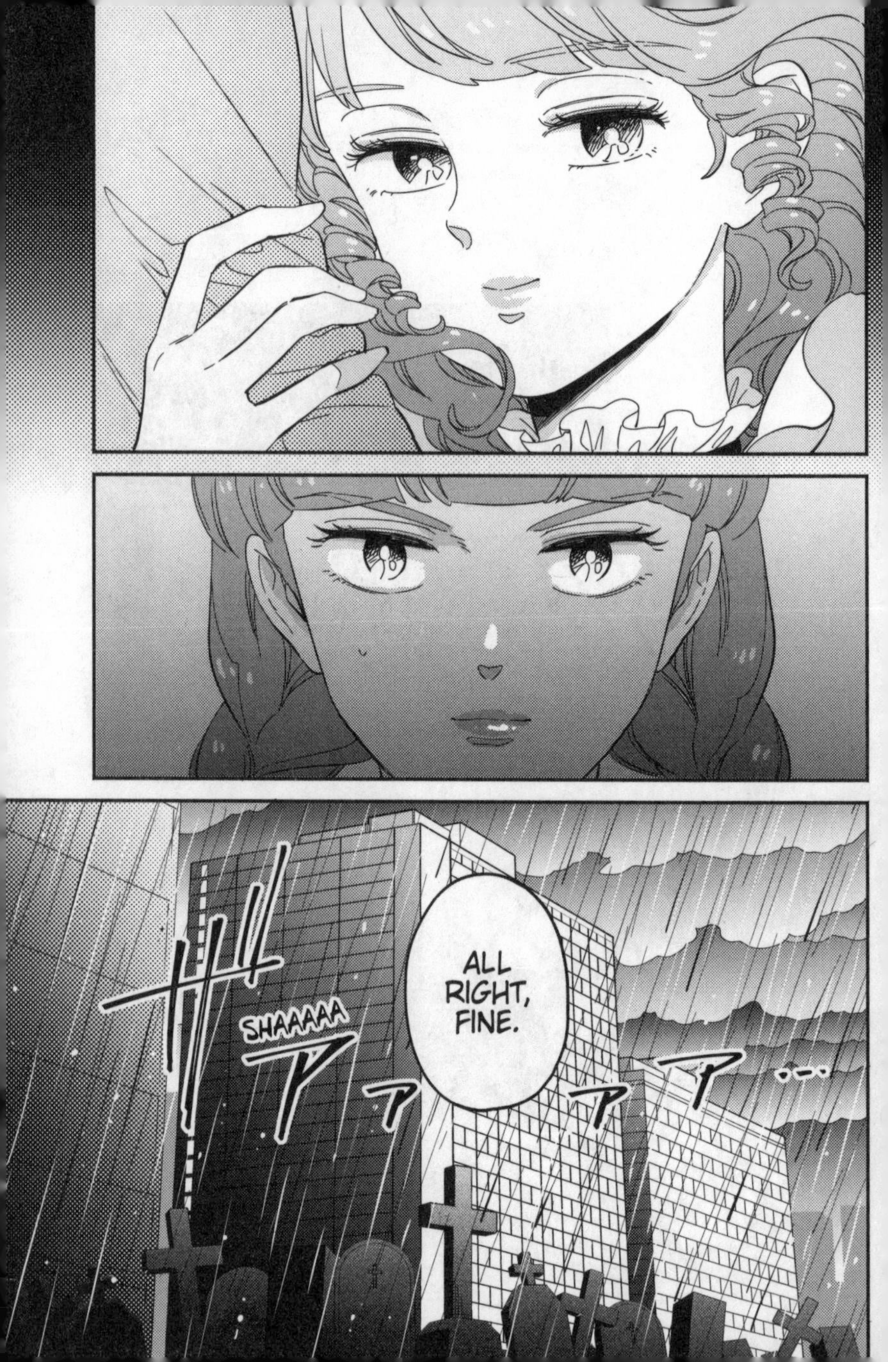
ALL RIGHT, FINE.
SHAAAAA

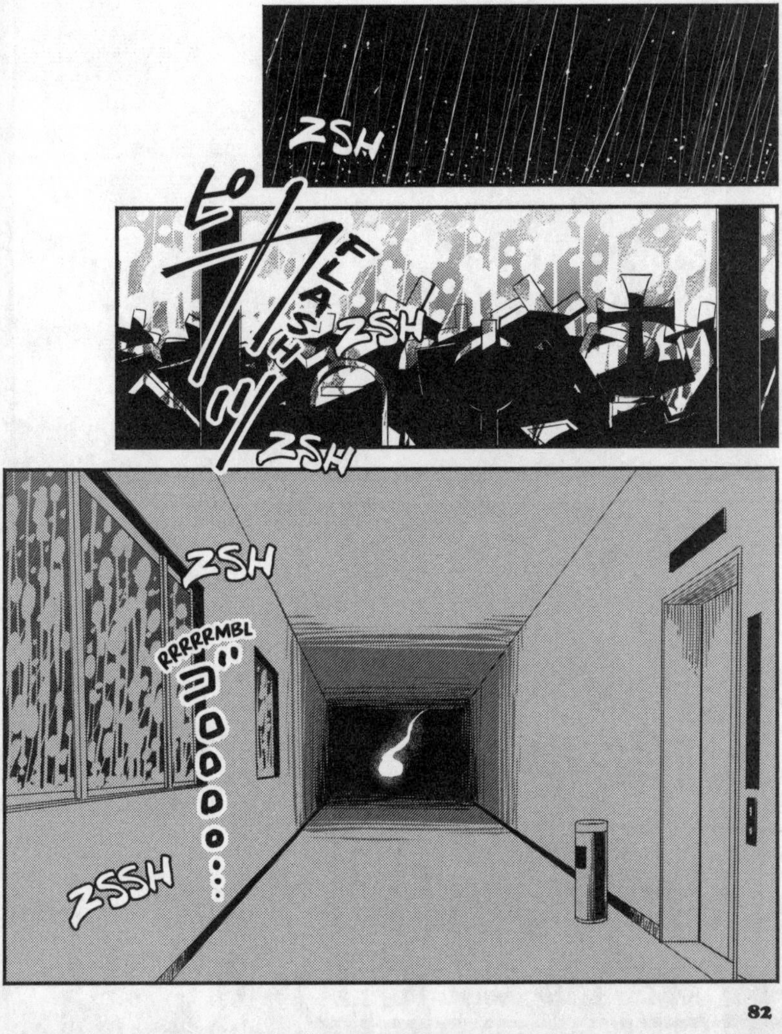
ZSH
ピカッ
FLASH
ZSH
ZSH
ZSH
RRRRRMBL
ゴロロロロロ…
ZSSH

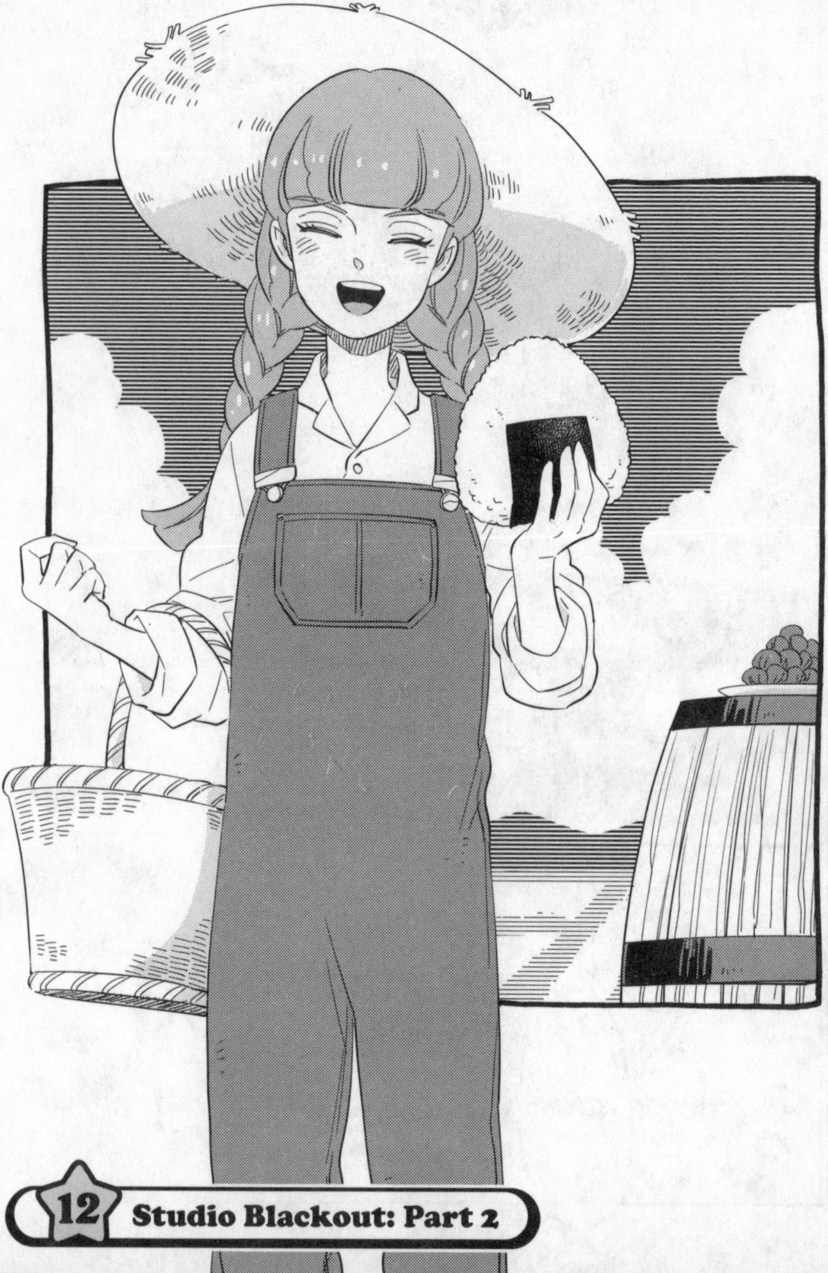

12 Studio Blackout: Part 2

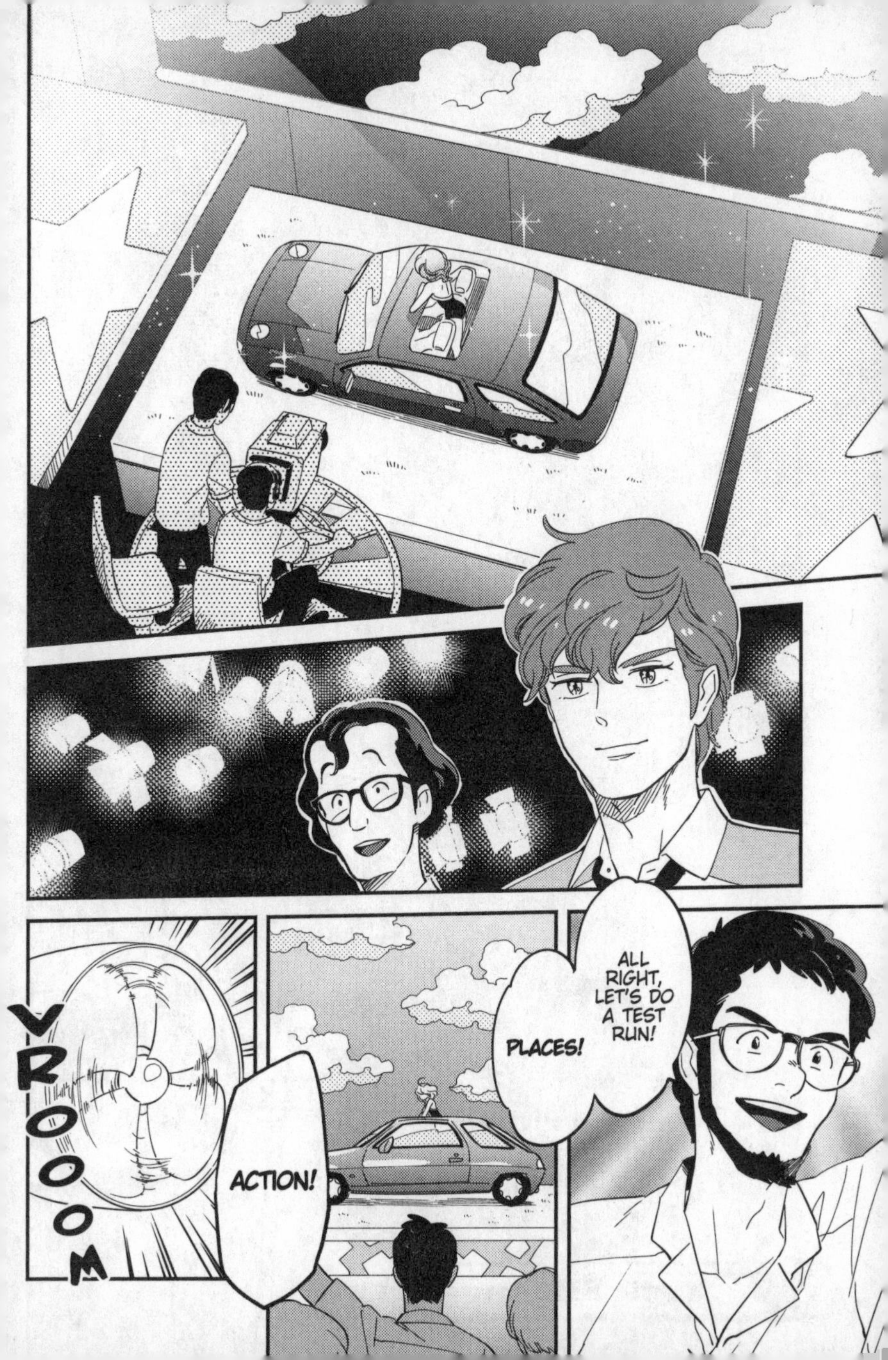
ALL RIGHT, LET'S DO A TEST RUN!
PLACES!
ACTION!
VROOOOM

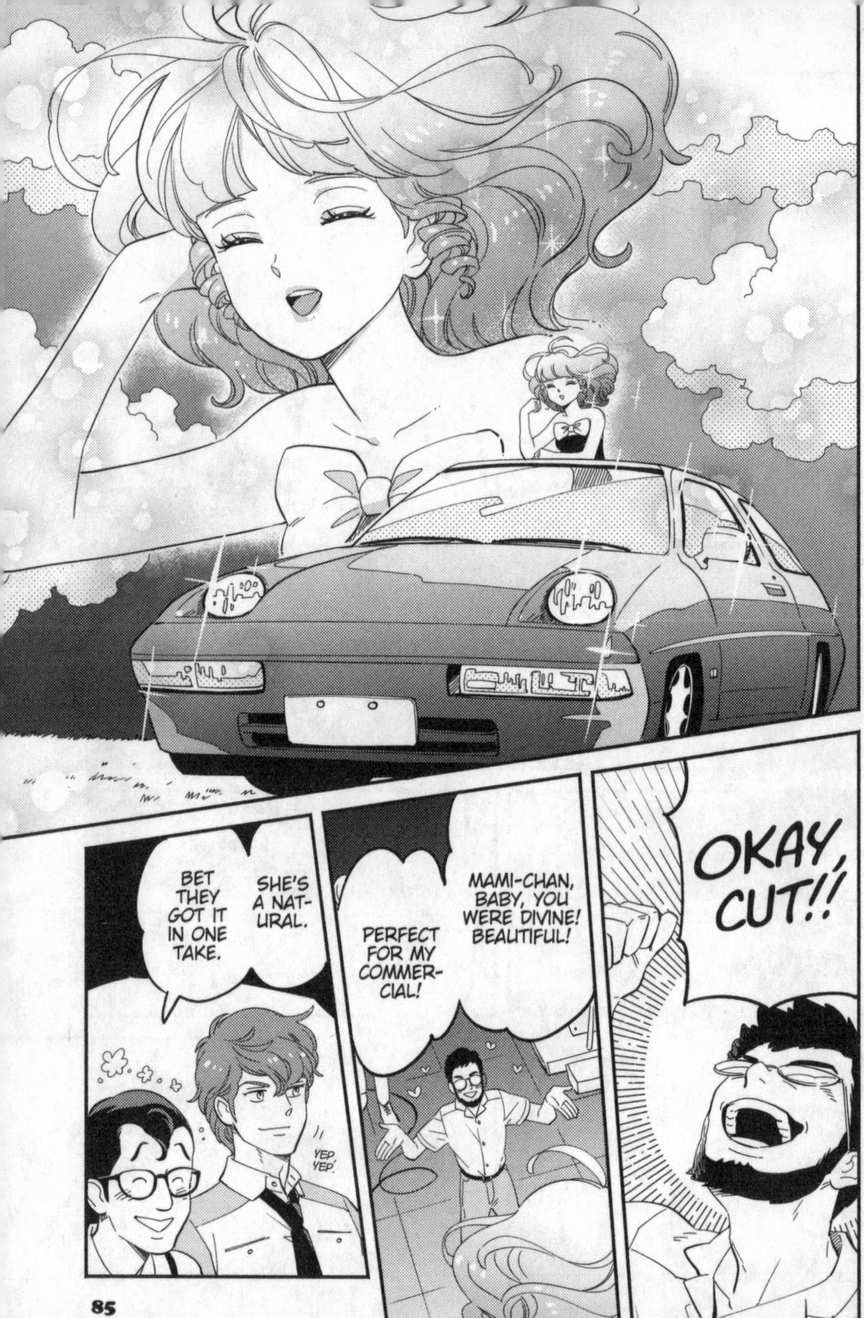
OKAY, CUT!!
MAMI-CHAN, BABY, YOU WERE DIVINE! BEAUTIFUL!
PERFECT FOR MY COMMERCIAL!
SHE'S A NATURAL.
BET THEY GOT IT IN ONE TAKE.
YEP, YEP.

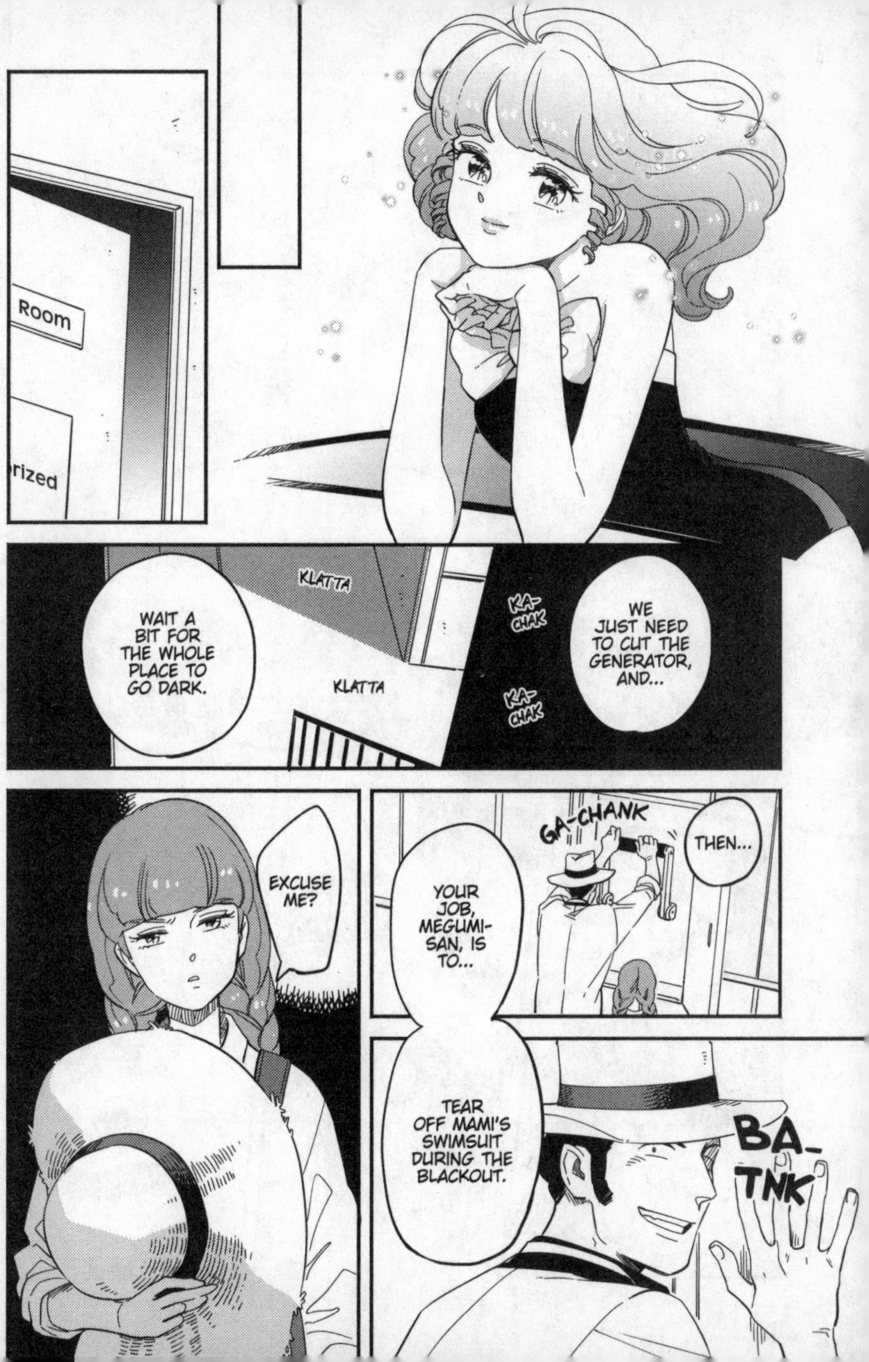

Room
rized
WE JUST NEED TO CUT THE GENERATOR, AND...
KA-CHAK
KA-CHAK
KLATTA
KLATTA
WAIT A BIT FOR THE WHOLE PLACE TO GO DARK.
THEN...
GA-CHANK
YOUR JOB, MEGUMI-SAN, IS TO...
TEAR OFF MAMI'S SWIMSUIT DURING THE BLACKOUT.
BA-TNK
EXCUSE ME?

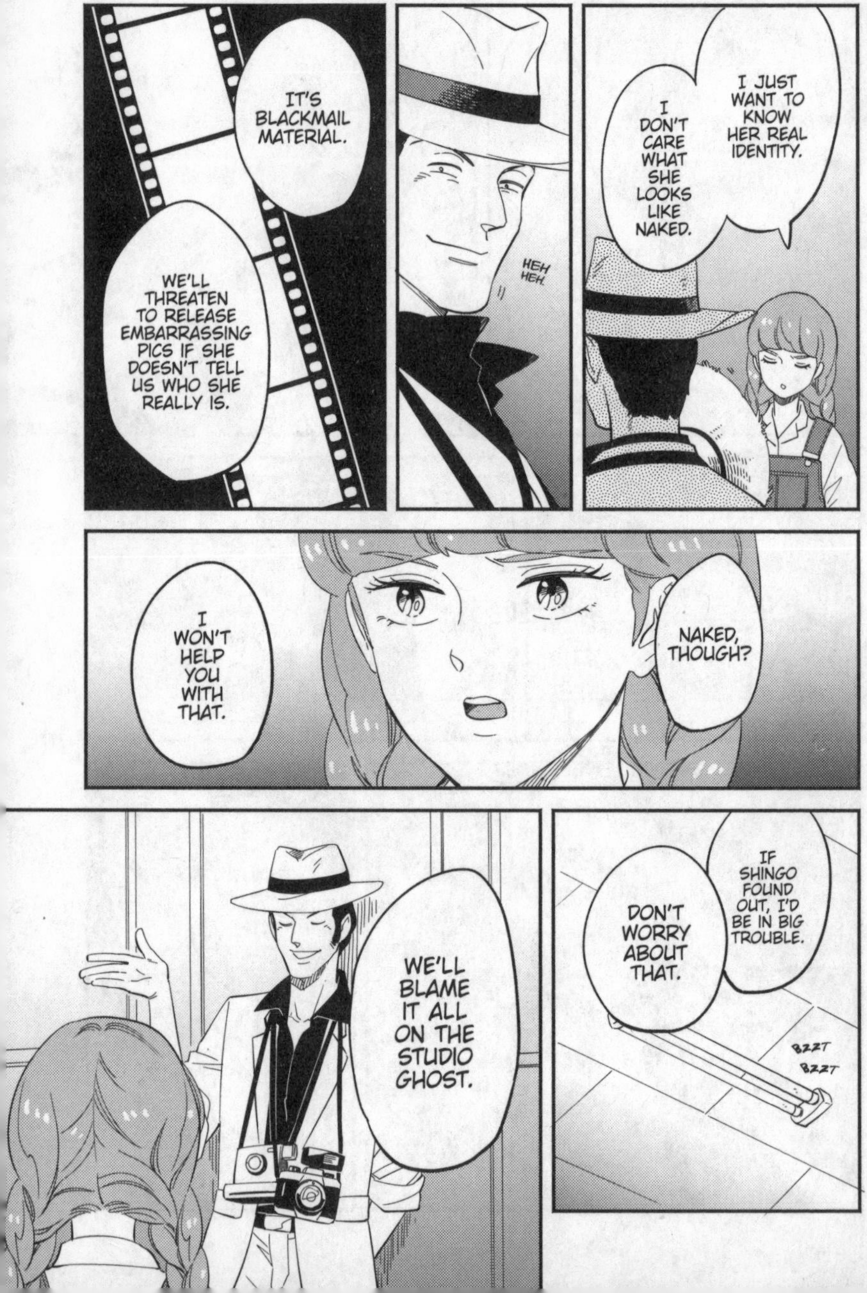
I JUST WANT TO KNOW HER REAL IDENTITY.
I DON'T CARE WHAT SHE LOOKS LIKE NAKED.
HEH HEH.
IT'S BLACKMAIL MATERIAL.
WE'LL THREATEN TO RELEASE EMBARRASSING PICS IF SHE DOESN'T TELL US WHO SHE REALLY IS.
NAKED, THOUGH?
I WON'T HELP YOU WITH THAT.
IF SHINGO FOUND OUT, I'D BE IN BIG TROUBLE.
DON'T WORRY ABOUT THAT.
BZZT
BZZT
WE'LL BLAME IT ALL ON THE STUDIO GHOST.

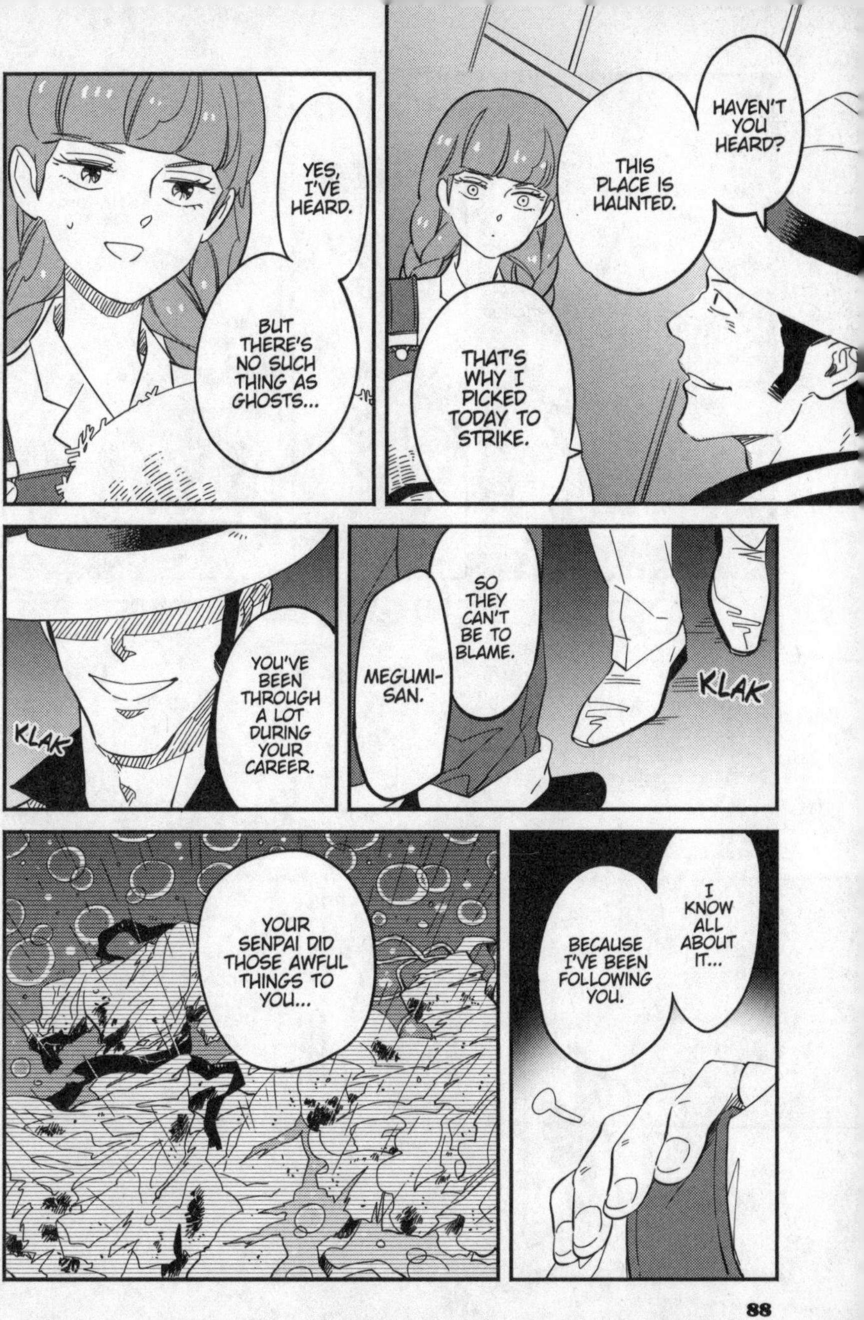
HAVEN'T YOU HEARD?
THIS PLACE IS HAUNTED.
THAT'S WHY I PICKED TODAY TO STRIKE.
YES, I'VE HEARD.
BUT THERE'S NO SUCH THING AS GHOSTS...
SO THEY CAN'T BE TO BLAME.
MEGUMI-SAN.
KLAK
YOU'VE BEEN THROUGH A LOT DURING YOUR CAREER.
KLAK
I KNOW ALL ABOUT IT...
BECAUSE I'VE BEEN FOLLOWING YOU.
YOUR SENPAI DID THOSE AWFUL THINGS TO YOU...

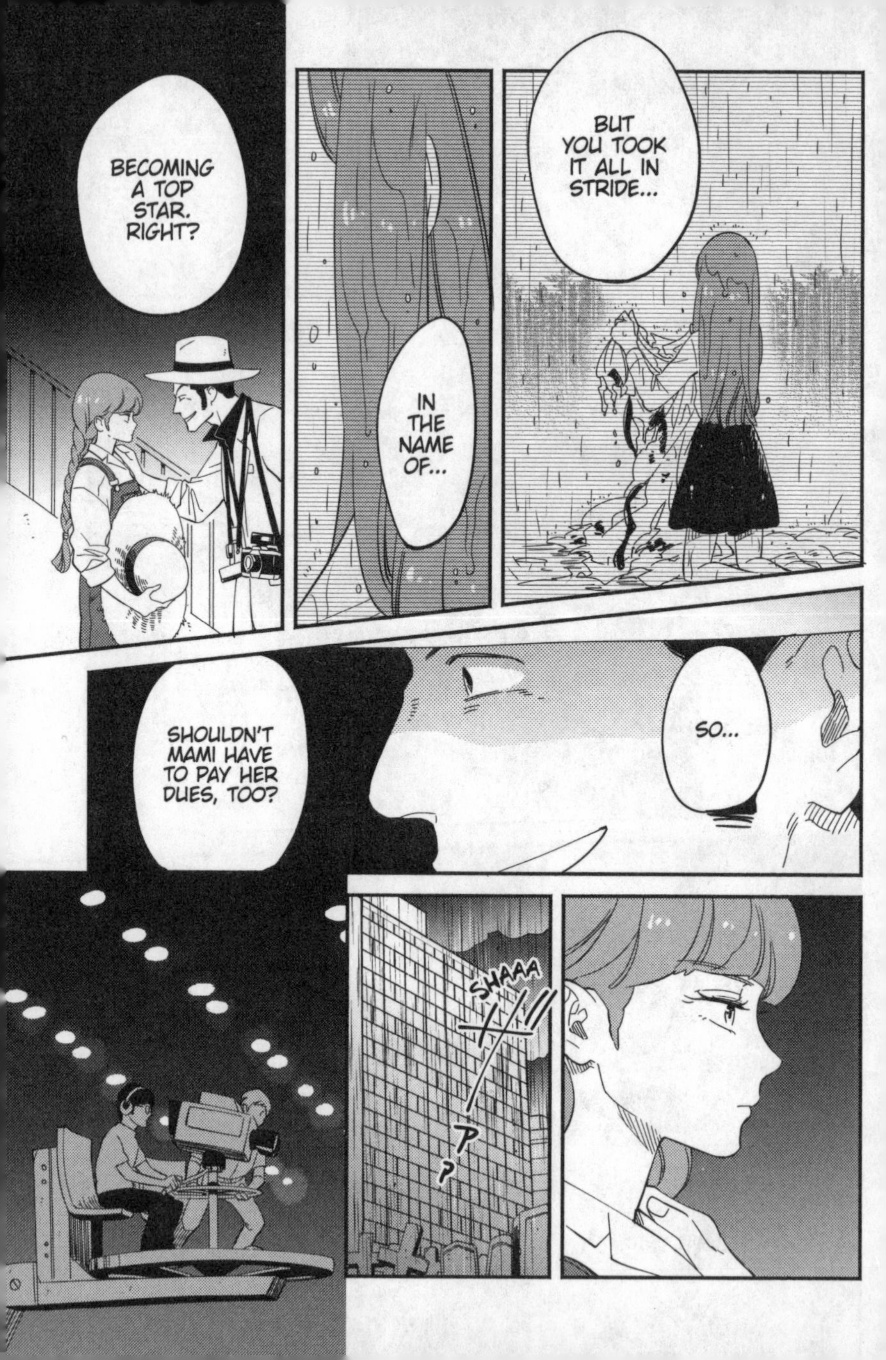
BUT YOU TOOK IT ALL IN STRIDE...
IN THE NAME OF...
BECOMING A TOP STAR. RIGHT?
SO...
SHOULDN'T MAMI HAVE TO PAY HER DUES, TOO?
SHAAA

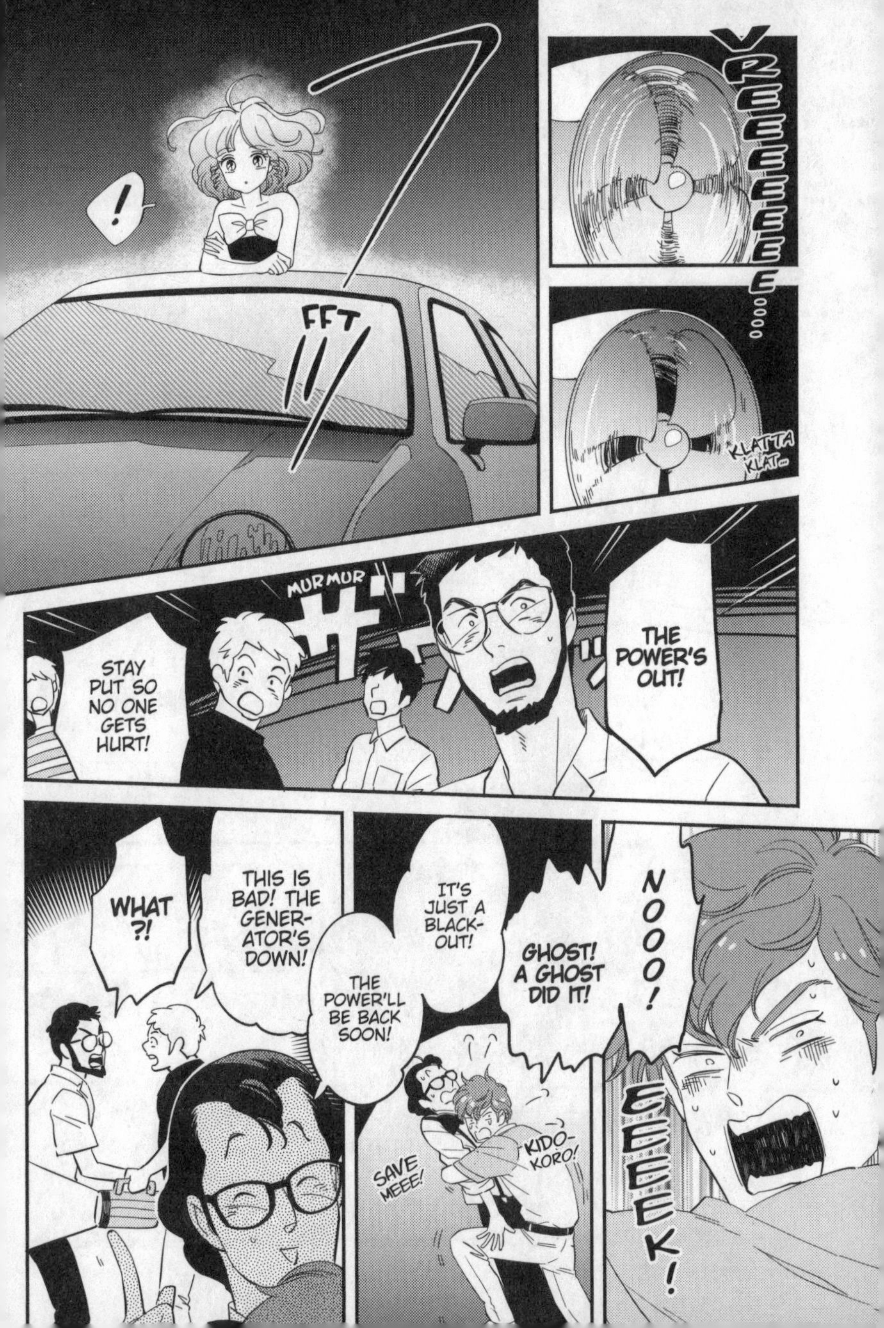
VREEEEEEEE...
KLATTA KLAT...
!
FFT
THE POWER'S OUT!
MURMUR
STAY PUT SO NO ONE GETS HURT!
NOOOO!
EEEEEK!
GHOST! A GHOST DID IT!
IT'S JUST A BLACK-OUT!
KIDO-KORO!
SAVE MEEE!
THIS IS BAD! THE GENER-ATOR'S DOWN!
WHAT?!
THE POWER'LL BE BACK SOON!

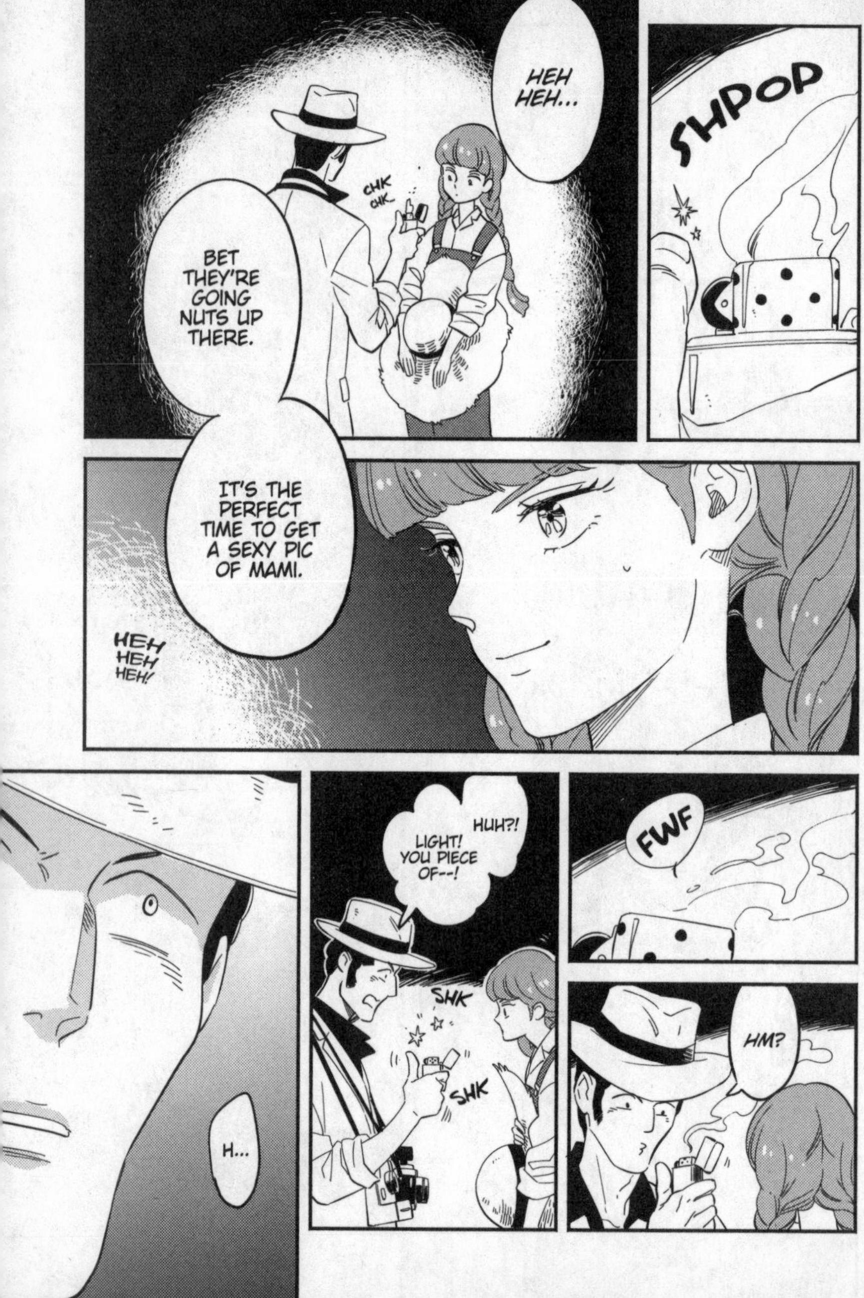
SHPOP
HEH HEH...
CHK CHK
BET THEY'RE GOING NUTS UP THERE.
IT'S THE PERFECT TIME TO GET A SEXY PIC OF MAMI.
HEH HEH HEH!
FWF
HM?
HUH?!
LIGHT! YOU PIECE OF--!
SHK
SHK
H...

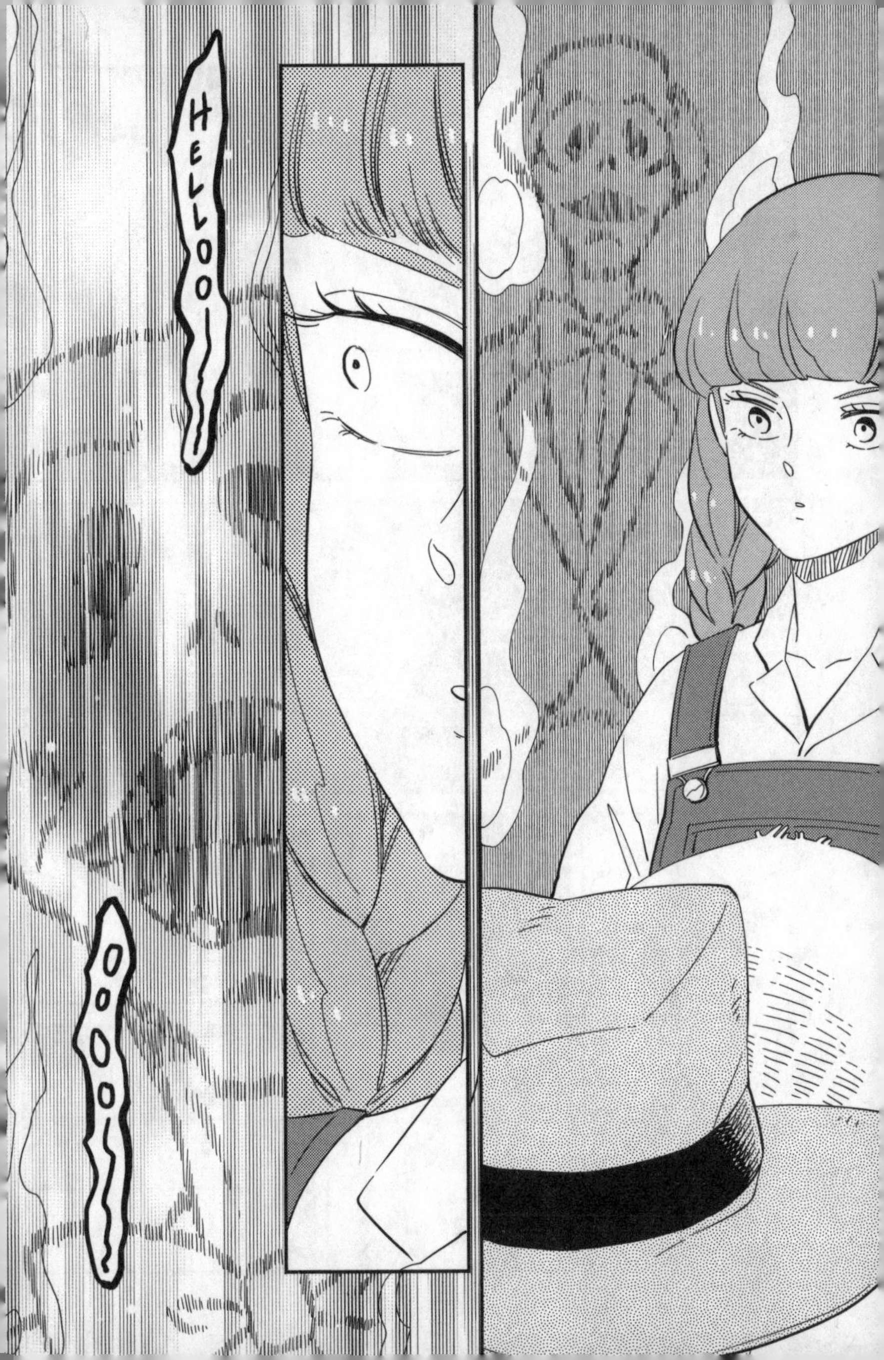
HELLOO
OOOOO

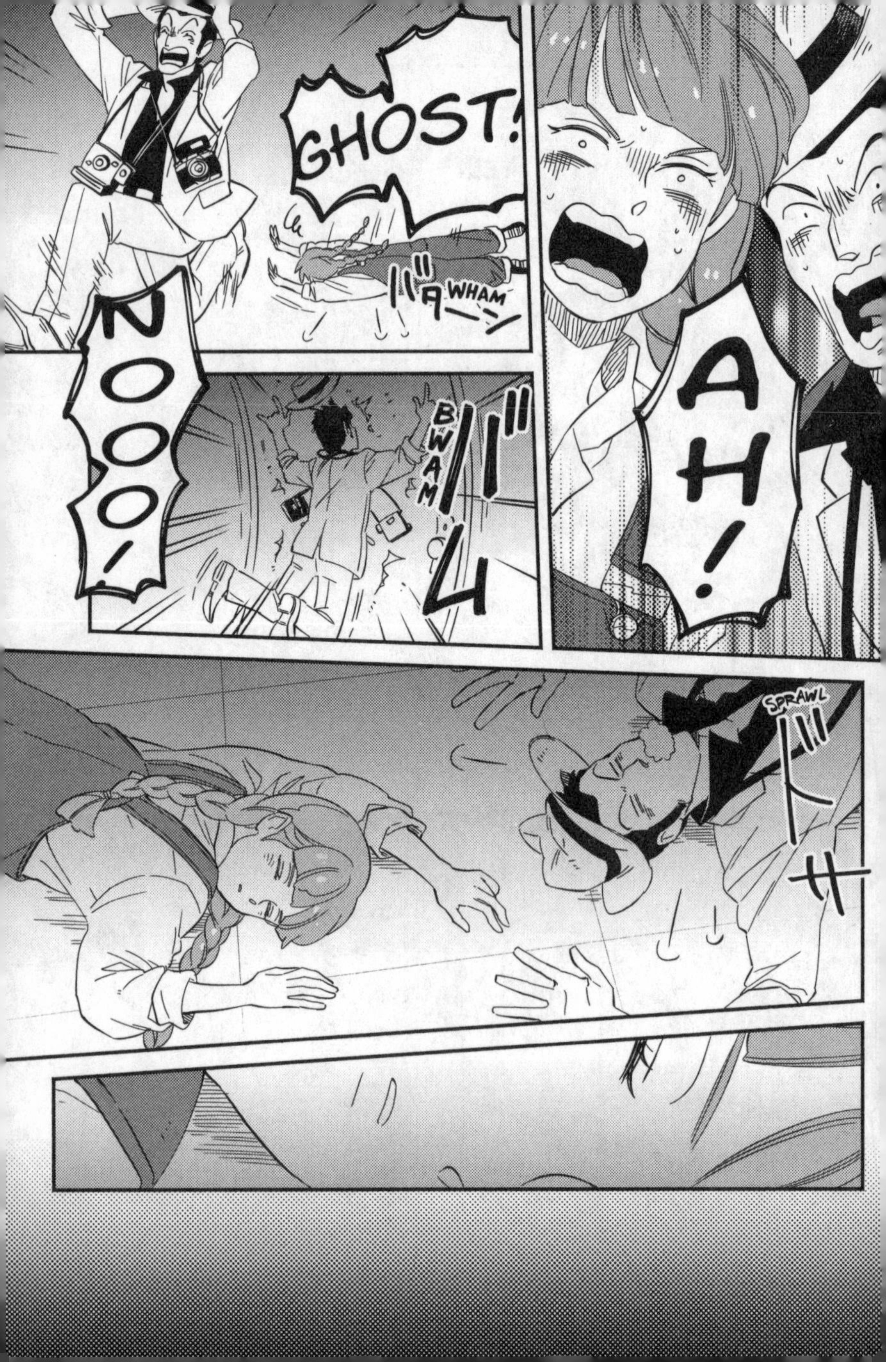
AH!
GHOST!
WHAM
NOOOO!
BWAM
SPRAWL

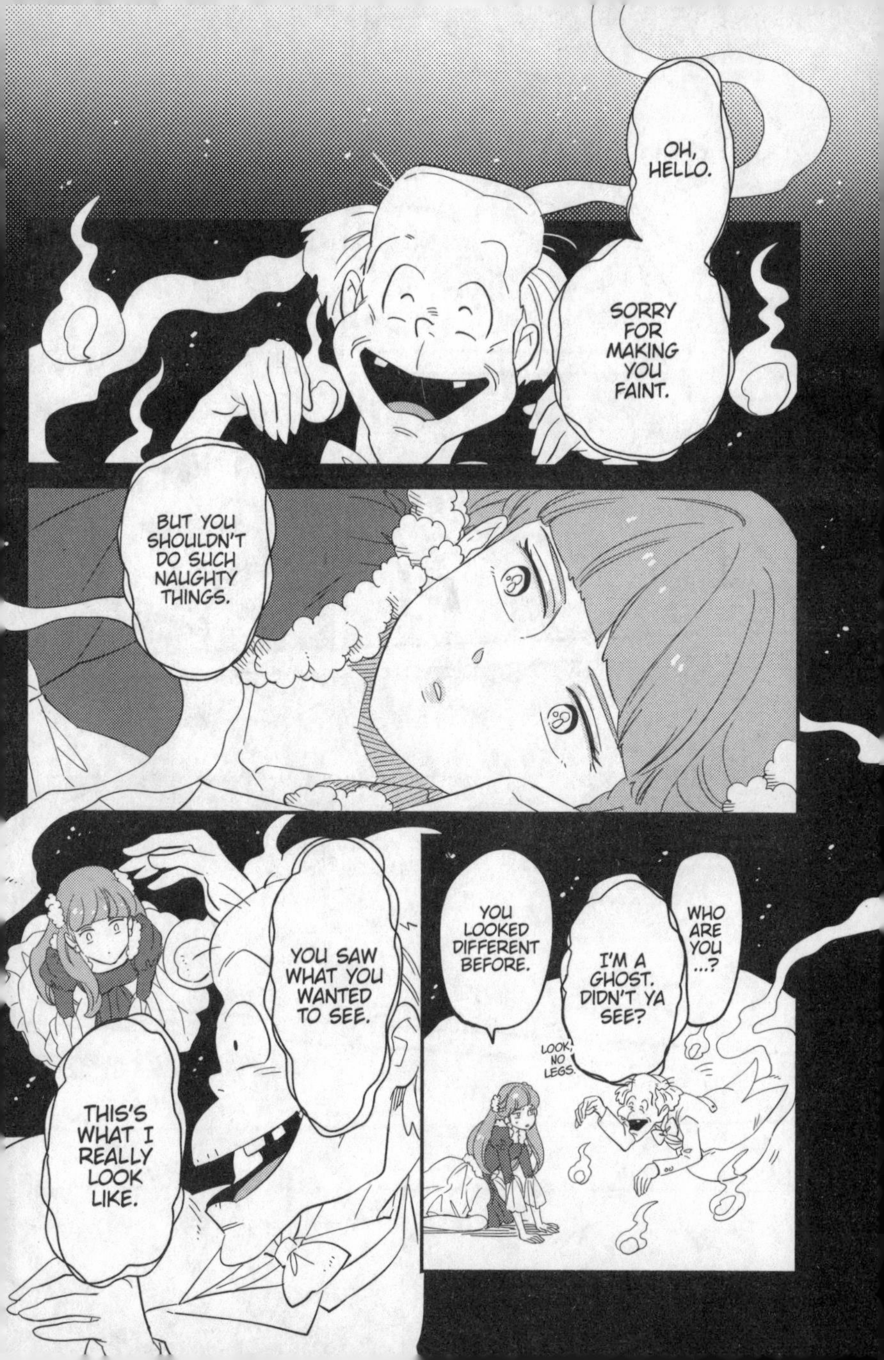
OH, HELLO.
SORRY FOR MAKING YOU FAINT.
BUT YOU SHOULDN'T DO SUCH NAUGHTY THINGS.
WHO ARE YOU ...?
I'M A GHOST. DIDN'T YA SEE?
LOOK, NO LEGS.
YOU LOOKED DIFFERENT BEFORE.
YOU SAW WHAT YOU WANTED TO SEE.
THIS'S WHAT I REALLY LOOK LIKE.

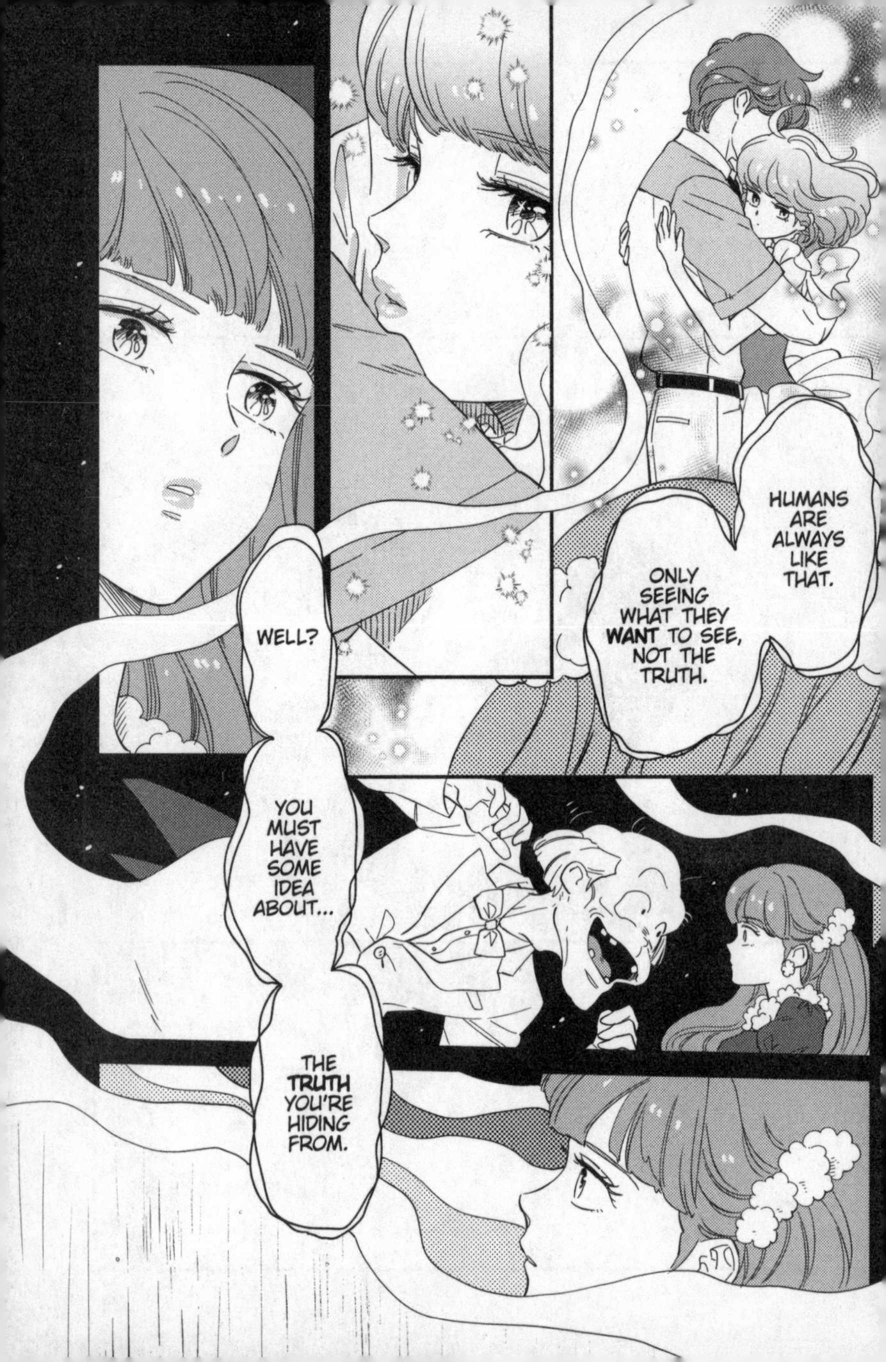
HUMANS ARE ALWAYS LIKE THAT.
ONLY SEEING WHAT THEY WANT TO SEE, NOT THE TRUTH.
WELL?
YOU MUST HAVE SOME IDEA ABOUT...
THE TRUTH YOU'RE HIDING FROM.

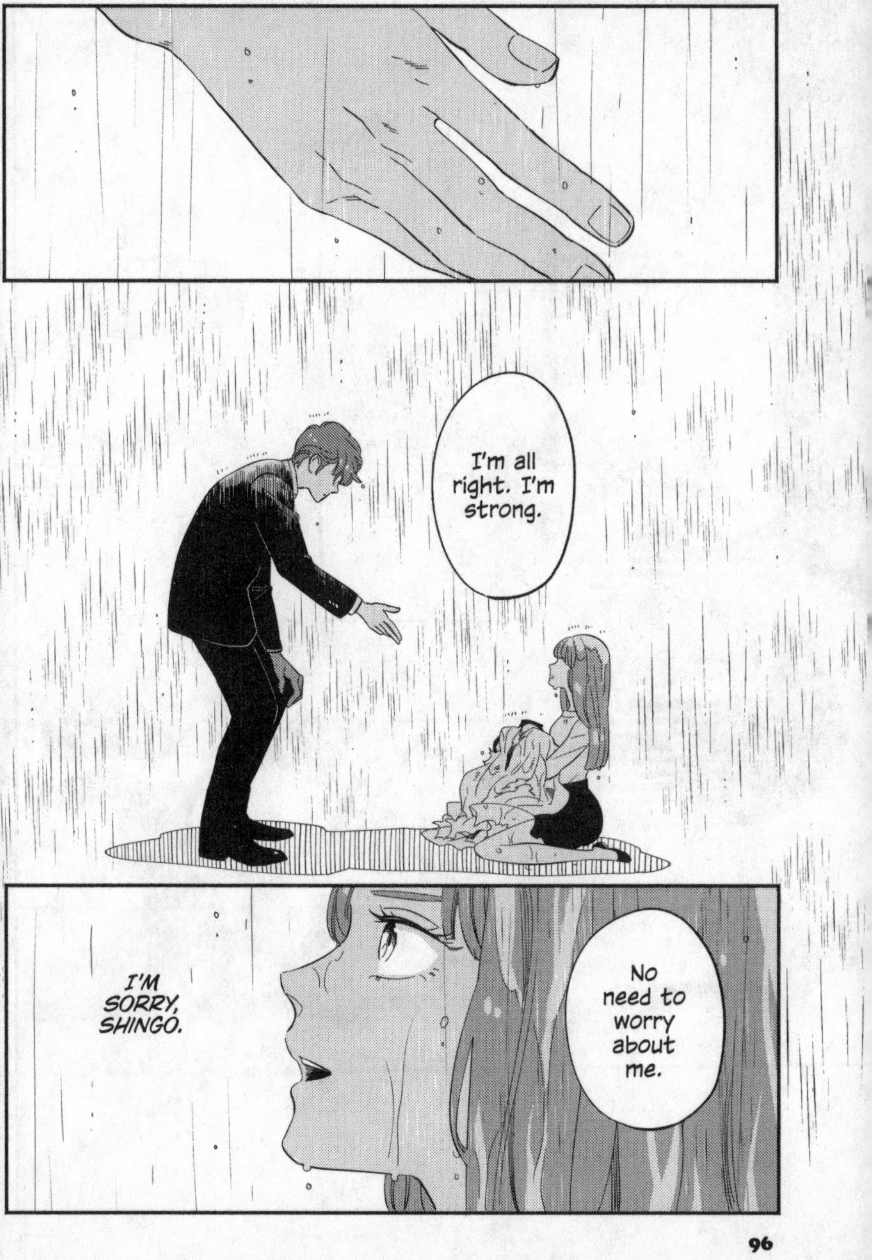
I'm all right. I'm strong.
No need to worry about me.
I'M SORRY, SHINGO.

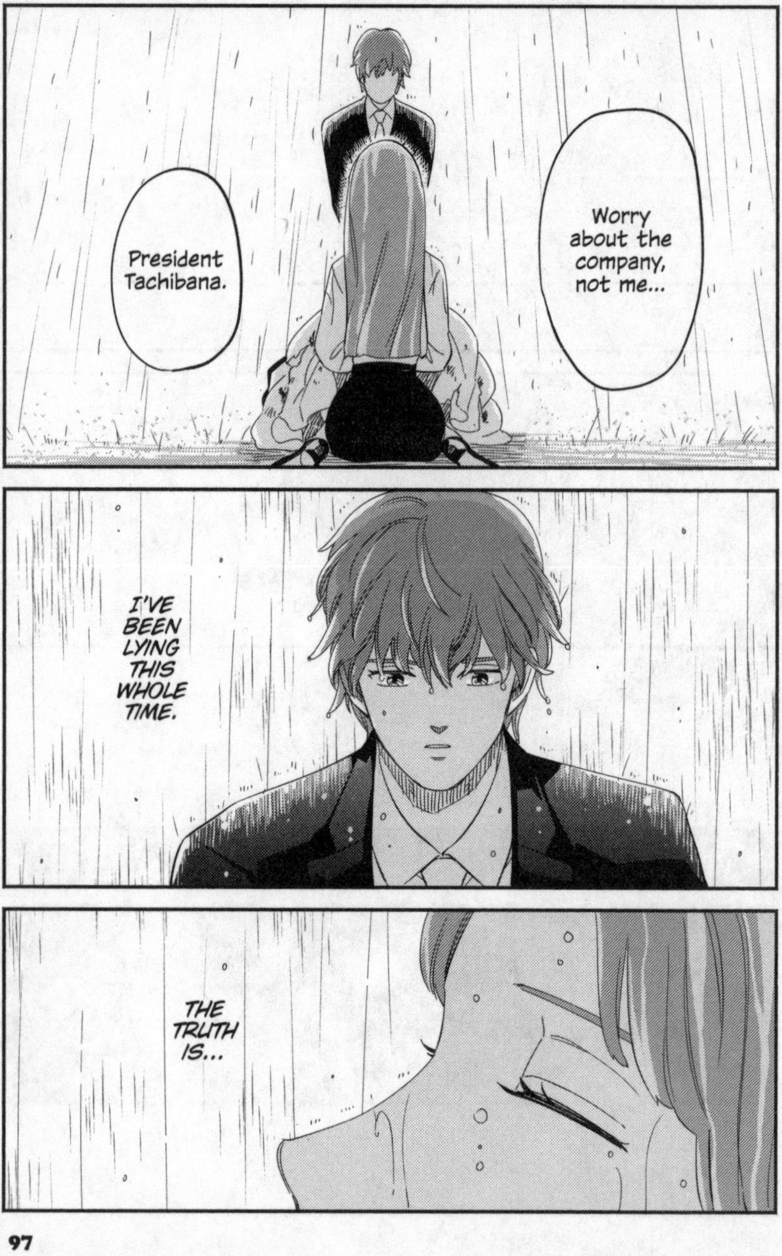
Worry about the company, not me...
President Tachibana.
I'VE BEEN LYING THIS WHOLE TIME.
THE TRUTH IS...

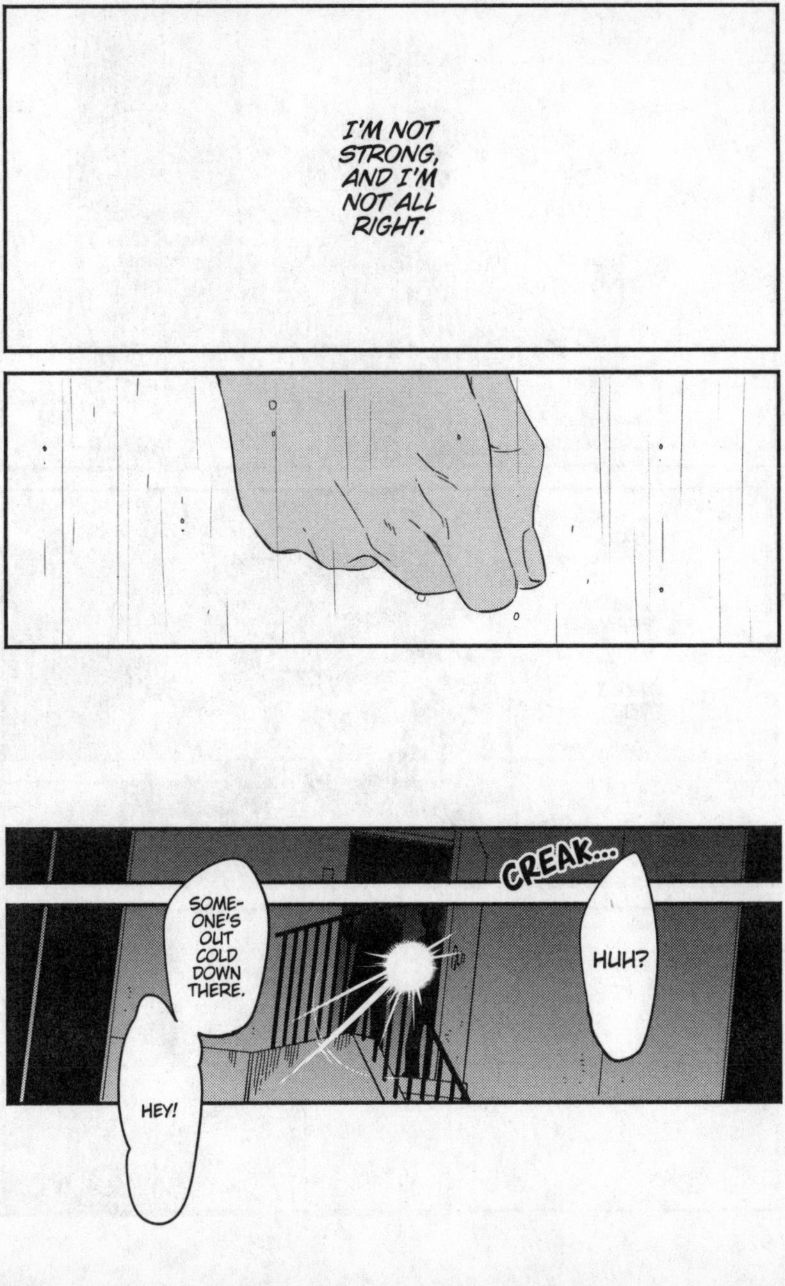
I'M NOT STRONG, AND I'M NOT ALL RIGHT.
CREAK...
HUH?
SOME-ONE'S OUT COLD DOWN THERE.
HEY!

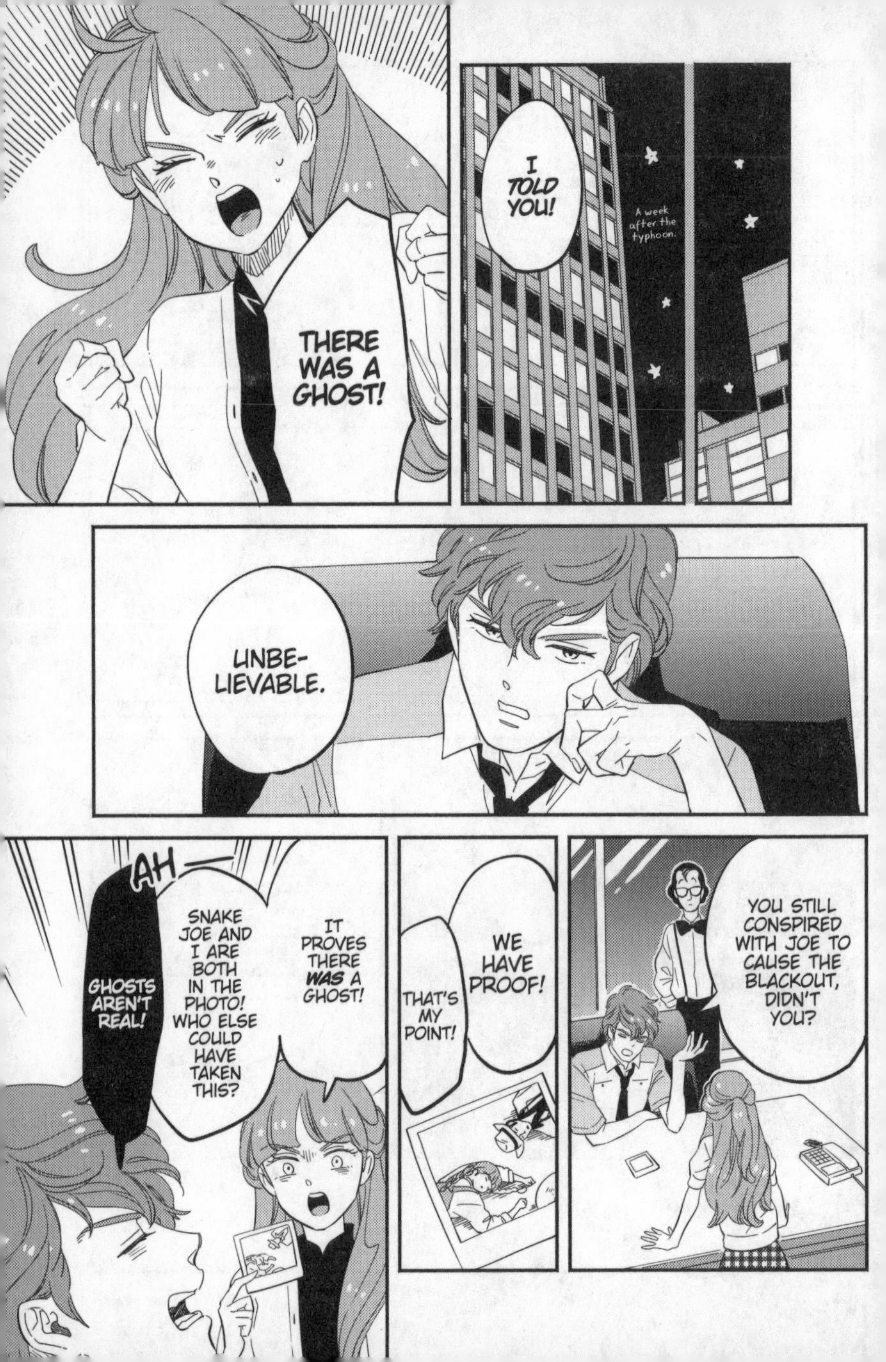
A week after the typhoon.
I TOLD YOU!
THERE WAS A GHOST!
UNBE-LIEVABLE.
YOU STILL CONSPIRED WITH JOE TO CAUSE THE BLACKOUT, DIDN'T YOU?
WE HAVE PROOF!
THAT'S MY POINT!
IT PROVES THERE *WAS* A GHOST!
SNAKE JOE AND I ARE BOTH IN THE PHOTO! WHO ELSE COULD HAVE TAKEN THIS?
AH—
GHOSTS AREN'T REAL!

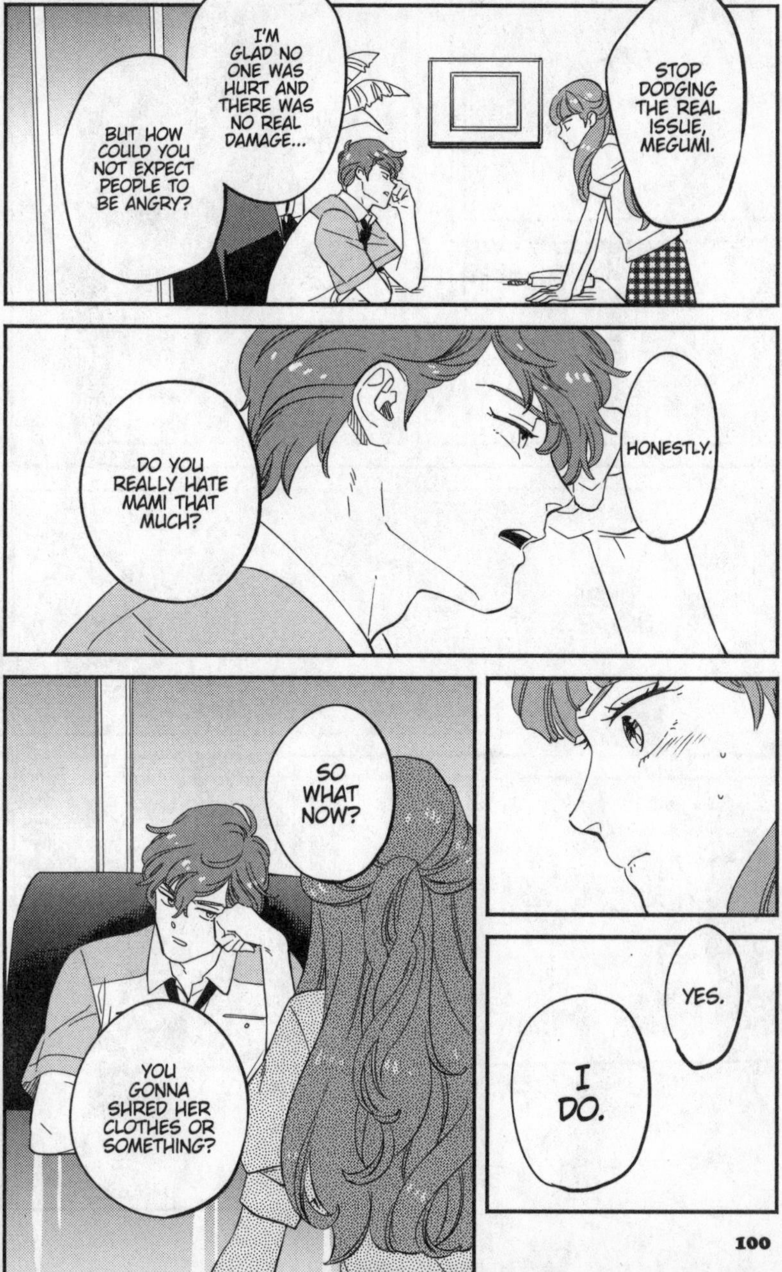
STOP DODGING THE REAL ISSUE, MEGUMI.
I'M GLAD NO ONE WAS HURT AND THERE WAS NO REAL DAMAGE...
BUT HOW COULD YOU NOT EXPECT PEOPLE TO BE ANGRY?
HONESTLY.
DO YOU REALLY HATE MAMI THAT MUCH?
YES.
I DO.
SO WHAT NOW?
YOU GONNA SHRED HER CLOTHES OR SOMETHING?

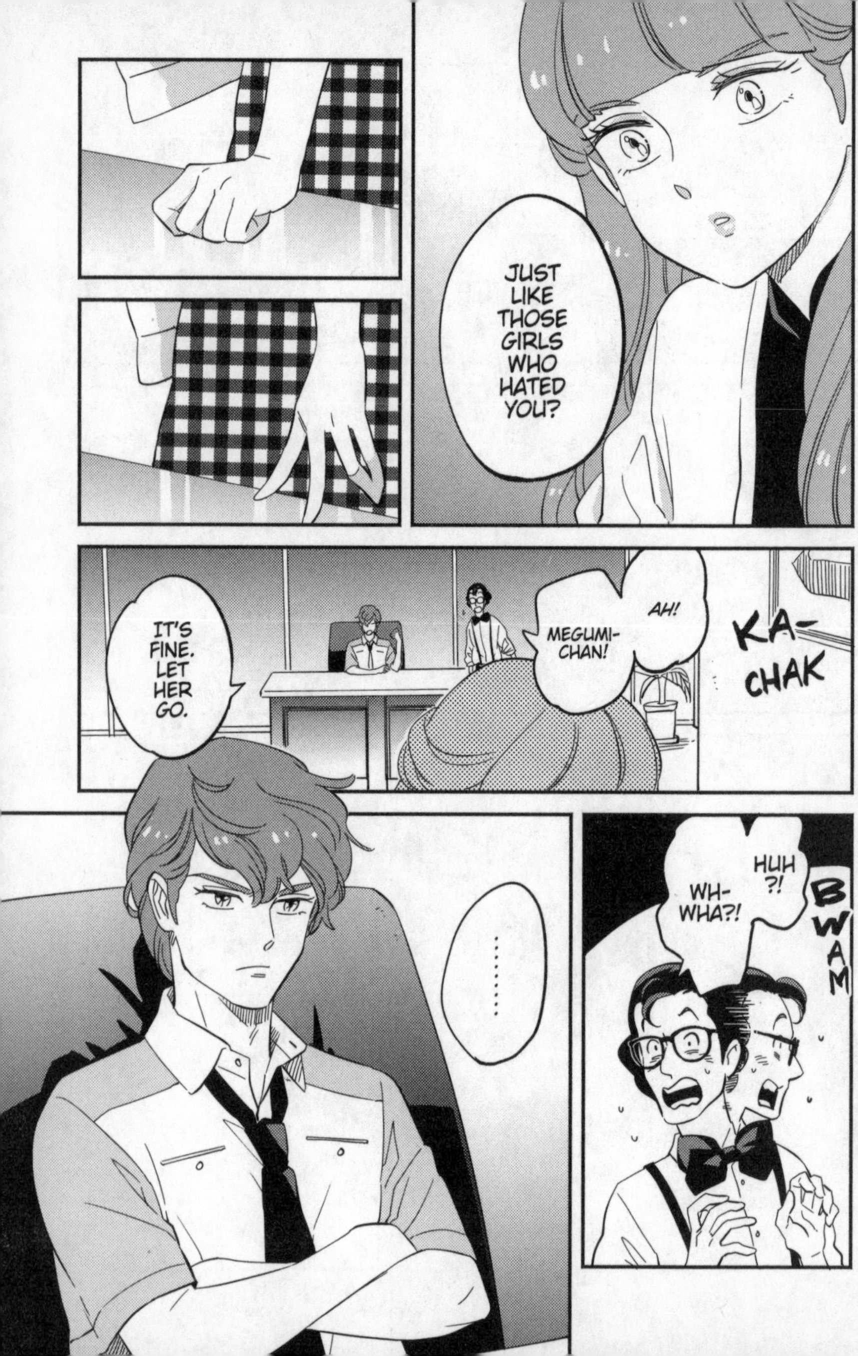
JUST LIKE THOSE GIRLS WHO HATED YOU?
KA-CHAK
AH!
MEGUMI-CHAN!
IT'S FINE. LET HER GO.
BWAM
HUH?!
WH-WHA?!
......

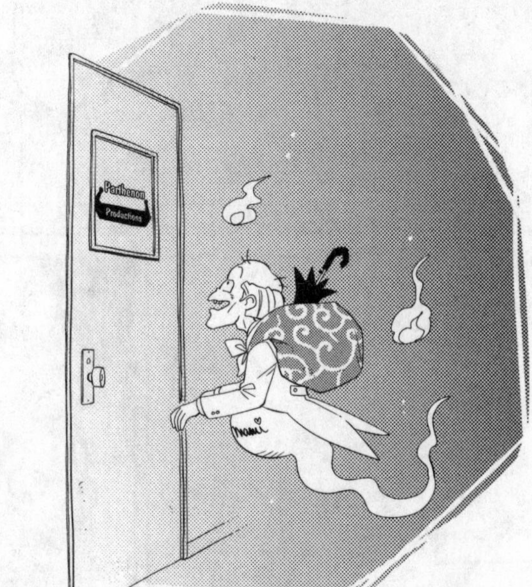

Parthenon
Productions

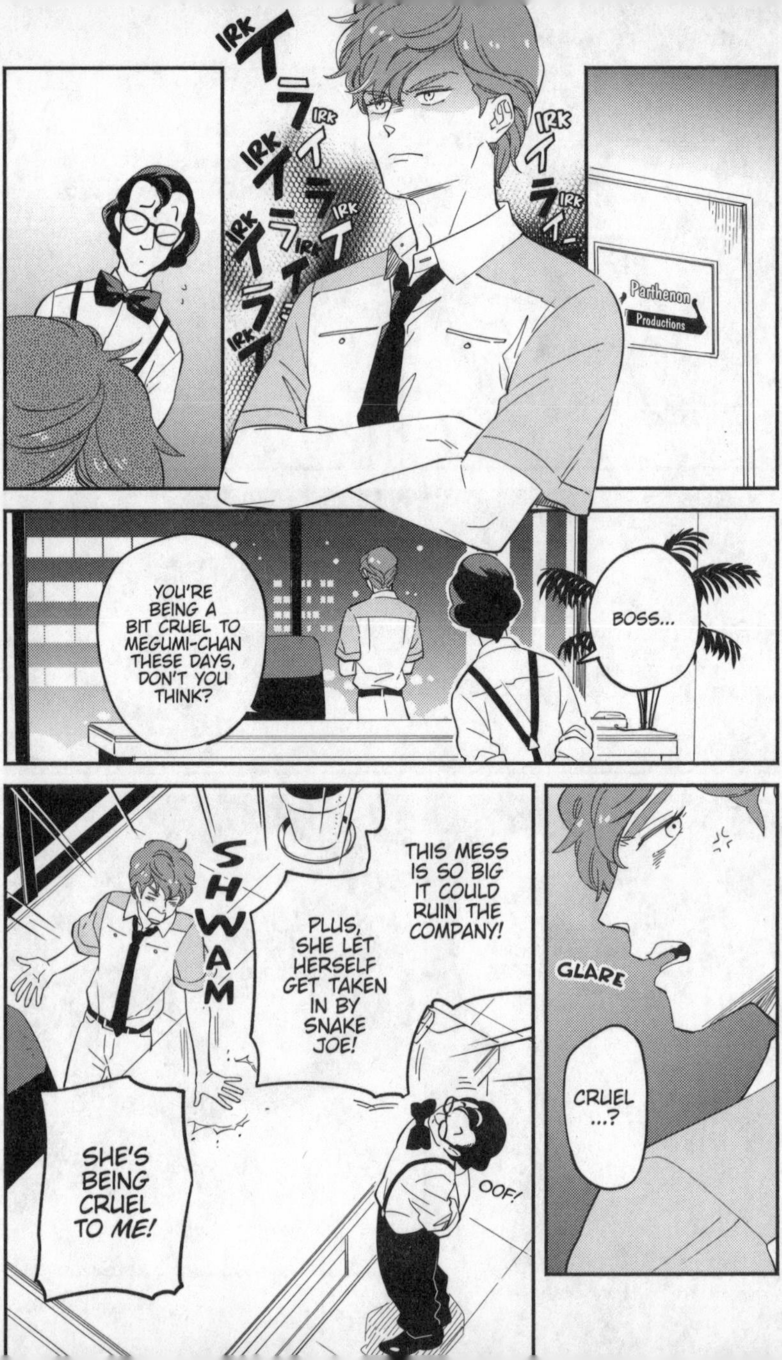
IRK
IRK
IRK
IRK
IRK
IRK
IRK
IRK
Parthenon Productions
BOSS...
YOU'RE BEING A BIT CRUEL TO MEGUMI-CHAN THESE DAYS, DON'T YOU THINK?
GLARE
CRUEL ...?
SHWAM
THIS MESS IS SO BIG IT COULD RUIN THE COMPANY!
PLUS, SHE LET HERSELF GET TAKEN IN BY SNAKE JOE!
SHE'S BEING CRUEL TO ME!
OOF!

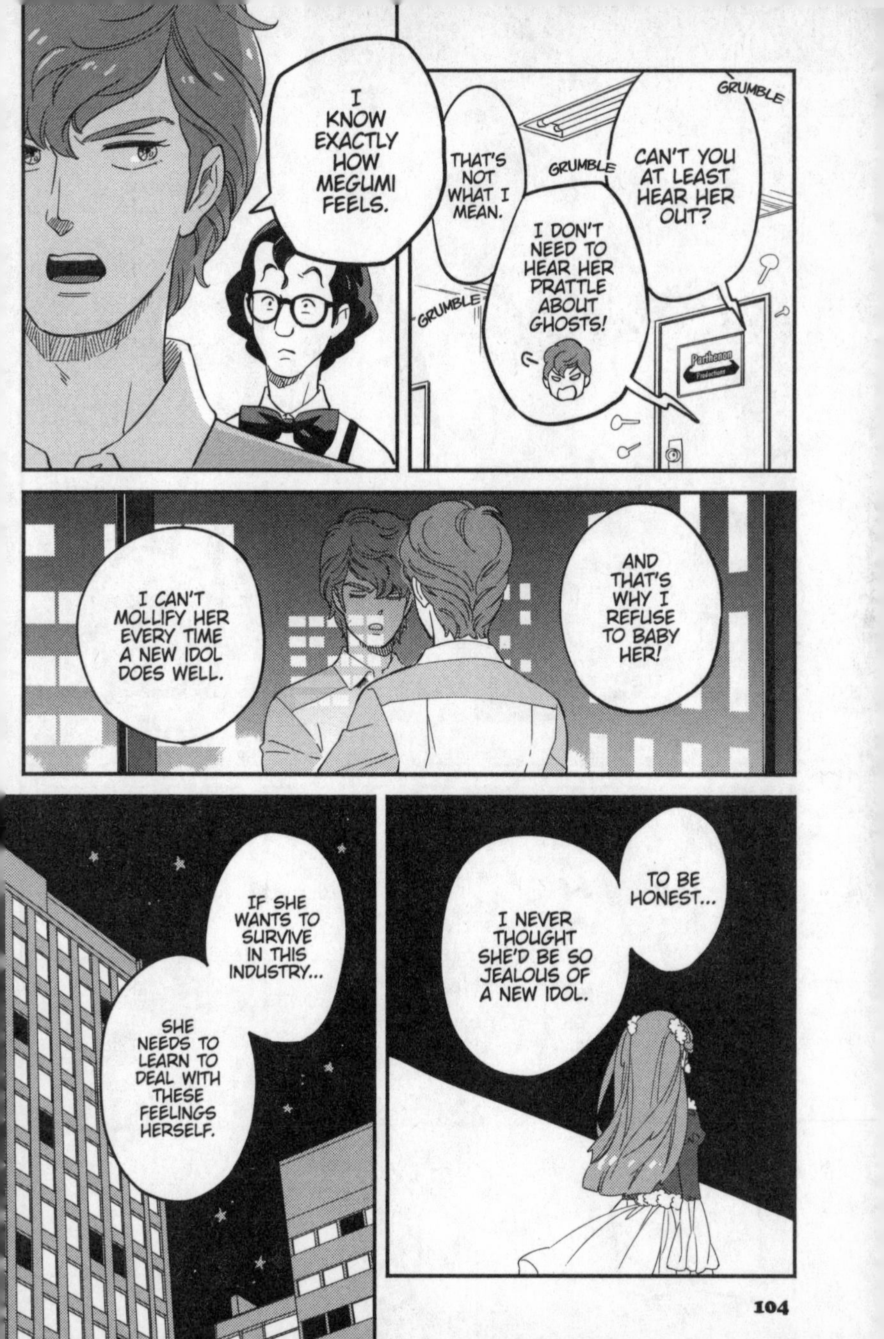
GRUMBLE
CAN'T YOU AT LEAST HEAR HER OUT?
GRUMBLE
I DON'T NEED TO HEAR HER PRATTLE ABOUT GHOSTS!
GRUMBLE
THAT'S NOT WHAT I MEAN.
Parthenon Productions
I KNOW EXACTLY HOW MEGUMI FEELS.
AND THAT'S WHY I REFUSE TO BABY HER!
I CAN'T MOLLIFY HER EVERY TIME A NEW IDOL DOES WELL.
TO BE HONEST...
I NEVER THOUGHT SHE'D BE SO JEALOUS OF A NEW IDOL.
IF SHE WANTS TO SURVIVE IN THIS INDUSTRY...
SHE NEEDS TO LEARN TO DEAL WITH THESE FEELINGS HERSELF.

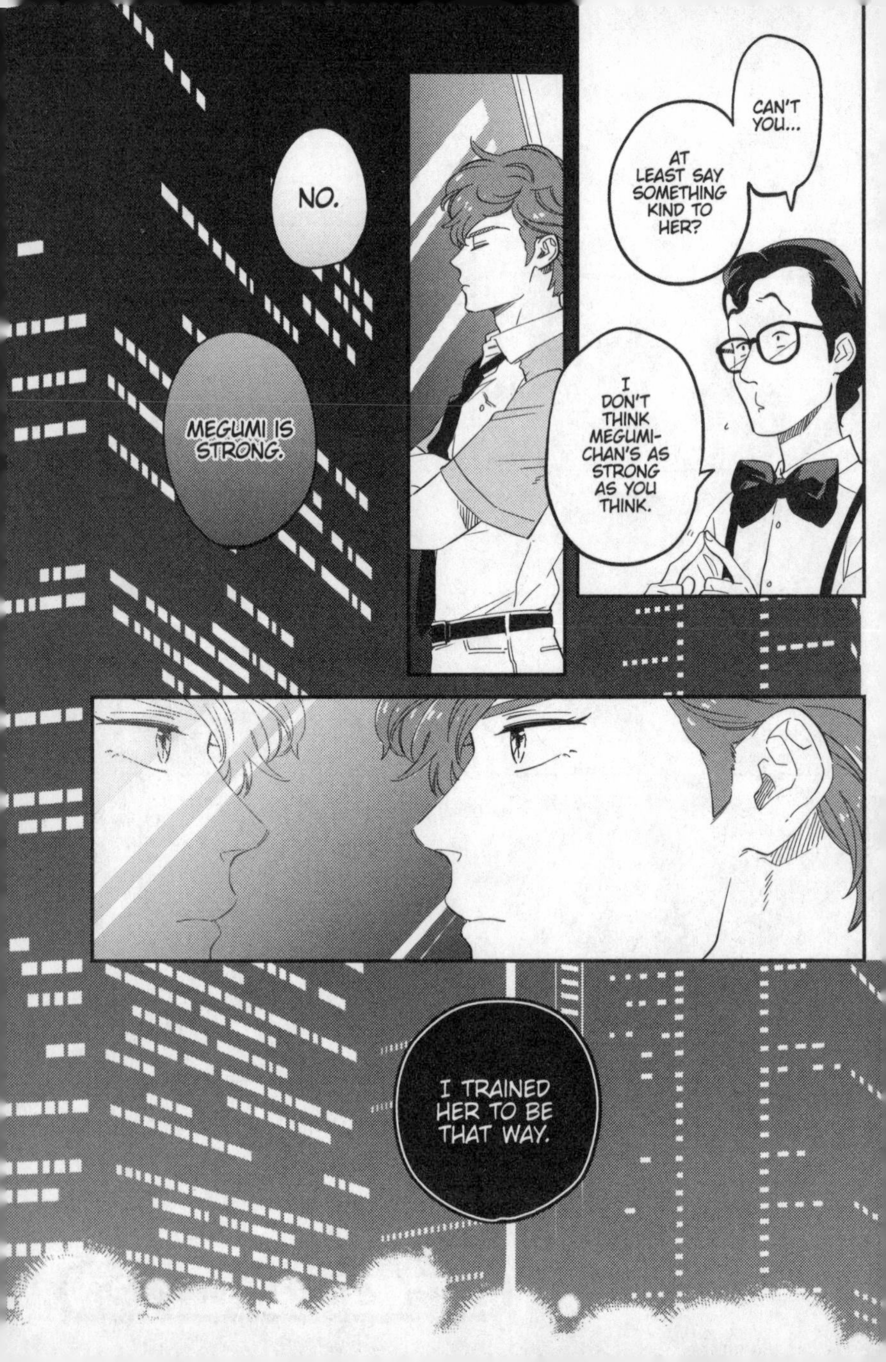
CAN'T YOU...
AT LEAST SAY SOMETHING KIND TO HER?
I DON'T THINK MEGUMI-CHAN'S AS STRONG AS YOU THINK.
NO.
MEGUMI IS STRONG.
I TRAINED HER TO BE THAT WAY.

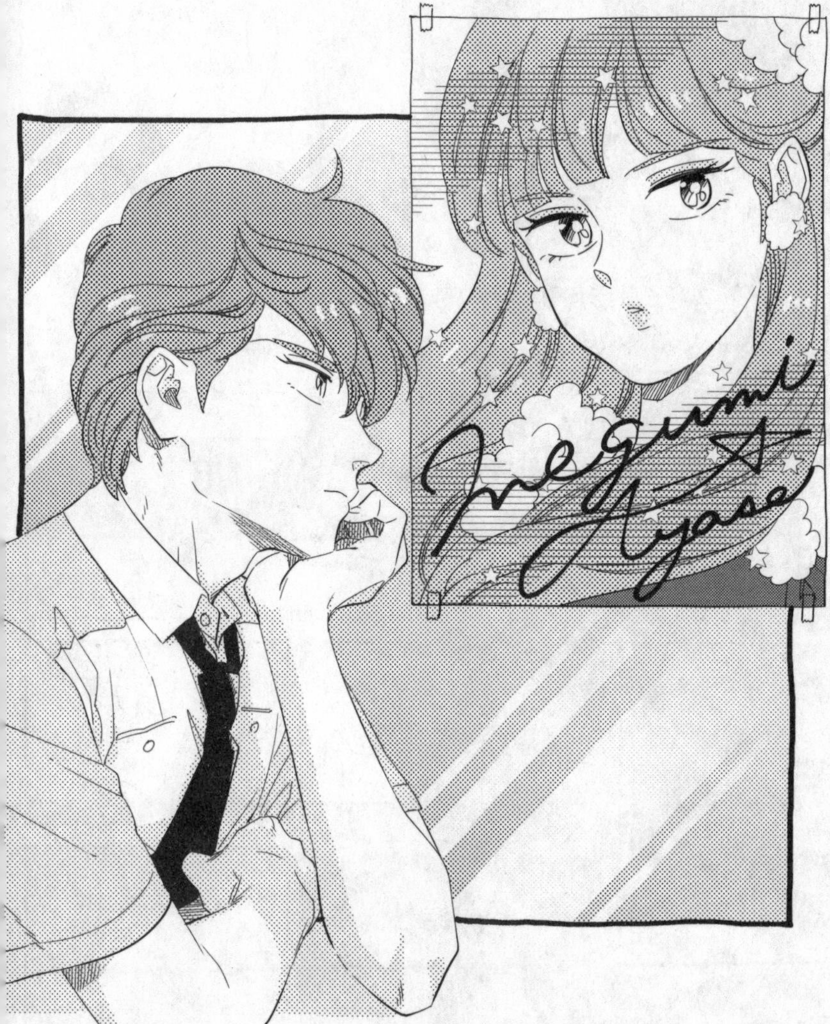
Megumi Ayase

13 A Star in the Rough

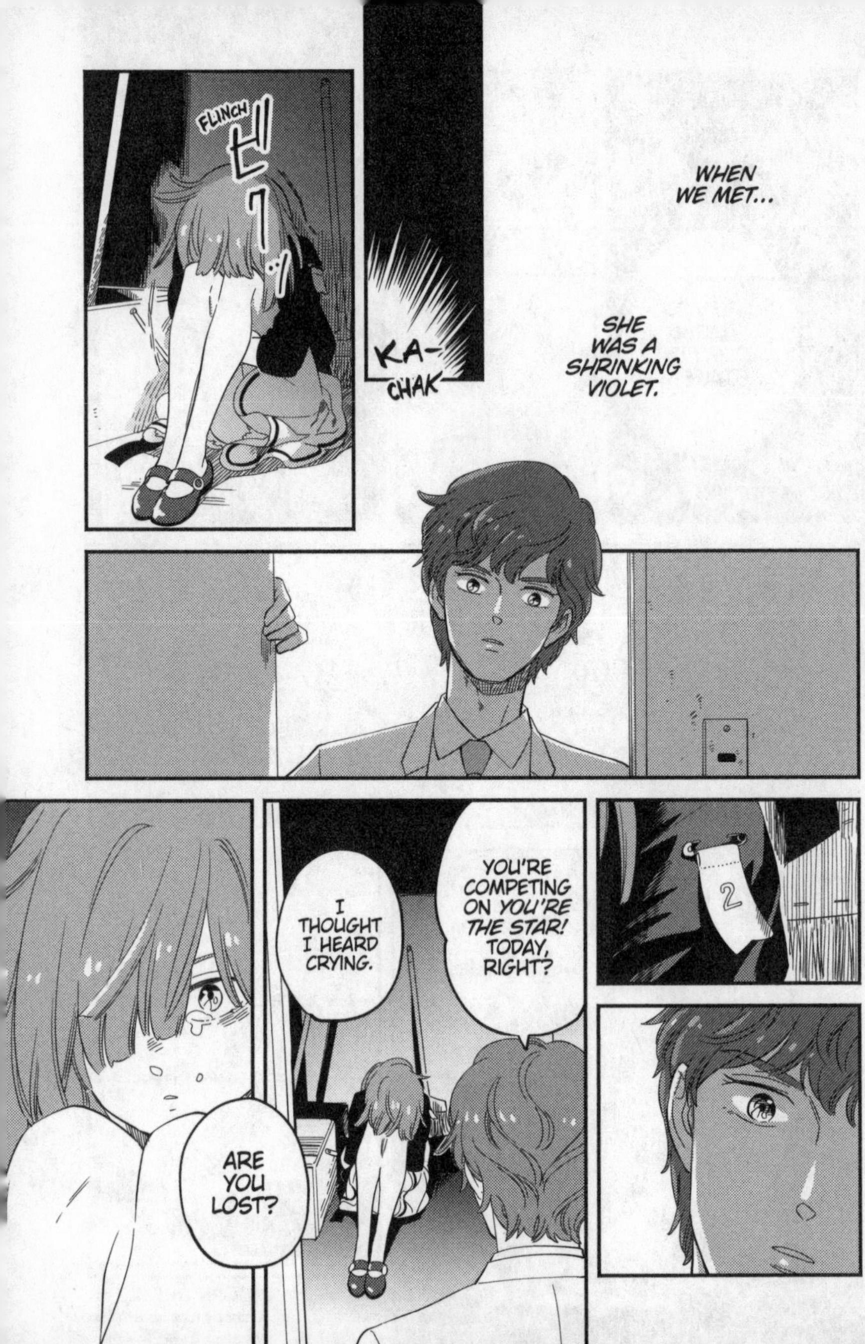
WHEN WE MET...
SHE WAS A SHRINKING VIOLET.
KA-CHAK
FLINCH
YOU'RE COMPETING ON *YOU'RE THE STAR!* TODAY, RIGHT?
I THOUGHT I HEARD CRYING.
ARE YOU LOST?

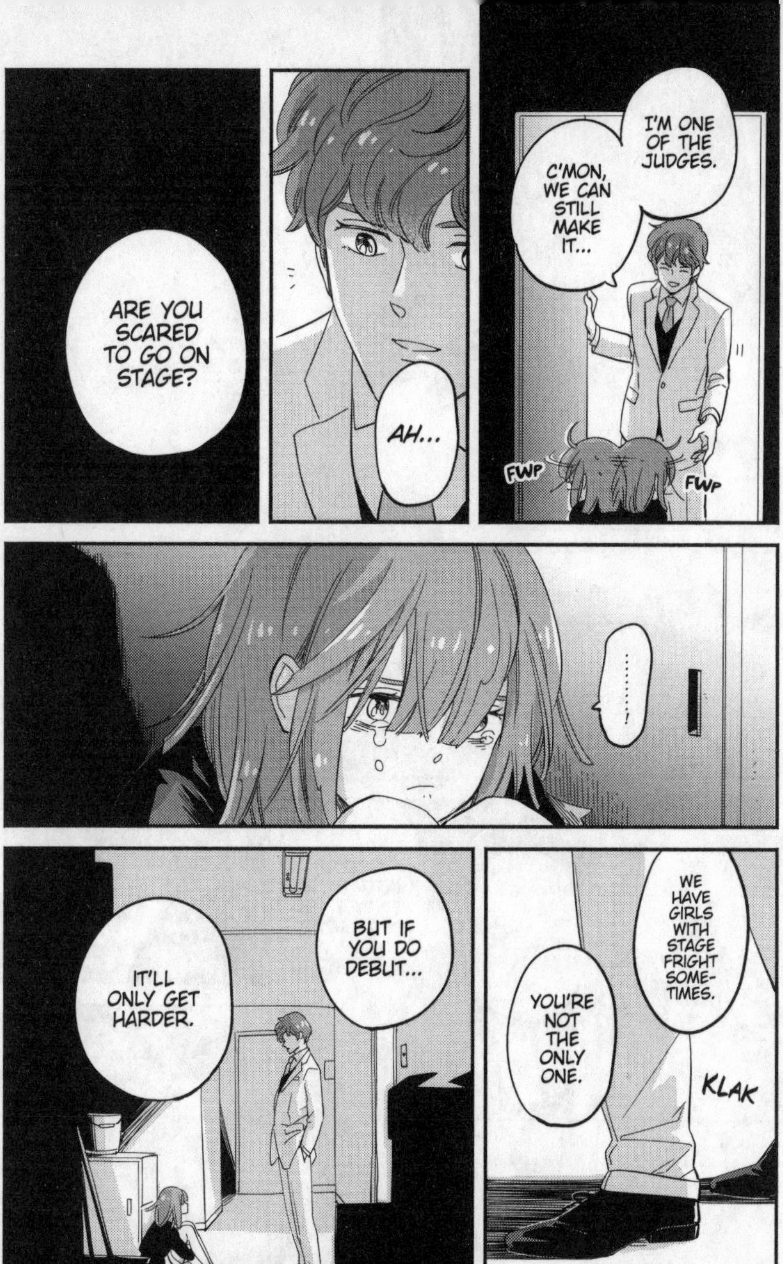
I'M ONE OF THE JUDGES.
C'MON, WE CAN STILL MAKE IT...
FWP
FWP
AH...
ARE YOU SCARED TO GO ON STAGE?
......!
WE HAVE GIRLS WITH STAGE FRIGHT SOME-TIMES.
YOU'RE NOT THE ONLY ONE.
KLAK
BUT IF YOU DO DEBUT...
IT'LL ONLY GET HARDER.

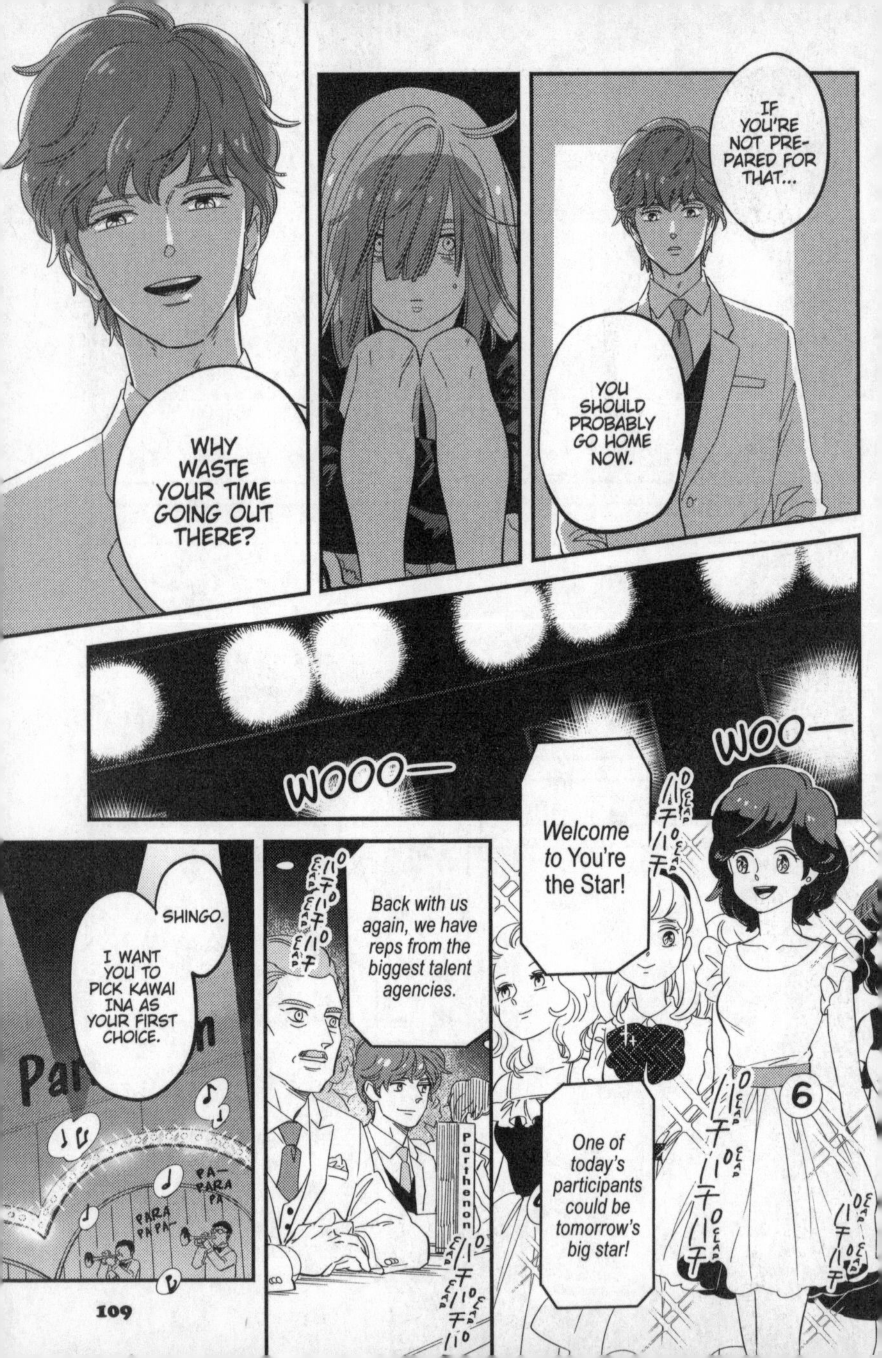
IF YOU'RE NOT PRE-PARED FOR THAT...
YOU SHOULD PROBABLY GO HOME NOW.
WHY WASTE YOUR TIME GOING OUT THERE?
WOO—
WOOO—
Welcome to You're the Star!
CLAP CLAP
One of today's participants could be tomorrow's big star!
CLAP CLAP
Back with us again, we have reps from the biggest talent agencies.
CLAP CLAP
Parthenon
SHINGO.
I WANT YOU TO PICK KAWAI INA AS YOUR FIRST CHOICE.
PA-PARA PA
PARA PAPA-

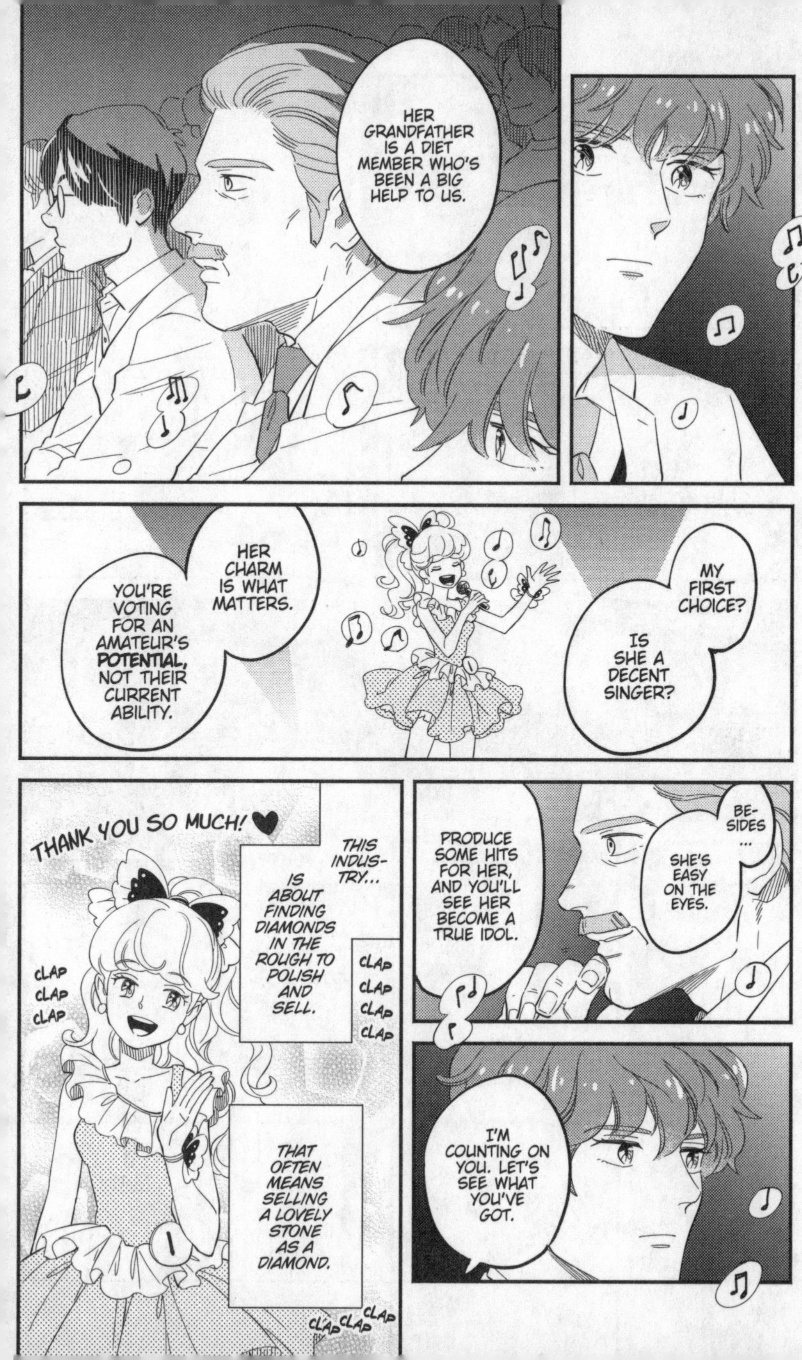
HER GRANDFATHER IS A DIET MEMBER WHO'S BEEN A BIG HELP TO US.
MY FIRST CHOICE?
IS SHE A DECENT SINGER?
HER CHARM IS WHAT MATTERS.
YOU'RE VOTING FOR AN AMATEUR'S POTENTIAL, NOT THEIR CURRENT ABILITY.
BE-SIDES...
SHE'S EASY ON THE EYES.
PRODUCE SOME HITS FOR HER, AND YOU'LL SEE HER BECOME A TRUE IDOL.
I'M COUNTING ON YOU. LET'S SEE WHAT YOU'VE GOT.
THIS INDUSTRY...
IS ABOUT FINDING DIAMONDS IN THE ROUGH TO POLISH AND SELL.
CLAP CLAP CLAP CLAP
THANK YOU SO MUCH! ♥
CLAP CLAP CLAP
THAT OFTEN MEANS SELLING A LOVELY STONE AS A DIAMOND.
CLAP CLAP CLAP

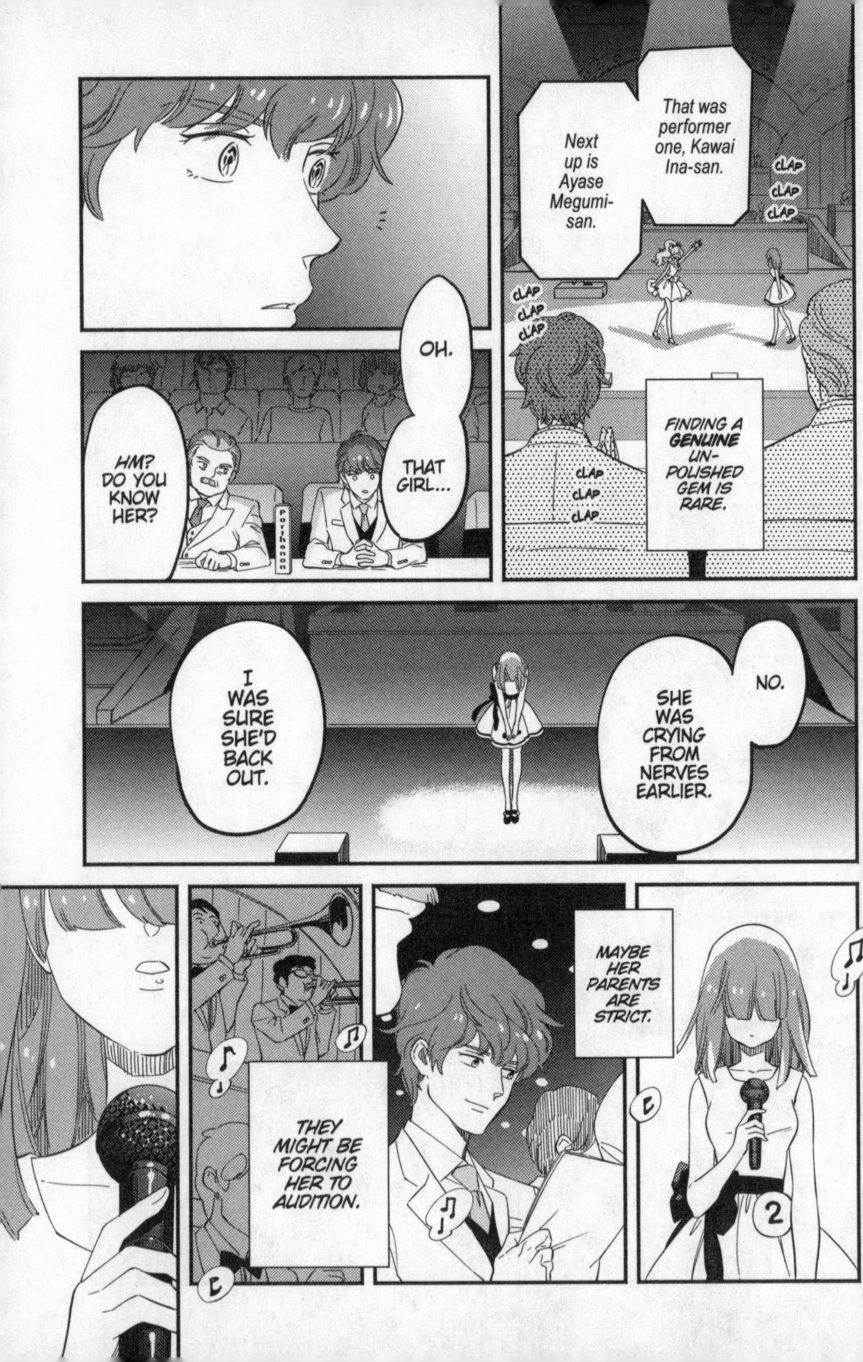
That was performer one, Kawai Ina-san.
Next up is Ayase Megumi-san.
CLAP CLAP CLAP
CLAP CLAP CLAP
FINDING A **GENUINE** UN-POLISHED GEM IS RARE.
CLAP CLAP CLAP
OH.
THAT GIRL...
HM? DO YOU KNOW HER?
Parthenon
NO.
SHE WAS CRYING FROM NERVES EARLIER.
I WAS SURE SHE'D BACK OUT.
2
MAYBE HER PARENTS ARE STRICT.
THEY MIGHT BE FORCING HER TO AUDITION.

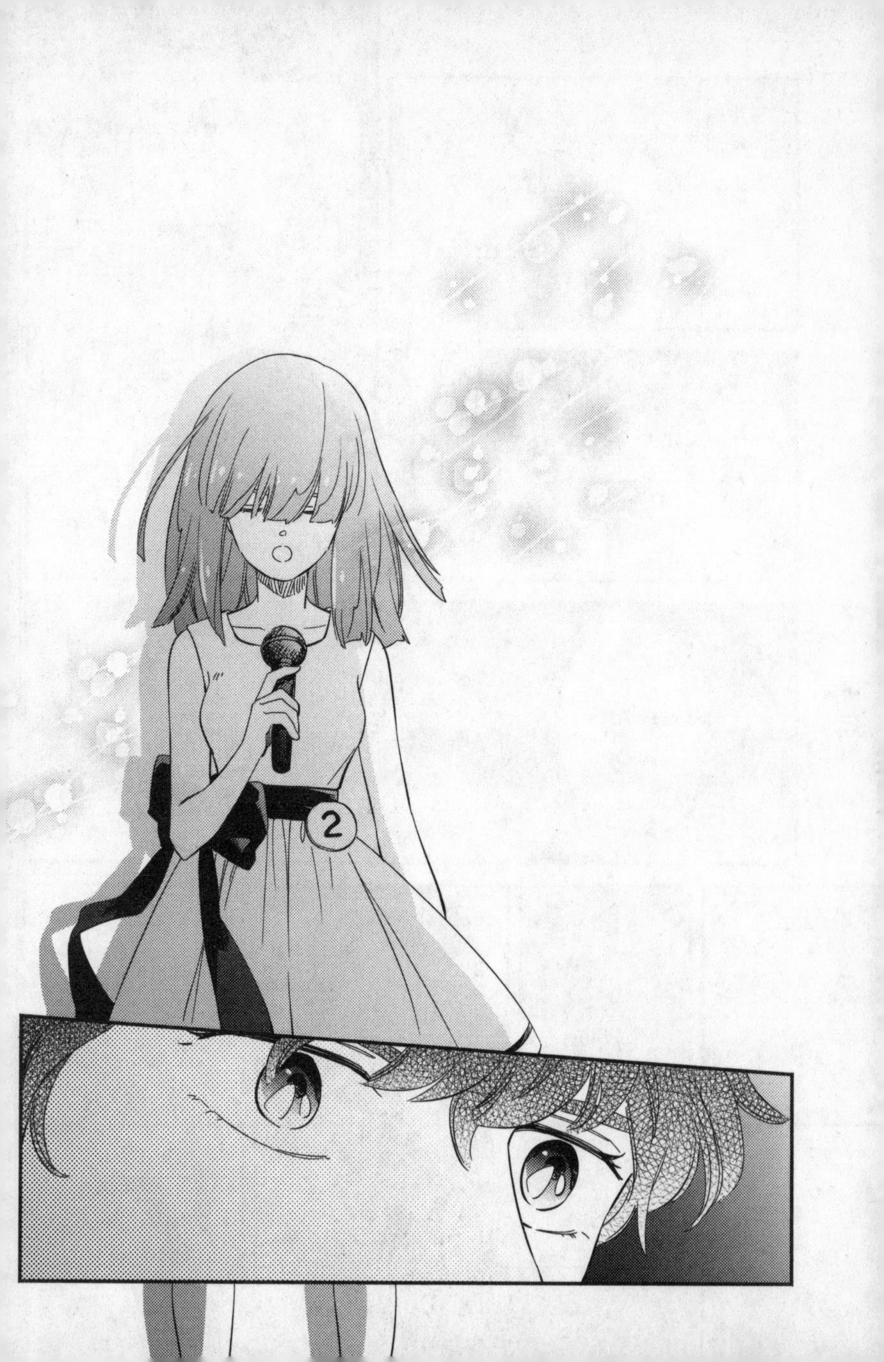
2

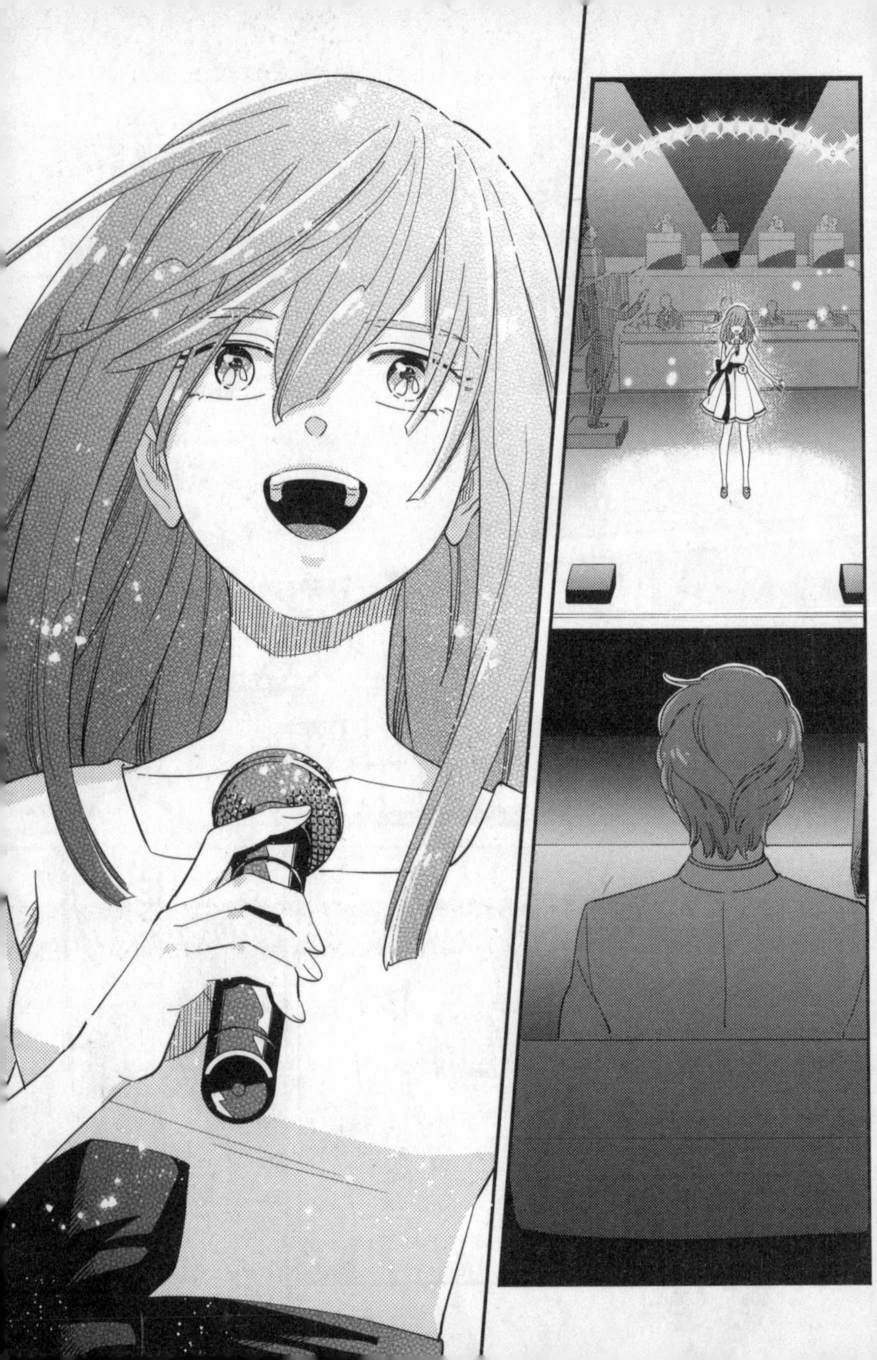

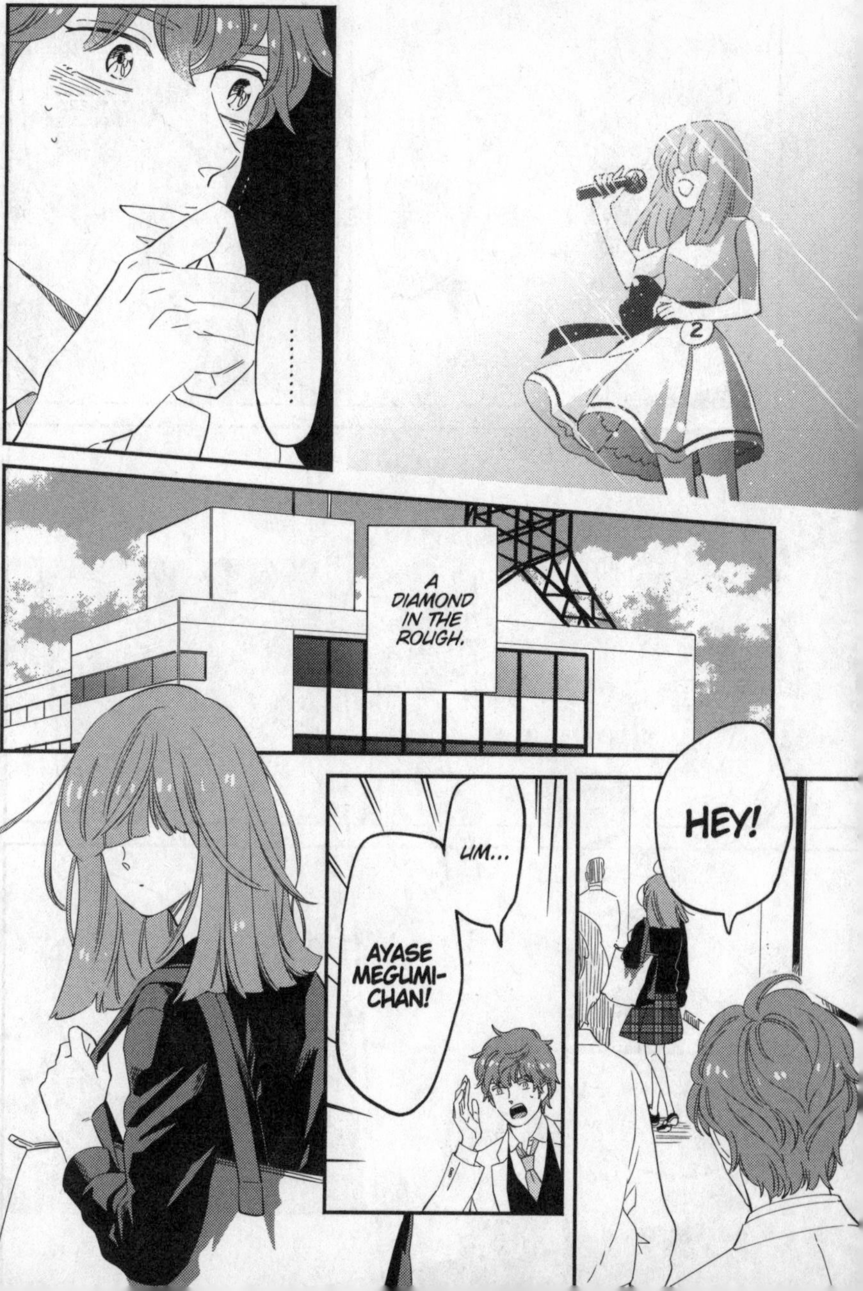
......
A DIAMOND IN THE ROUGH.
HEY!
UM...
AYASE MEGUMI-CHAN!

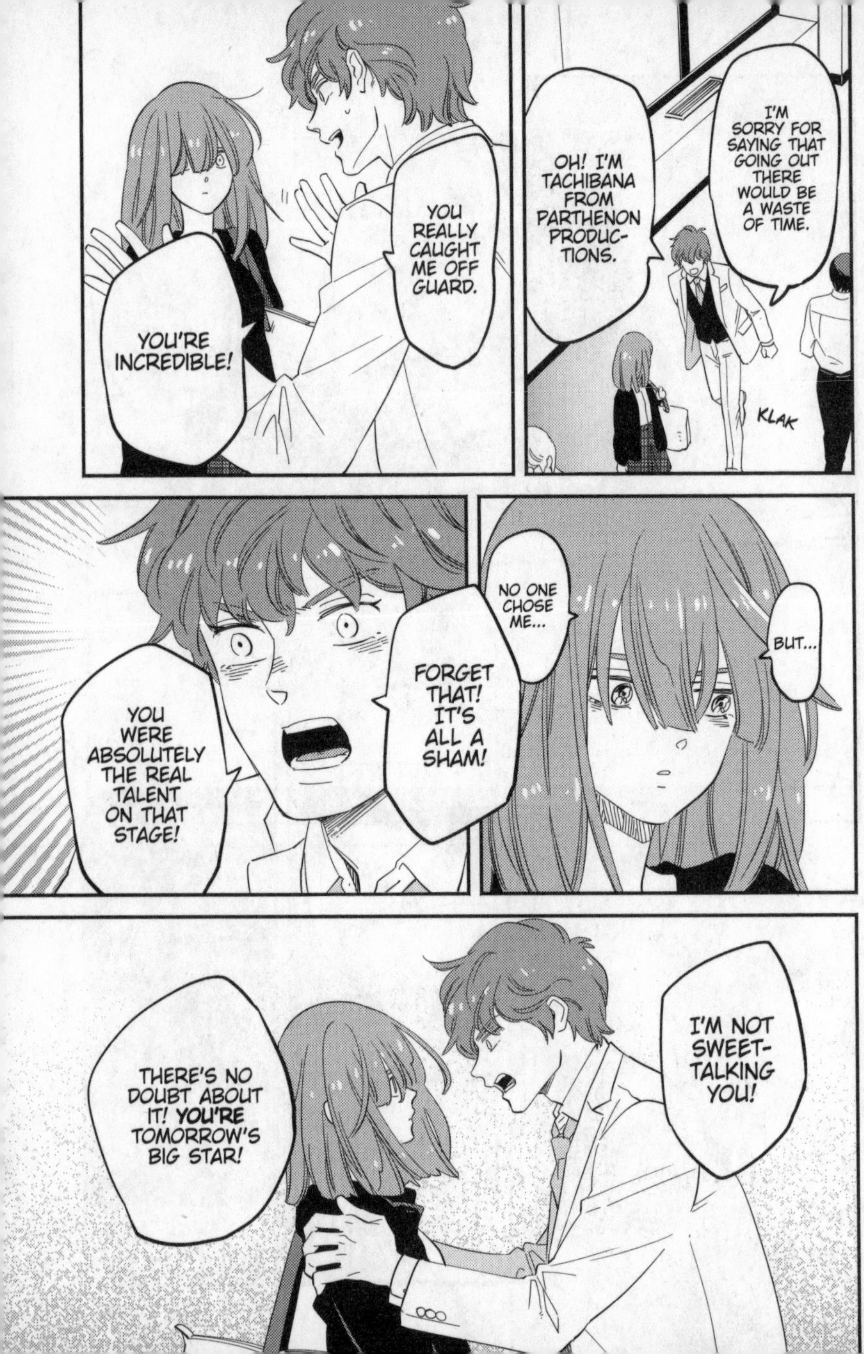
I'M SORRY FOR SAYING THAT GOING OUT THERE WOULD BE A WASTE OF TIME.
OH! I'M TACHIBANA FROM PARTHENON PRODUC-TIONS.
KLAK
YOU REALLY CAUGHT ME OFF GUARD.
YOU'RE INCREDIBLE!
NO ONE CHOSE ME...
BUT...
FORGET THAT! IT'S ALL A SHAM!
YOU WERE ABSOLUTELY THE REAL TALENT ON THAT STAGE!
I'M NOT SWEET-TALKING YOU!
THERE'S NO DOUBT ABOUT IT! **YOU'RE** TOMORROW'S BIG STAR!

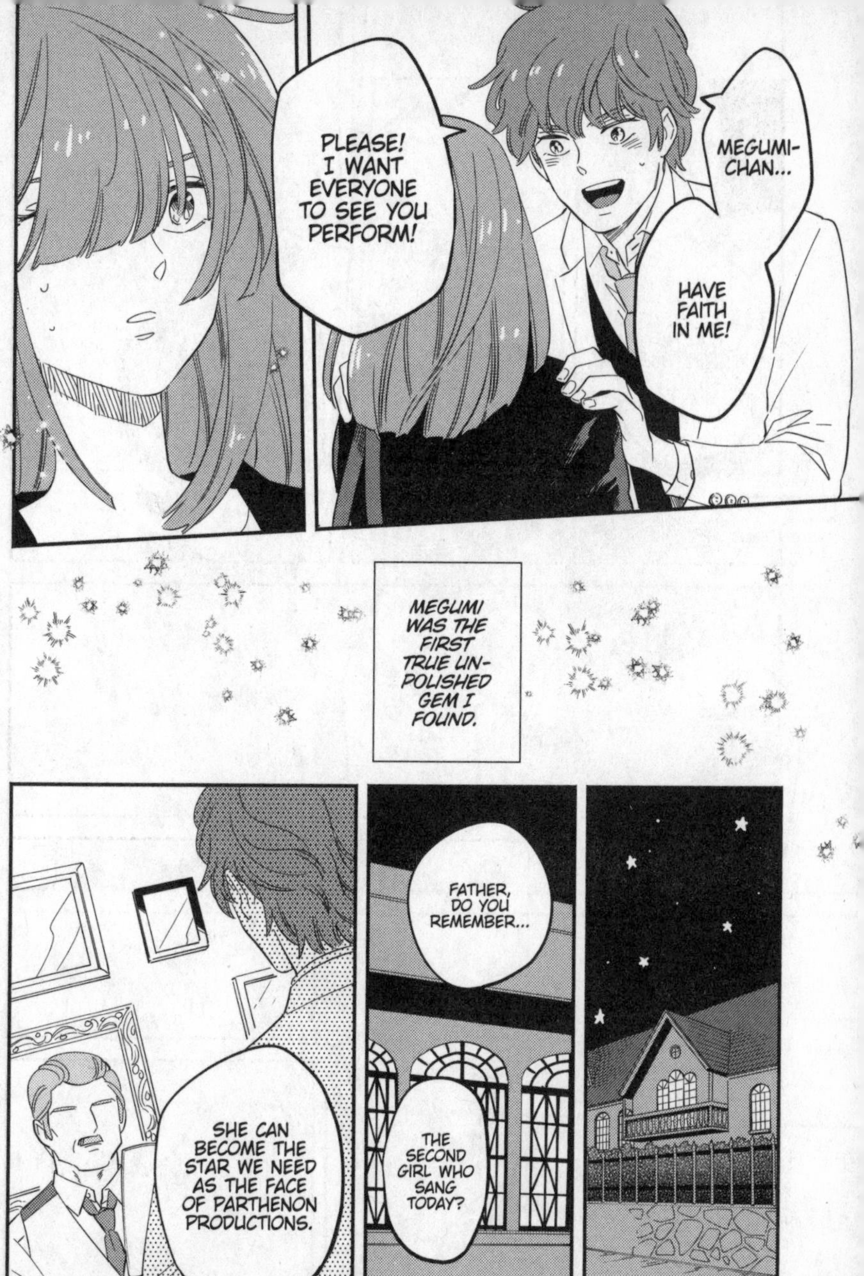
MEGUMI-CHAN...
HAVE FAITH IN ME!
PLEASE! I WANT EVERYONE TO SEE YOU PERFORM!
MEGUMI WAS THE FIRST TRUE UN-POLISHED GEM I FOUND.
FATHER, DO YOU REMEMBER...
THE SECOND GIRL WHO SANG TODAY?
SHE CAN BECOME THE STAR WE NEED AS THE FACE OF PARTHENON PRODUCTIONS.

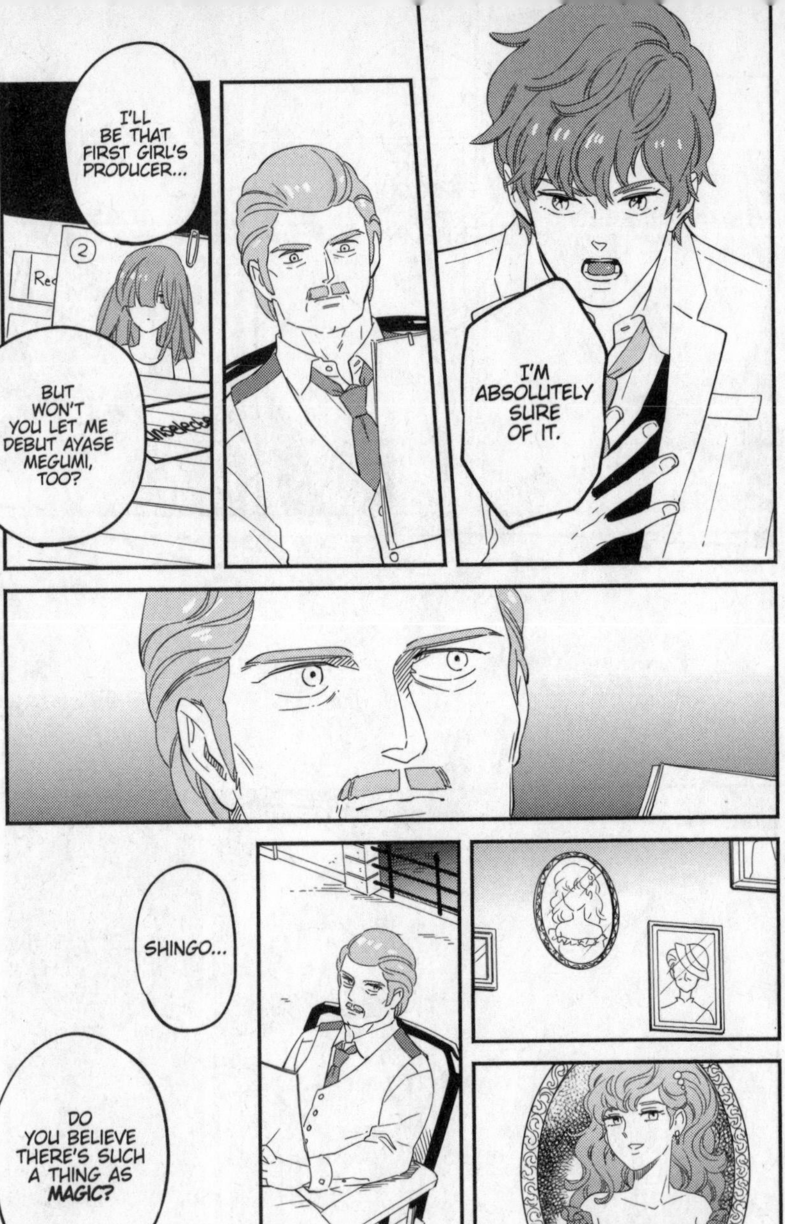
I'M ABSOLUTELY SURE OF IT.
I'LL BE THAT FIRST GIRL'S PRODUCER...
BUT WON'T YOU LET ME DEBUT AYASE MEGUMI, TOO?
SHINGO...
DO YOU BELIEVE THERE'S SUCH A THING AS **MAGIC?**

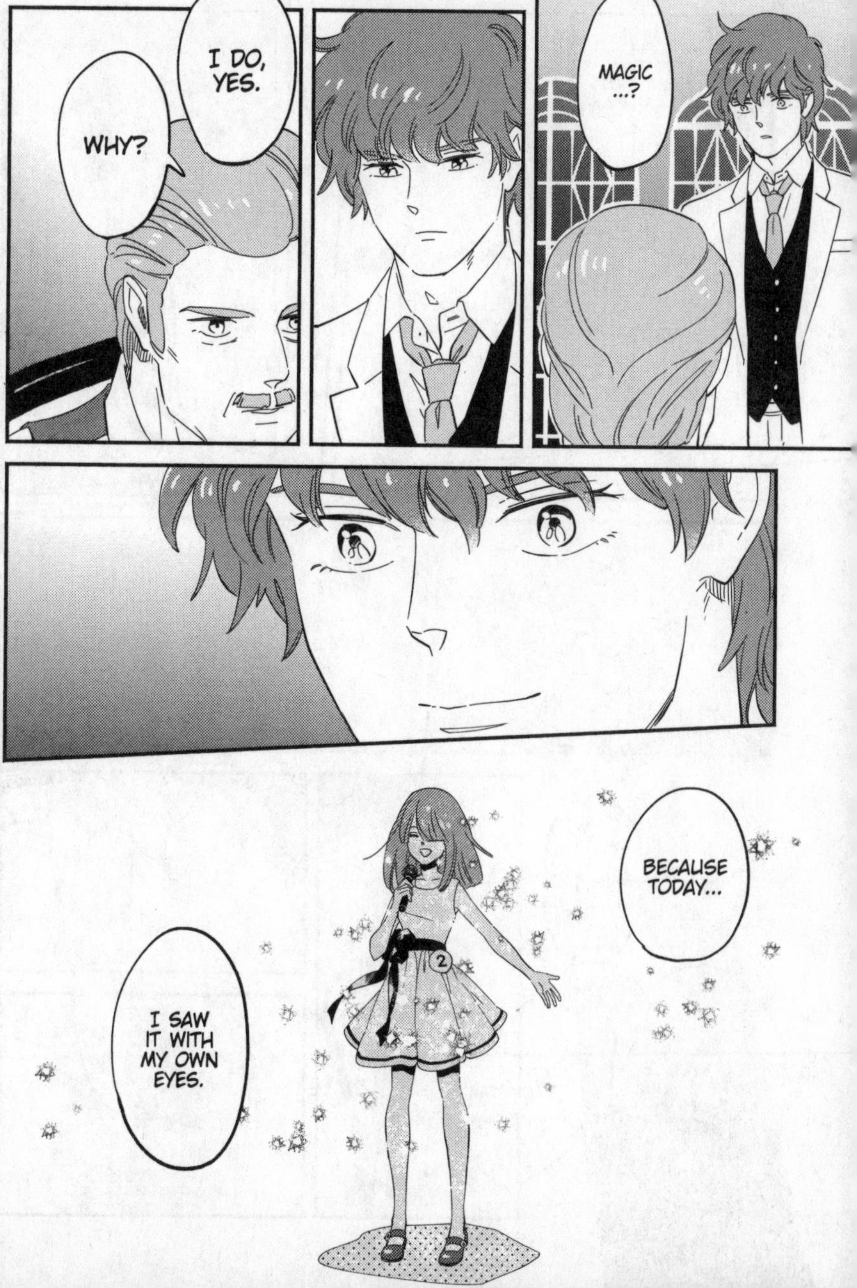
MAGIC ...?
I DO, YES.
WHY?
BECAUSE TODAY...
I SAW IT WITH MY OWN EYES.

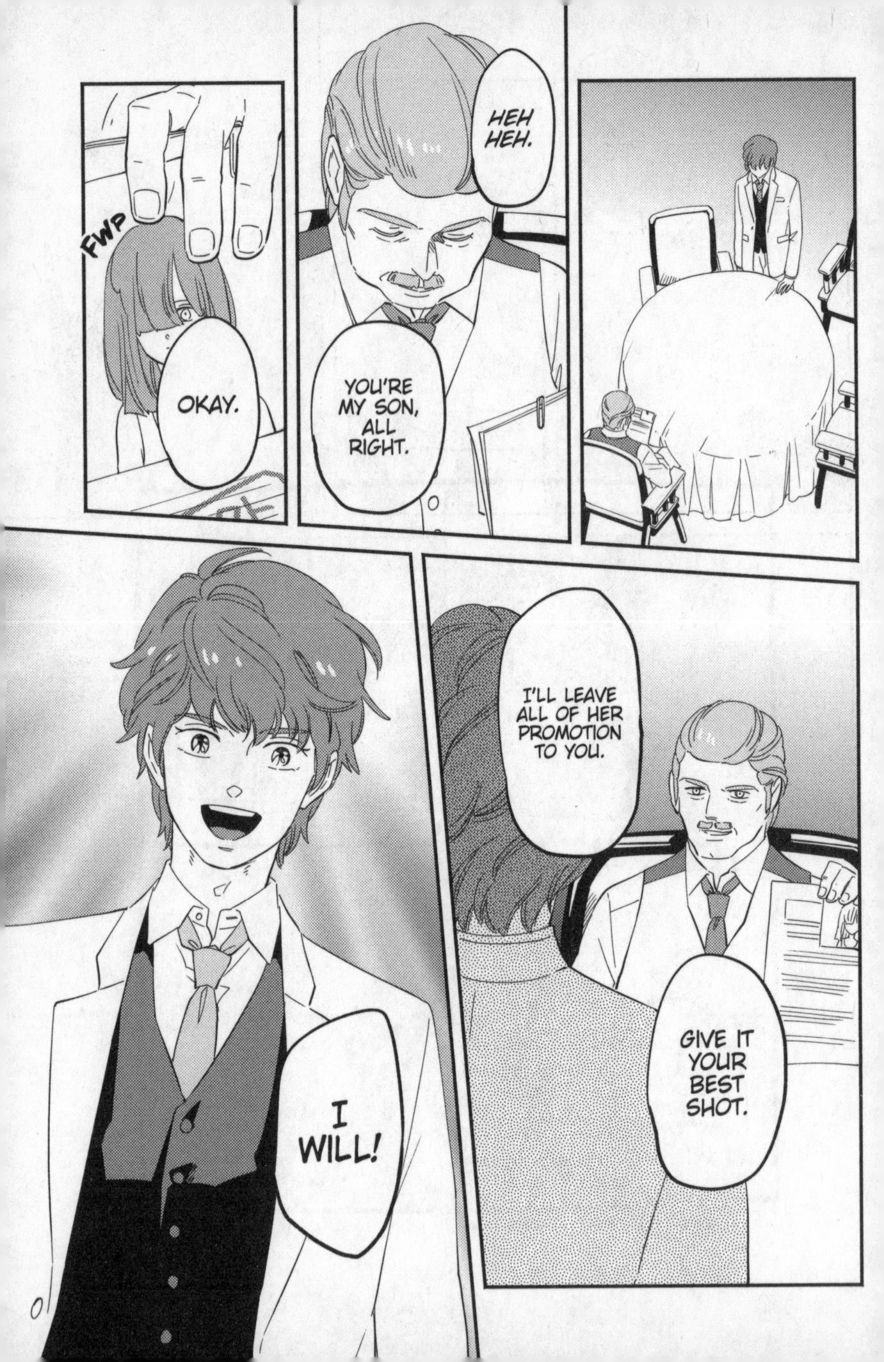
HEH HEH.
YOU'RE MY SON, ALL RIGHT.
FWP
OKAY.
I'LL LEAVE ALL OF HER PROMOTION TO YOU.
GIVE IT YOUR BEST SHOT.
I WILL!

People of the '80s

I WANNA GO SEE CATS!
YOU HAVE TO WORK!
I WANNA RIDE THE TOHOKU BULLET TRAIN LINE!
YOU HAVE TO WORK!
JUST RELAX WITH THESE WAVE SOUNDS.
ZSSSH

First Japanese performance in '83.

The line opened in '82.

The Walkman came out in '79 and the compact "cassette size" premiered in '83.

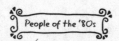

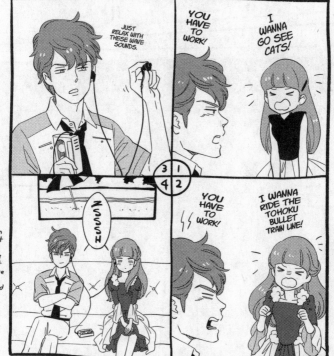

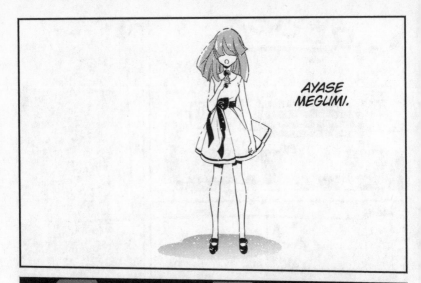

AYASE MEGUMI.

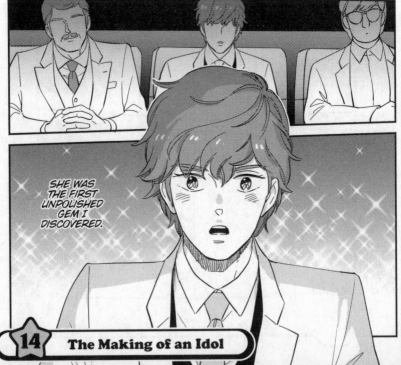

SHE WAS THE FIRST UNPOLISHED GEM I DISCOVERED.

14 The Making of an Idol

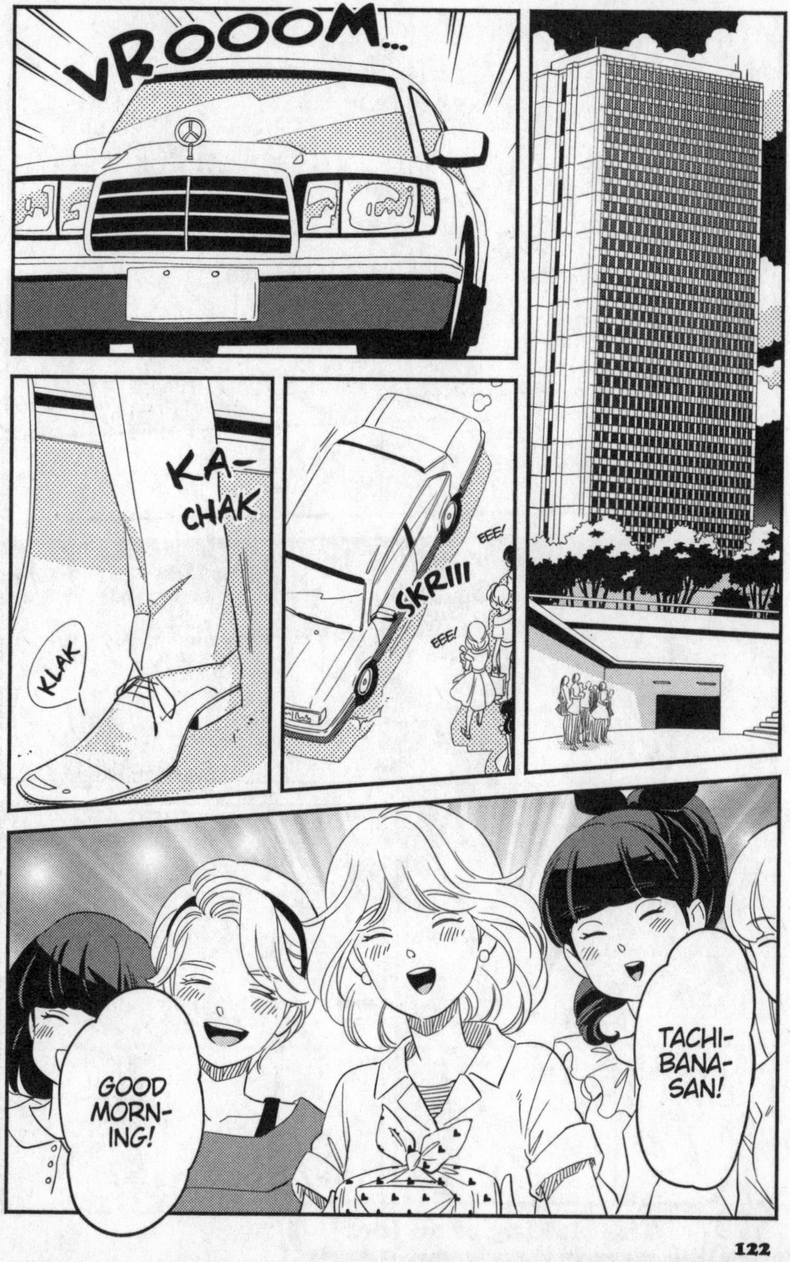
VROOOM...
EEE!
SKRIII
EEE!
KA-CHAK
KLAK
TACHI-BANA-SAN!
GOOD MORN-ING!

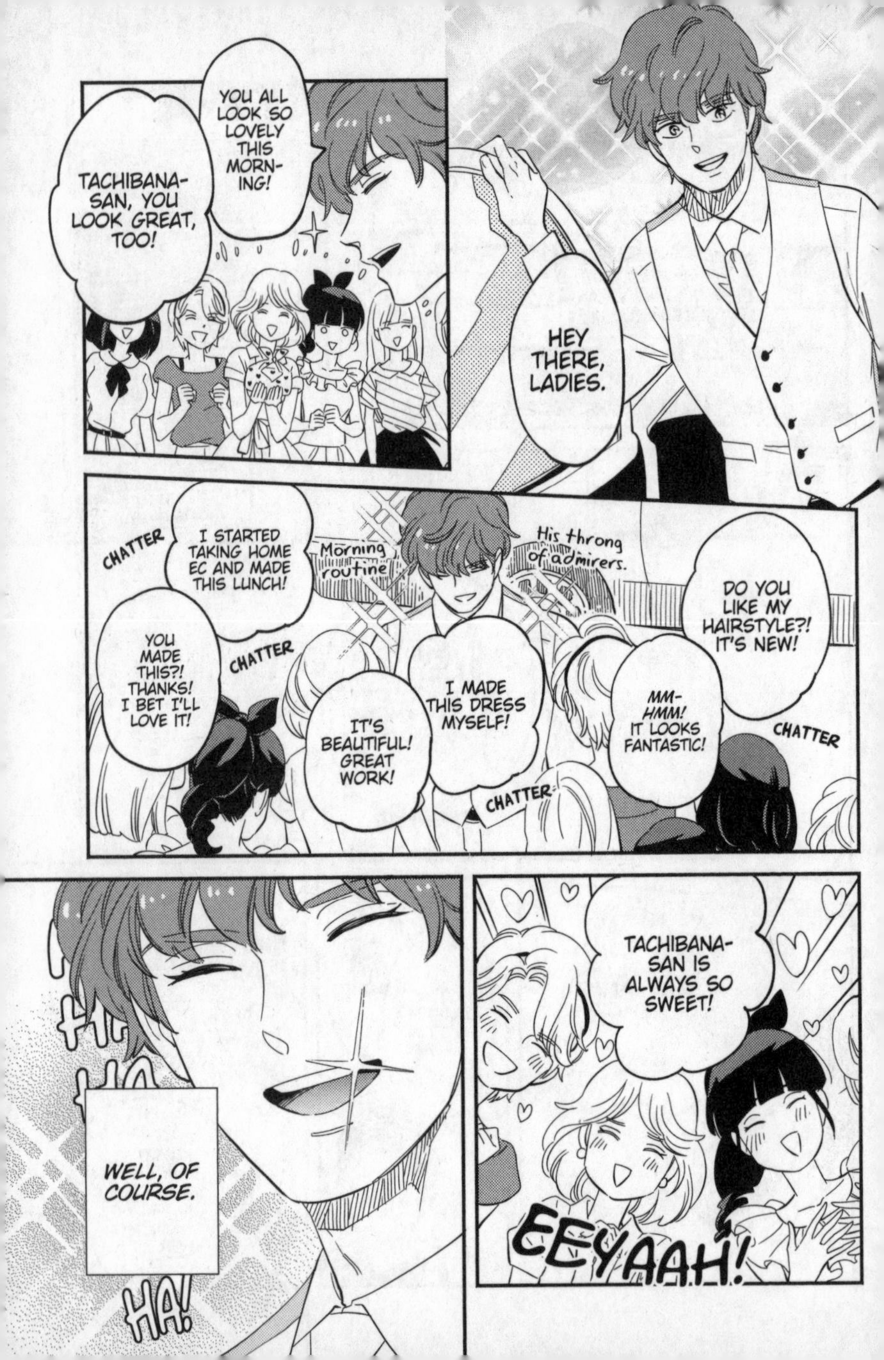
HEY THERE, LADIES.
YOU ALL LOOK SO LOVELY THIS MORNING!
TACHIBANA-SAN, YOU LOOK GREAT, TOO!
His throng of admirers.
DO YOU LIKE MY HAIRSTYLE?! IT'S NEW!
CHATTER
MM-HMM! IT LOOKS FANTASTIC!
I MADE THIS DRESS MYSELF!
IT'S BEAUTIFUL! GREAT WORK!
CHATTER
Morning routine
I STARTED TAKING HOME EC AND MADE THIS LUNCH!
CHATTER
YOU MADE THIS?! THANKS! I BET I'LL LOVE IT!
CHATTER
TACHIBANA-SAN IS ALWAYS SO SWEET!
EEYAAH!
WELL, OF COURSE.
HA!

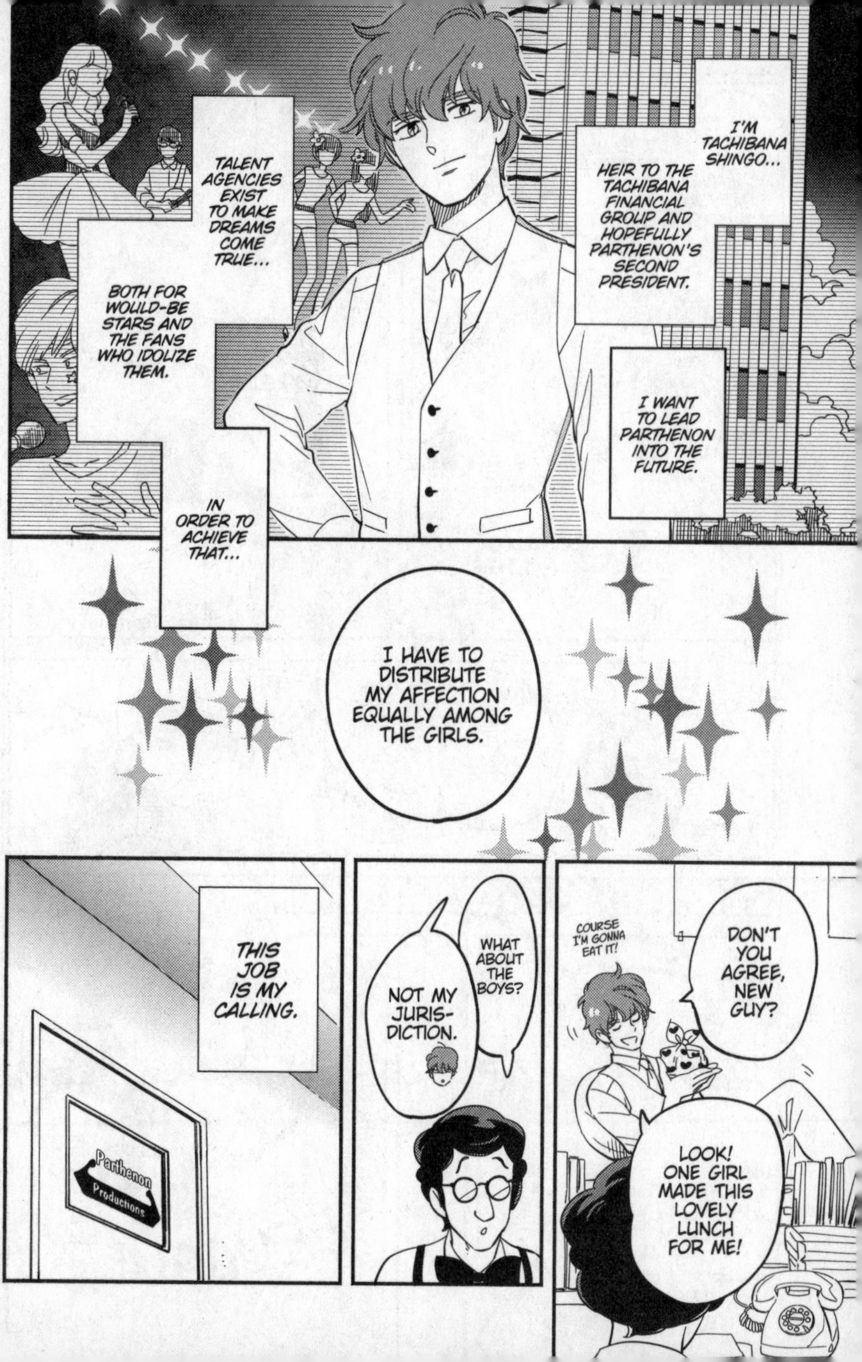
I'M TACHIBANA SHINGO...
HEIR TO THE TACHIBANA FINANCIAL GROUP AND HOPEFULLY PARTHENON'S SECOND PRESIDENT.
I WANT TO LEAD PARTHENON INTO THE FUTURE.
TALENT AGENCIES EXIST TO MAKE DREAMS COME TRUE...
BOTH FOR WOULD-BE STARS AND THE FANS WHO IDOLIZE THEM.
IN ORDER TO ACHIEVE THAT...
I HAVE TO DISTRIBUTE MY AFFECTION EQUALLY AMONG THE GIRLS.
DON'T YOU AGREE, NEW GUY?
COURSE I'M GONNA EAT IT!
LOOK! ONE GIRL MADE THIS LOVELY LUNCH FOR ME!
WHAT ABOUT THE BOYS?
NOT MY JURIS-DICTION.
THIS JOB IS MY CALLING.
Parthenon Productions
...

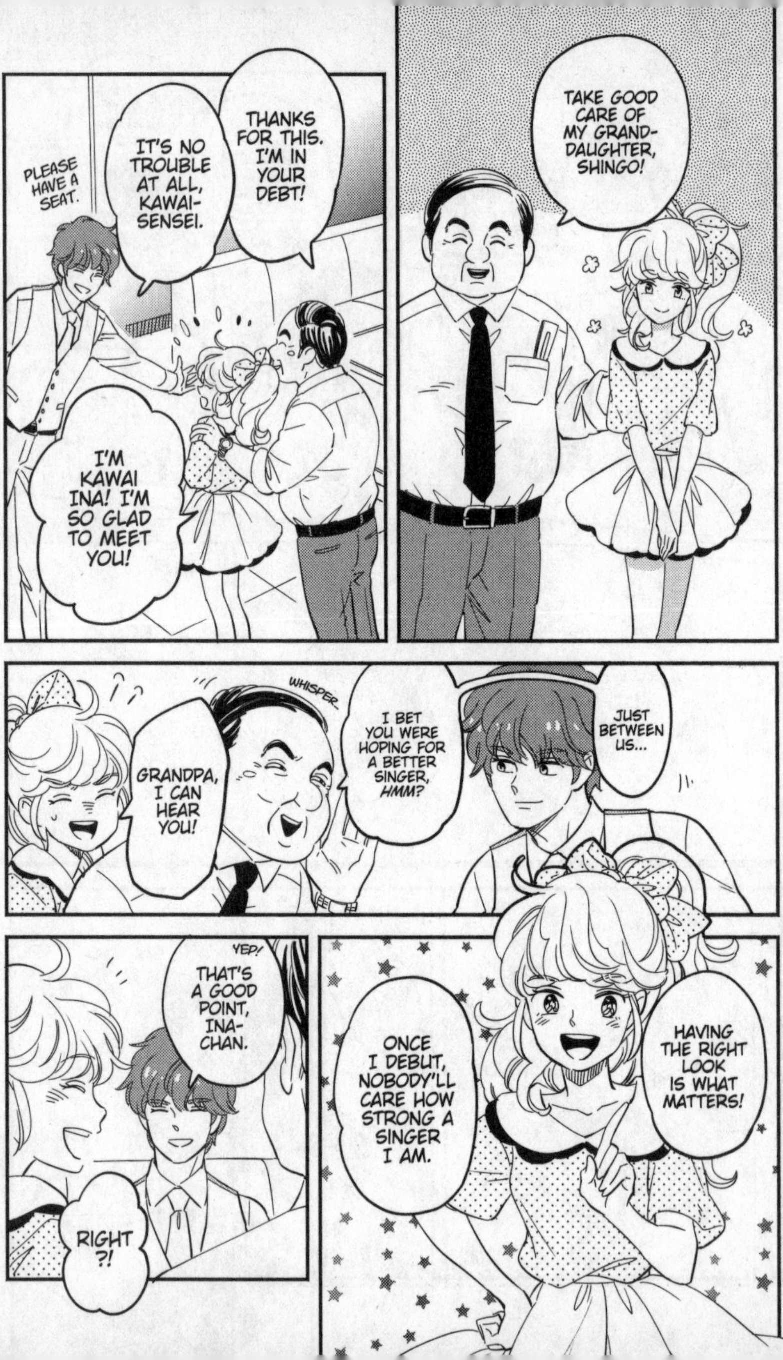
TAKE GOOD CARE OF MY GRAND-DAUGHTER, SHINGO!
THANKS FOR THIS. I'M IN YOUR DEBT!
IT'S NO TROUBLE AT ALL, KAWAI-SENSEI.
PLEASE HAVE A SEAT.
I'M KAWAI INA! I'M SO GLAD TO MEET YOU!
JUST BETWEEN US...
WHISPER
I BET YOU WERE HOPING FOR A BETTER SINGER, *HMM?*
GRANDPA, I CAN HEAR YOU!
HAVING THE RIGHT LOOK IS WHAT MATTERS!
ONCE I DEBUT, NOBODY'LL CARE HOW STRONG A SINGER I AM.
YEP!
THAT'S A GOOD POINT, INA-CHAN.
RIGHT?!

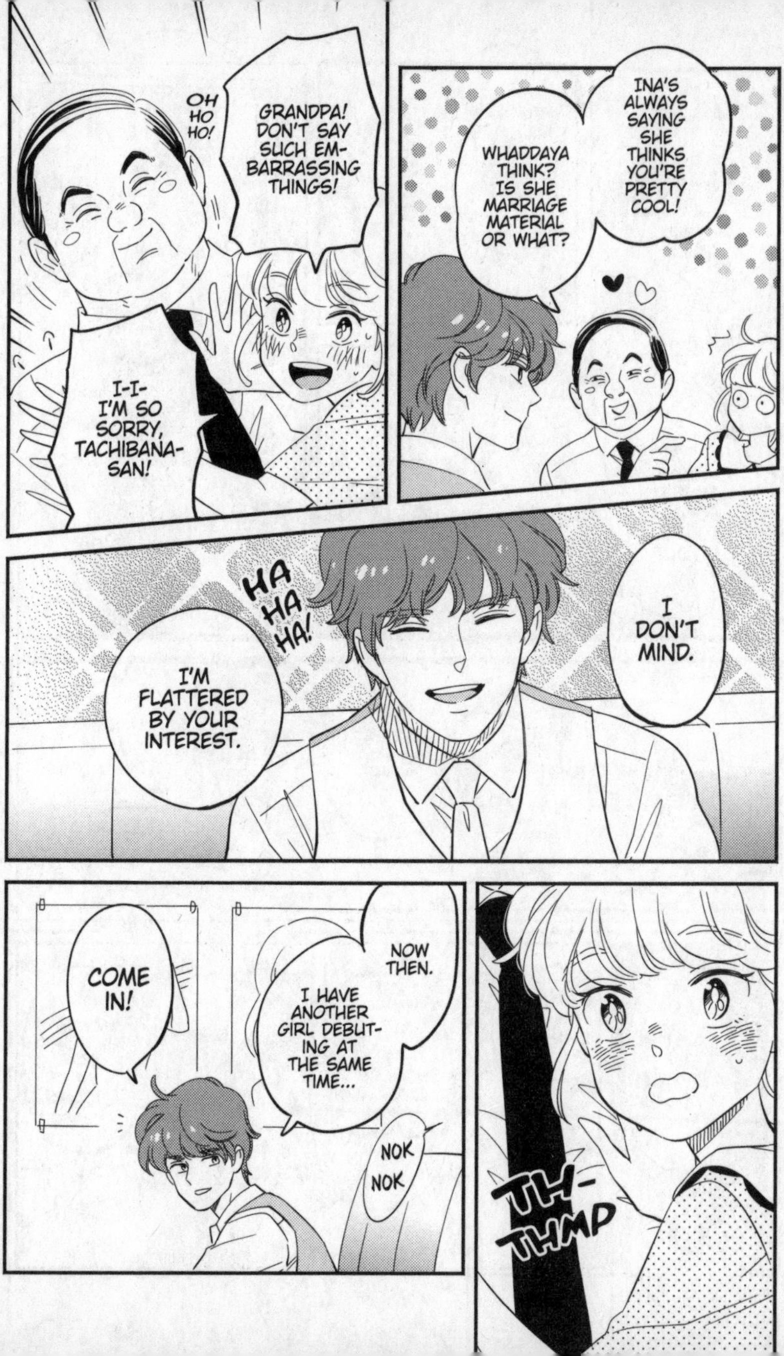
INA'S ALWAYS SAYING SHE THINKS YOU'RE PRETTY COOL!
WHADDAYA THINK? IS SHE MARRIAGE MATERIAL OR WHAT?
GRANDPA! DON'T SAY SUCH EM-BARRASSING THINGS!
OH HO HO!
I-I- I'M SO SORRY, TACHIBANA-SAN!
I DON'T MIND.
HA HA HA!
I'M FLATTERED BY YOUR INTEREST.
TH-THUMP
NOW THEN.
I HAVE ANOTHER GIRL DEBUT-ING AT THE SAME TIME...
NOK NOK
COME IN!

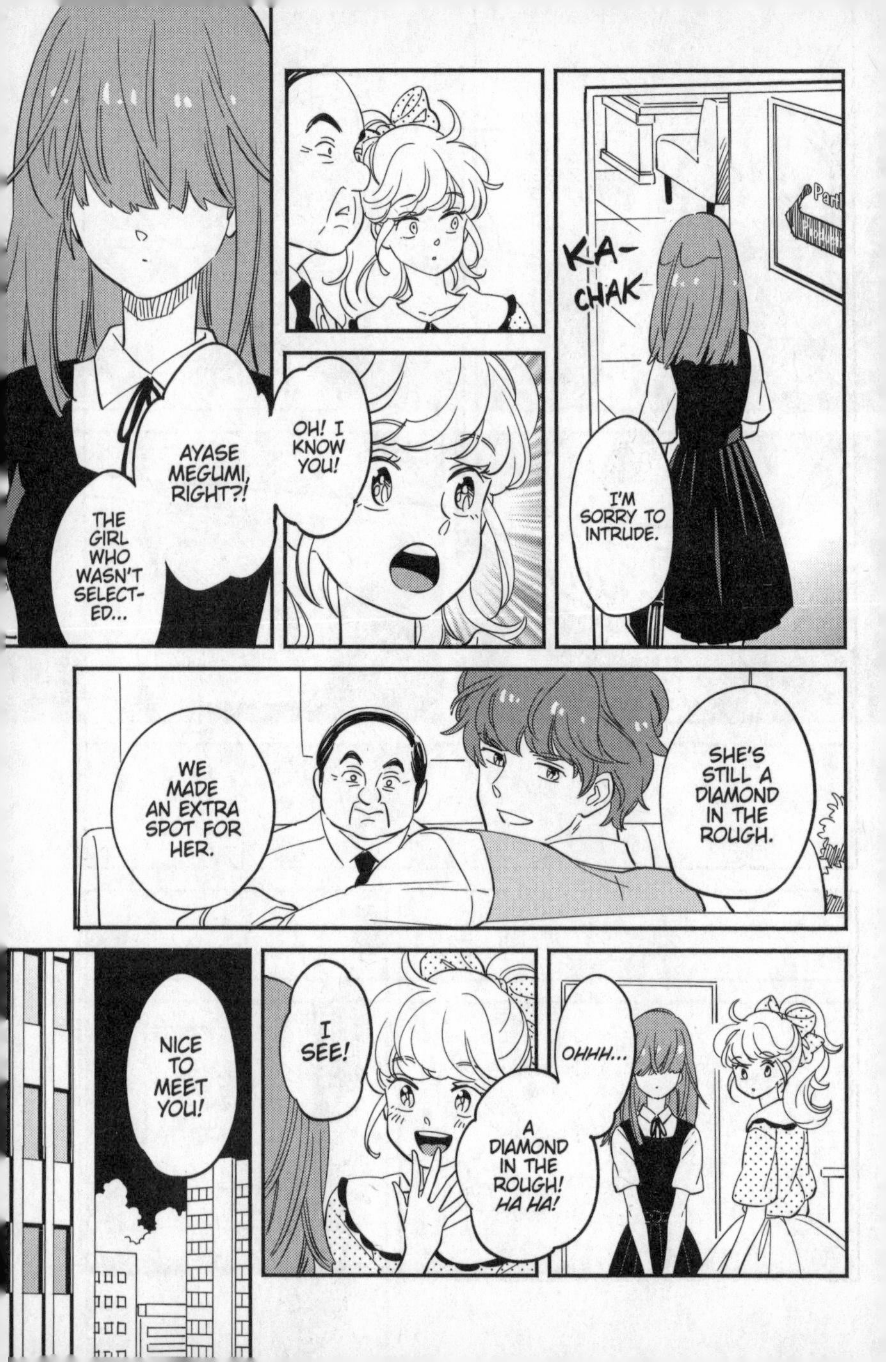
KA-CHAK
I'M SORRY TO INTRUDE.
OH! I KNOW YOU!
AYASE MEGUMI, RIGHT?!
THE GIRL WHO WASN'T SELECT-ED...
SHE'S STILL A DIAMOND IN THE ROUGH.
WE MADE AN EXTRA SPOT FOR HER.
OHHH...
A DIAMOND IN THE ROUGH! HA HA!
I SEE!
NICE TO MEET YOU!

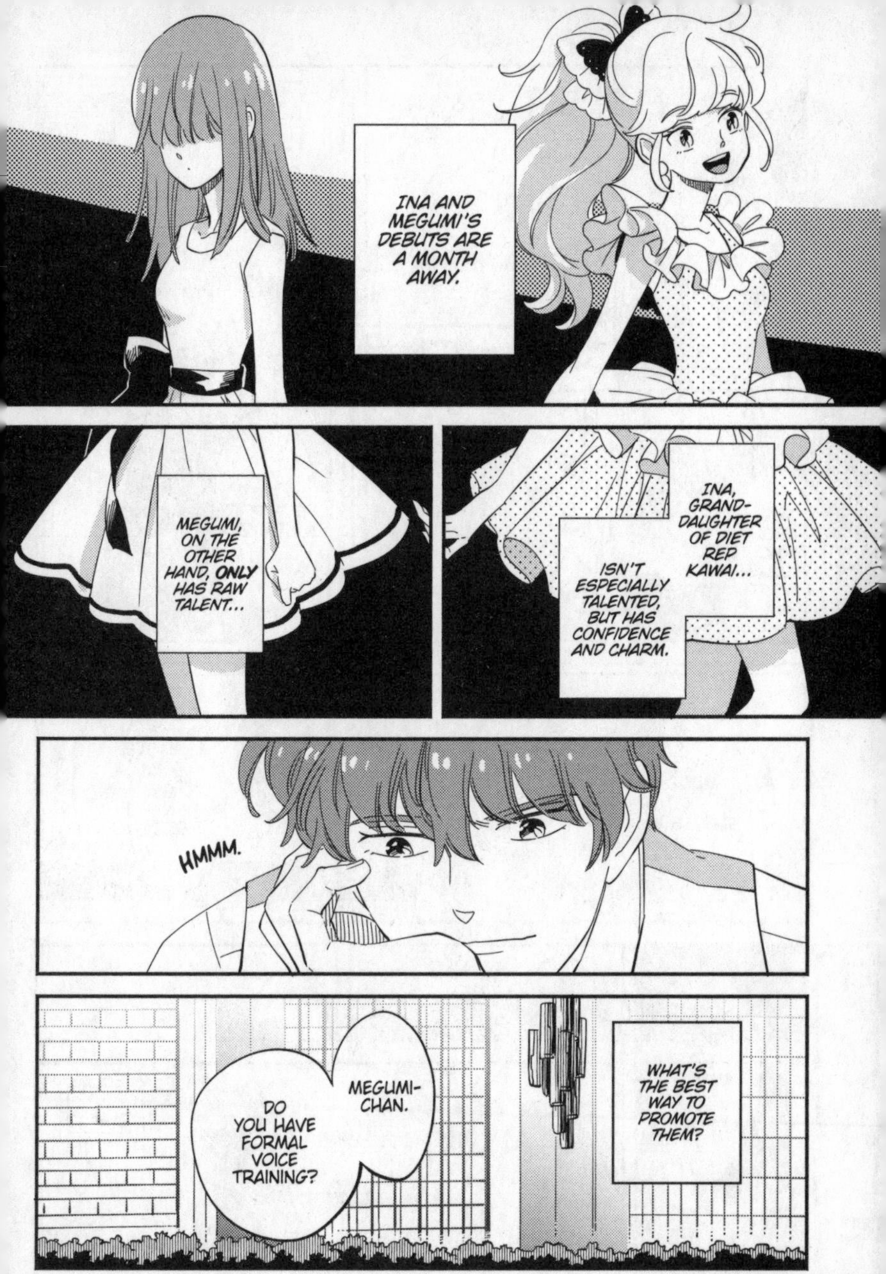
INA AND MEGUMI'S DEBUTS ARE A MONTH AWAY.
INA, GRAND-DAUGHTER OF DIET REP KAWAI...
ISN'T ESPECIALLY TALENTED, BUT HAS CONFIDENCE AND CHARM.
MEGUMI, ON THE OTHER HAND, ONLY HAS RAW TALENT...
HMMM.
WHAT'S THE BEST WAY TO PROMOTE THEM?
MEGUMI-CHAN.
DO YOU HAVE FORMAL VOICE TRAINING?

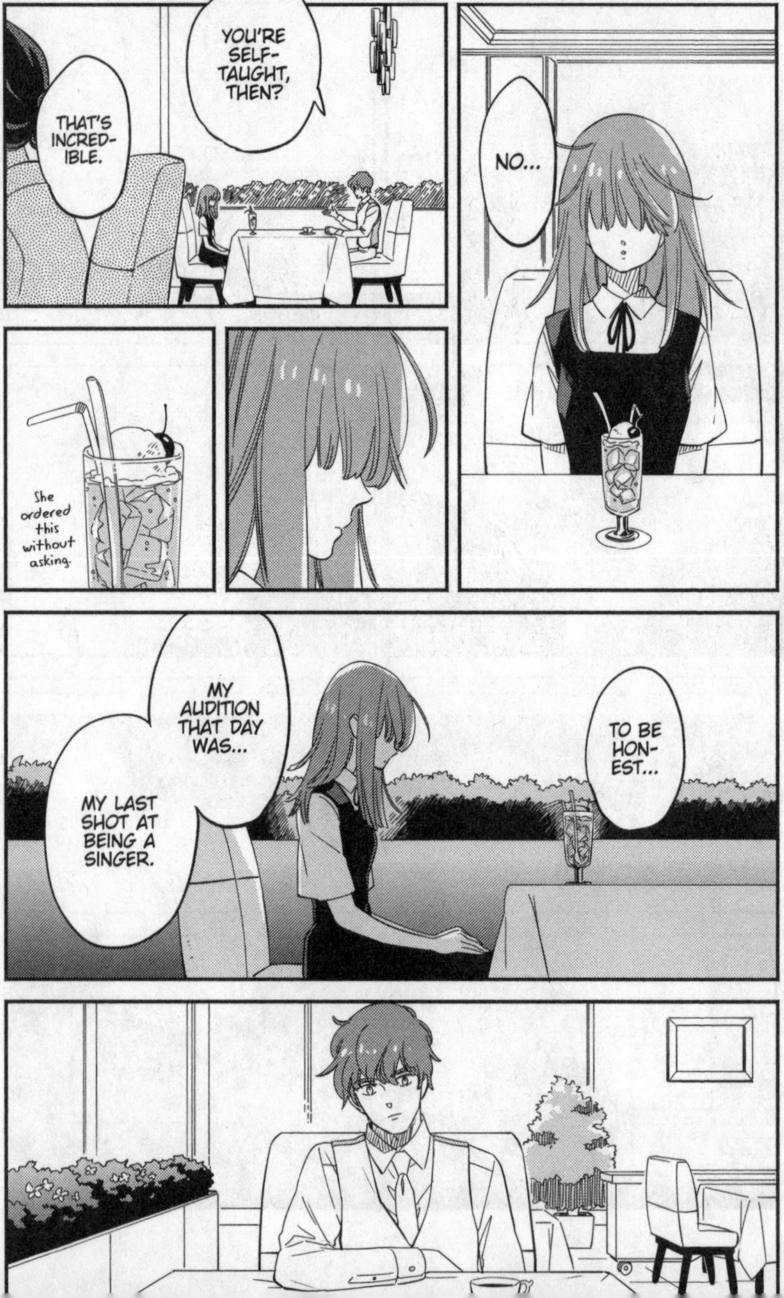
YOU'RE SELF-TAUGHT, THEN?
THAT'S INCREDIBLE.
NO...
She ordered this without asking.
TO BE HONEST...
MY AUDITION THAT DAY WAS...
MY LAST SHOT AT BEING A SINGER.

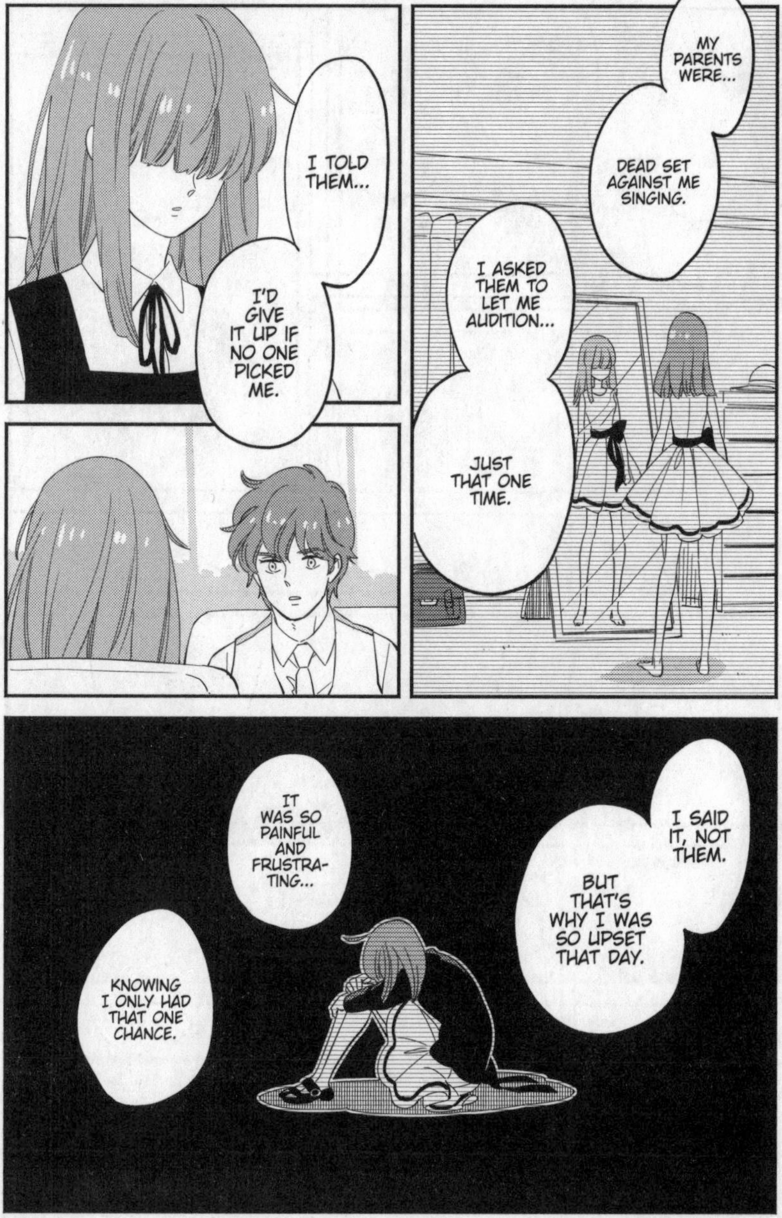
MY PARENTS WERE...
DEAD SET AGAINST ME SINGING.
I ASKED THEM TO LET ME AUDITION...
JUST THAT ONE TIME.
I TOLD THEM...
I'D GIVE IT UP IF NO ONE PICKED ME.
I SAID IT, NOT THEM.
BUT THAT'S WHY I WAS SO UPSET THAT DAY.
IT WAS SO PAINFUL AND FRUSTRATING...
KNOWING I ONLY HAD THAT ONE CHANCE.

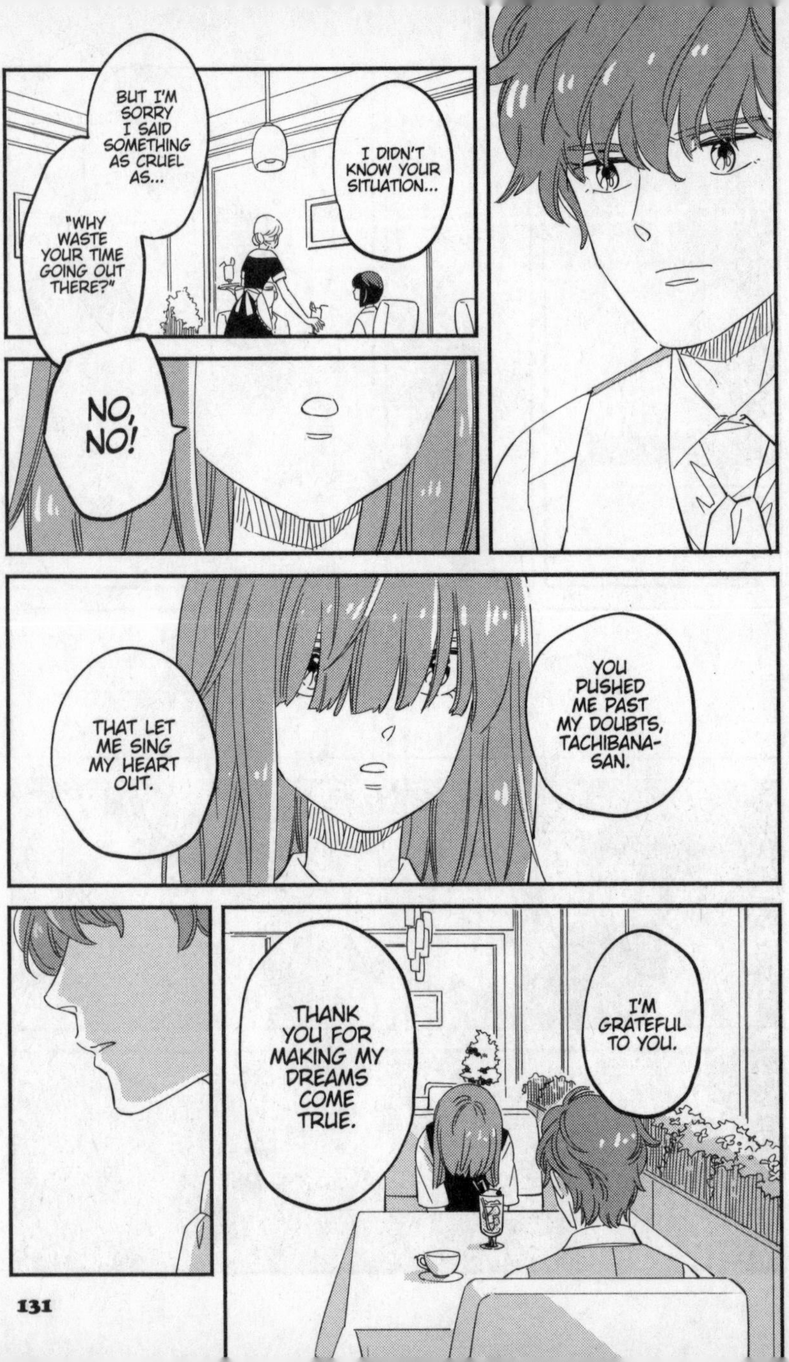
I DIDN'T KNOW YOUR SITUATION...
BUT I'M SORRY I SAID SOMETHING AS CRUEL AS...
"WHY WASTE YOUR TIME GOING OUT THERE?"
NO, NO!
YOU PUSHED ME PAST MY DOUBTS, TACHIBANA-SAN.
THAT LET ME SING MY HEART OUT.
I'M GRATEFUL TO YOU.
THANK YOU FOR MAKING MY DREAMS COME TRUE.

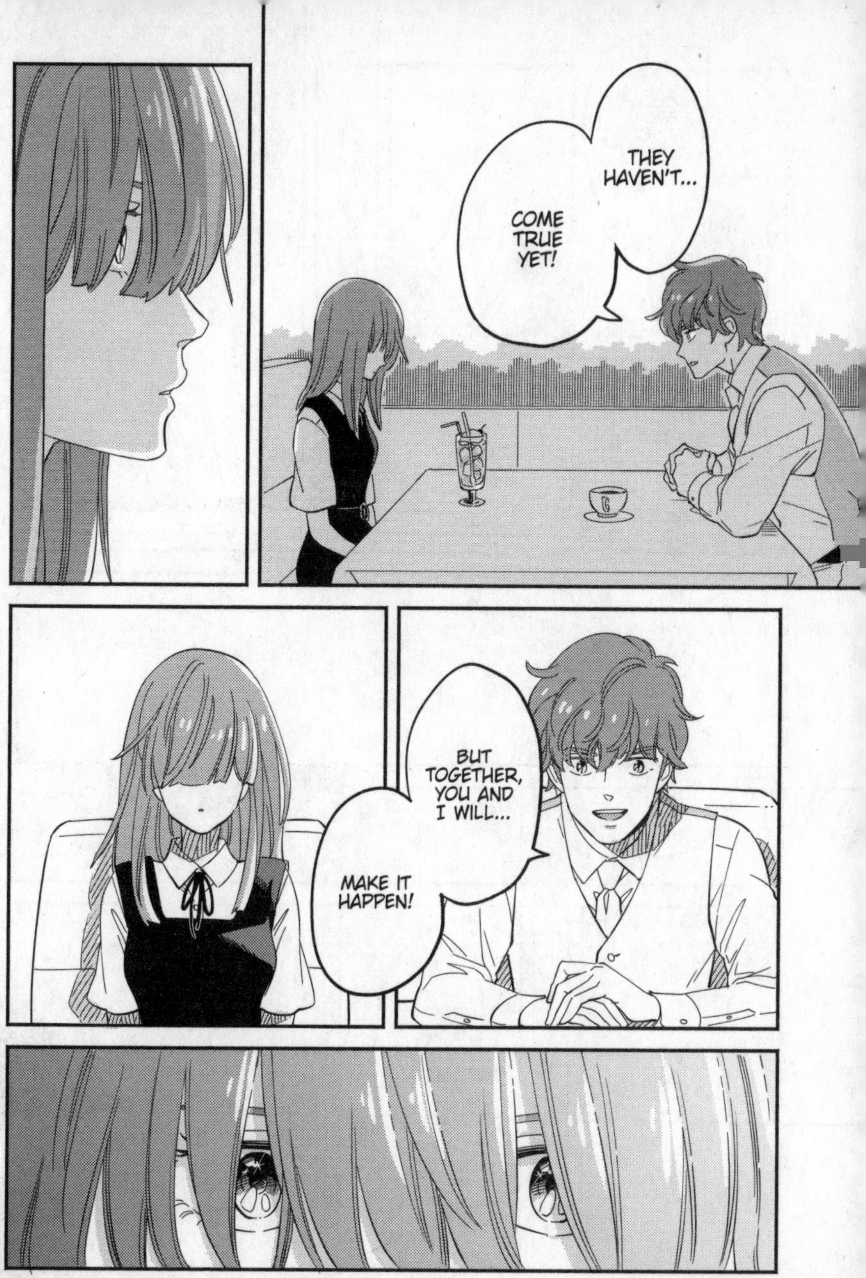
THEY HAVEN'T...
COME TRUE YET!
BUT TOGETHER, YOU AND I WILL...
MAKE IT HAPPEN!

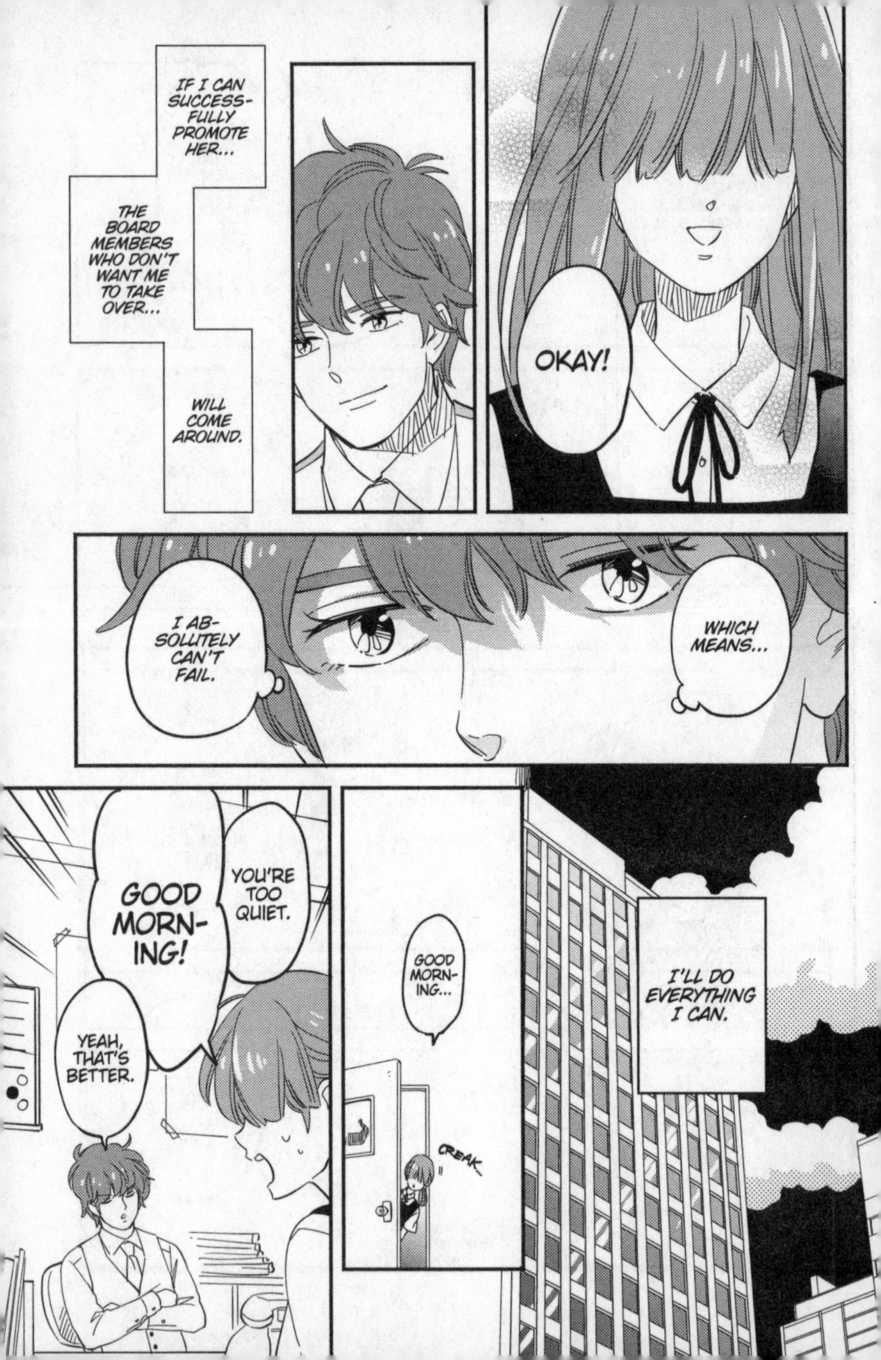
OKAY!
IF I CAN SUCCESSFULLY PROMOTE HER...
THE BOARD MEMBERS WHO DON'T WANT ME TO TAKE OVER...
WILL COME AROUND.
WHICH MEANS...
I ABSOLUTELY CAN'T FAIL.
I'LL DO EVERYTHING I CAN.
GOOD MORNING...
CREAK...
YOU'RE TOO QUIET.
GOOD MORNING!
YEAH, THAT'S BETTER.

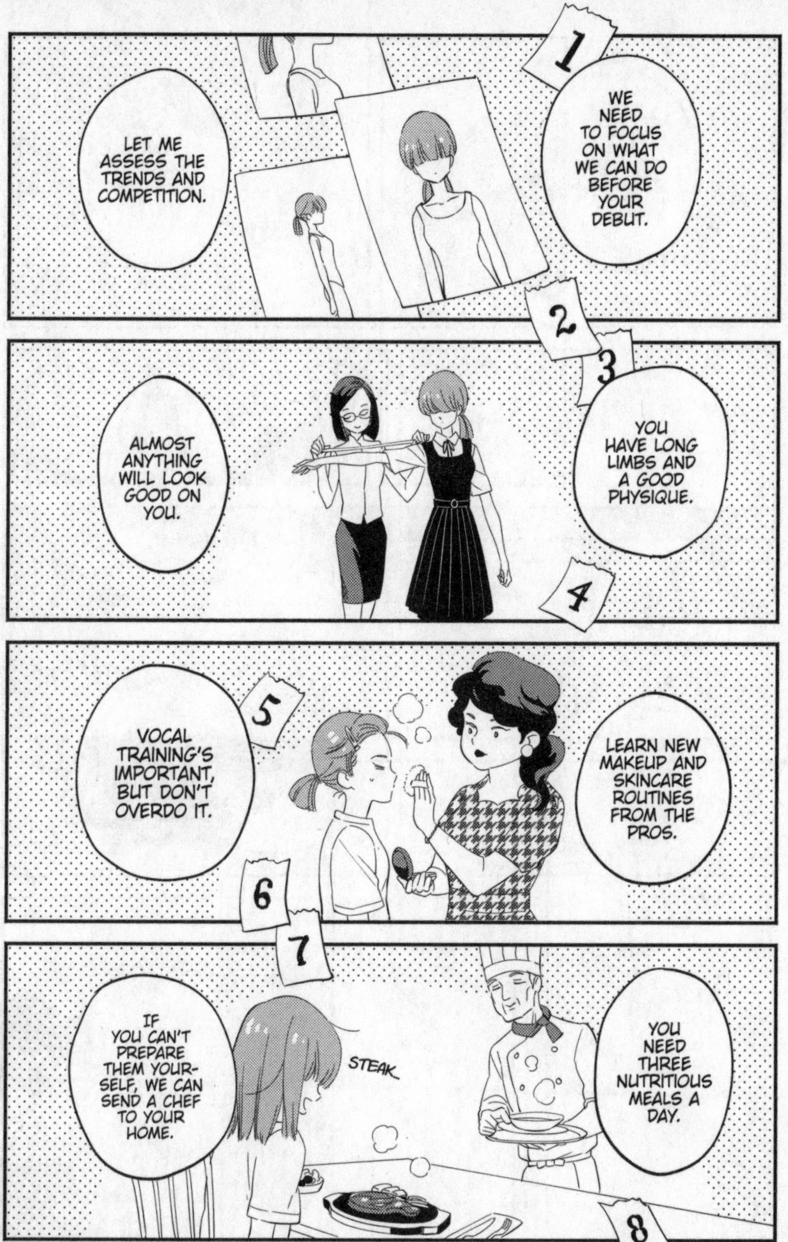
1
WE NEED TO FOCUS ON WHAT WE CAN DO BEFORE YOUR DEBUT.
LET ME ASSESS THE TRENDS AND COMPETITION.
2
3
YOU HAVE LONG LIMBS AND A GOOD PHYSIQUE.
ALMOST ANYTHING WILL LOOK GOOD ON YOU.
4
LEARN NEW MAKEUP AND SKINCARE ROUTINES FROM THE PROS.
5
VOCAL TRAINING'S IMPORTANT, BUT DON'T OVERDO IT.
6
7
YOU NEED THREE NUTRITIOUS MEALS A DAY.
STEAK...
IF YOU CAN'T PREPARE THEM YOURSELF, WE CAN SEND A CHEF TO YOUR HOME.
8

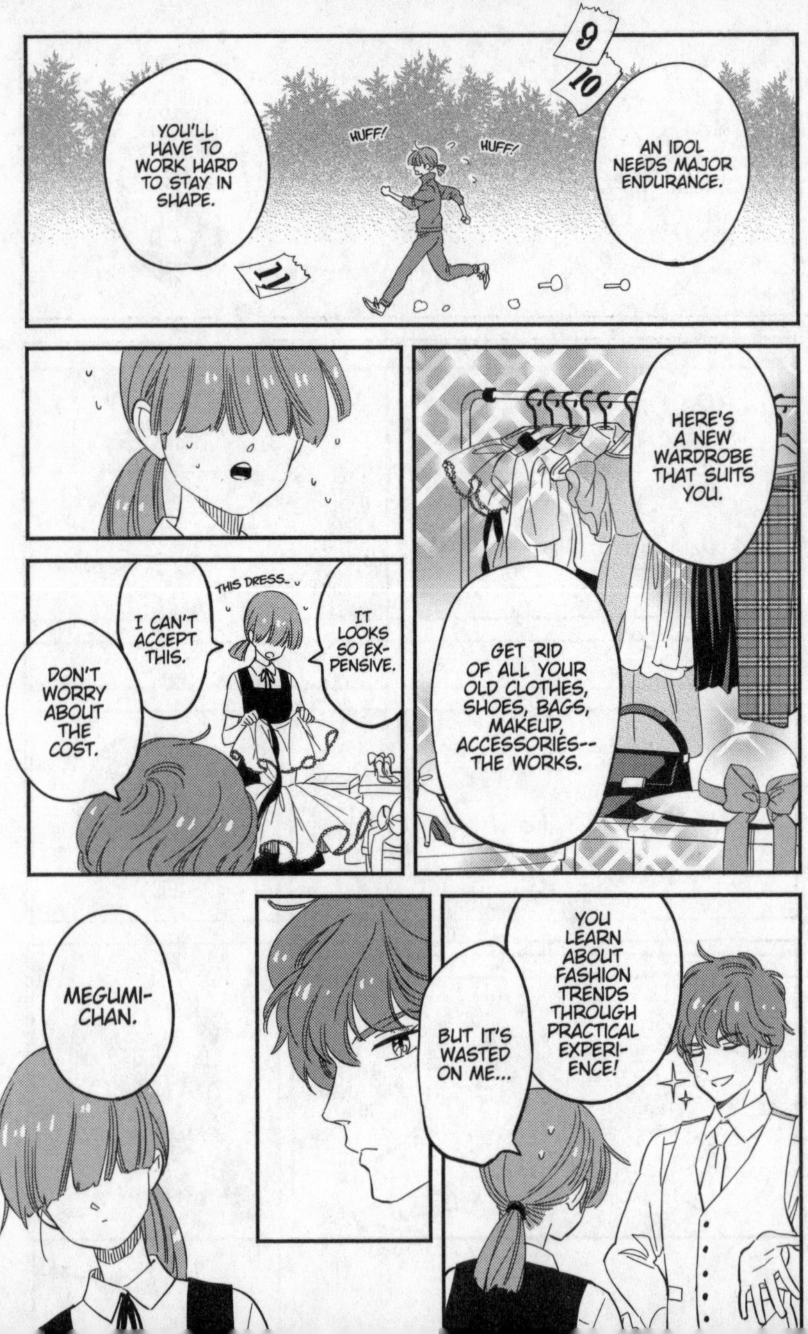
9
10
AN IDOL NEEDS MAJOR ENDURANCE.
HUFF!
HUFF!
YOU'LL HAVE TO WORK HARD TO STAY IN SHAPE.
11
HERE'S A NEW WARDROBE THAT SUITS YOU.
GET RID OF ALL YOUR OLD CLOTHES, SHOES, BAGS, MAKEUP, ACCESSORIES-- THE WORKS.
IT LOOKS SO EX-PENSIVE.
THIS DRESS...
I CAN'T ACCEPT THIS.
DON'T WORRY ABOUT THE COST.
YOU LEARN ABOUT FASHION TRENDS THROUGH PRACTICAL EXPERI-ENCE!
BUT IT'S WASTED ON ME...
MEGUMI-CHAN.

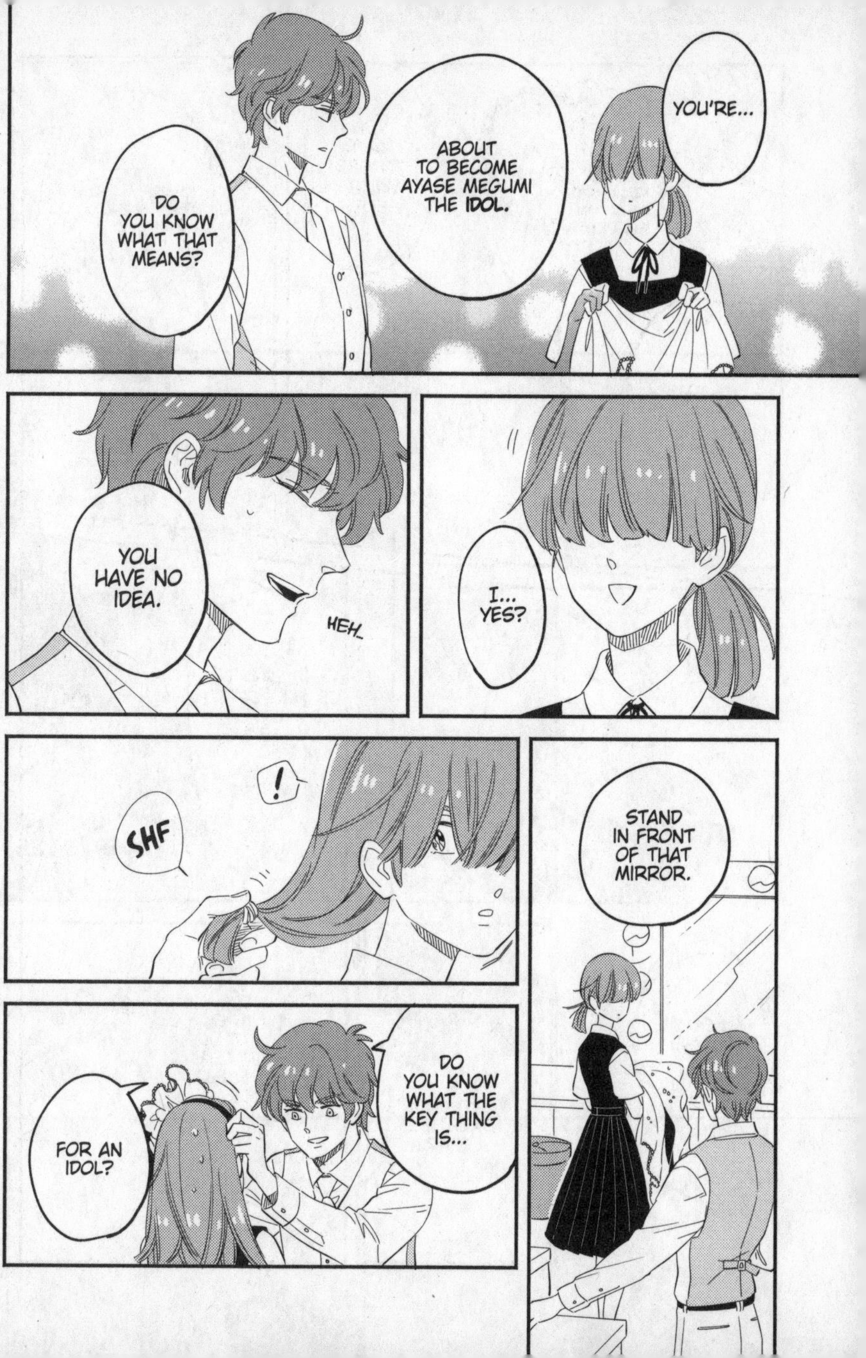
YOU'RE...
ABOUT TO BECOME AYASE MEGUMI THE IDOL.
DO YOU KNOW WHAT THAT MEANS?
I... YES?
YOU HAVE NO IDEA.
HEH.
STAND IN FRONT OF THAT MIRROR.
!
SHF
DO YOU KNOW WHAT THE KEY THING IS...
FOR AN IDOL?

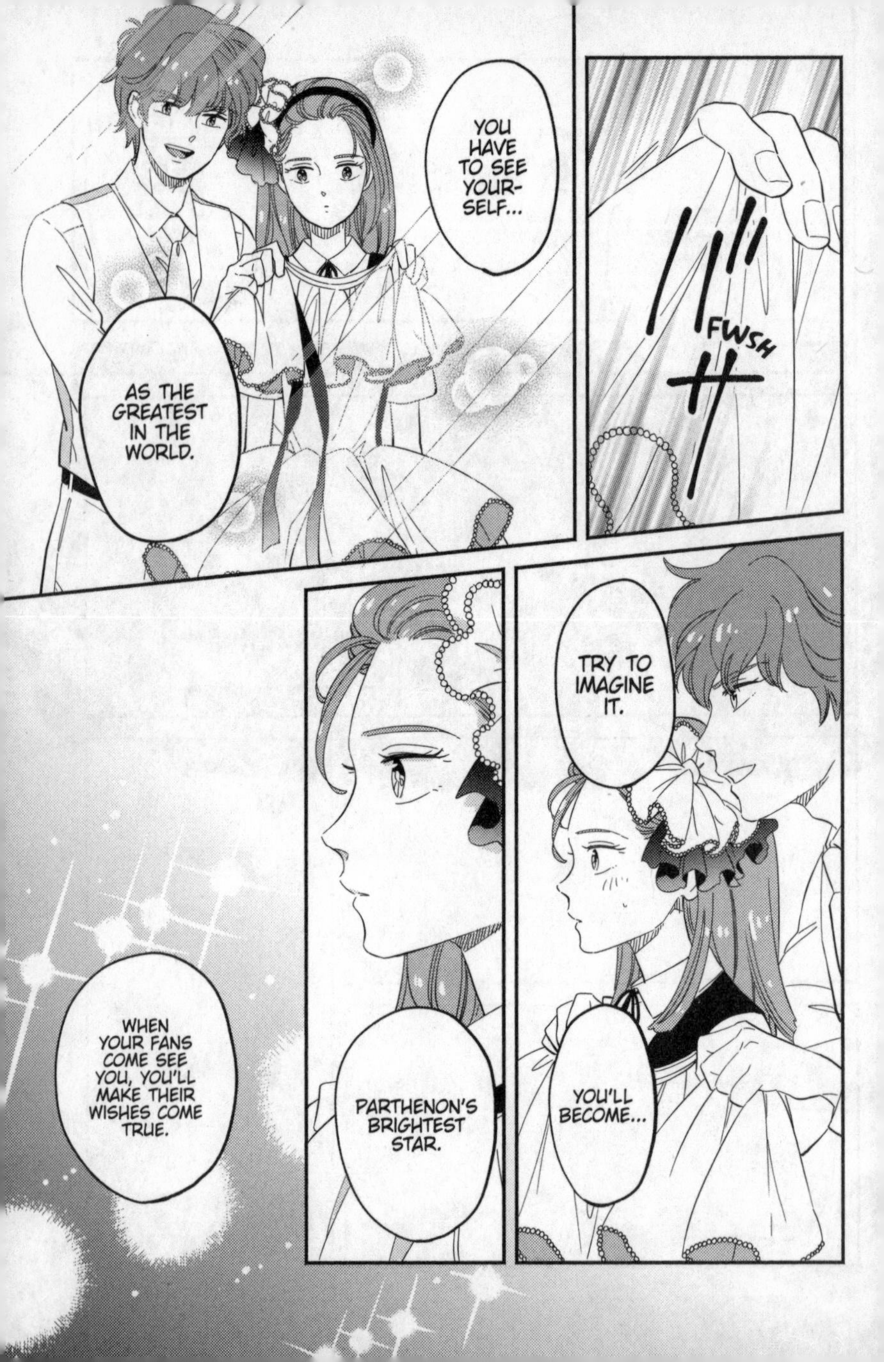
FWSH
YOU HAVE TO SEE YOUR-SELF...
AS THE GREATEST IN THE WORLD.
TRY TO IMAGINE IT.
YOU'LL BECOME...
PARTHENON'S BRIGHTEST STAR.
WHEN YOUR FANS COME SEE YOU, YOU'LL MAKE THEIR WISHES COME TRUE.

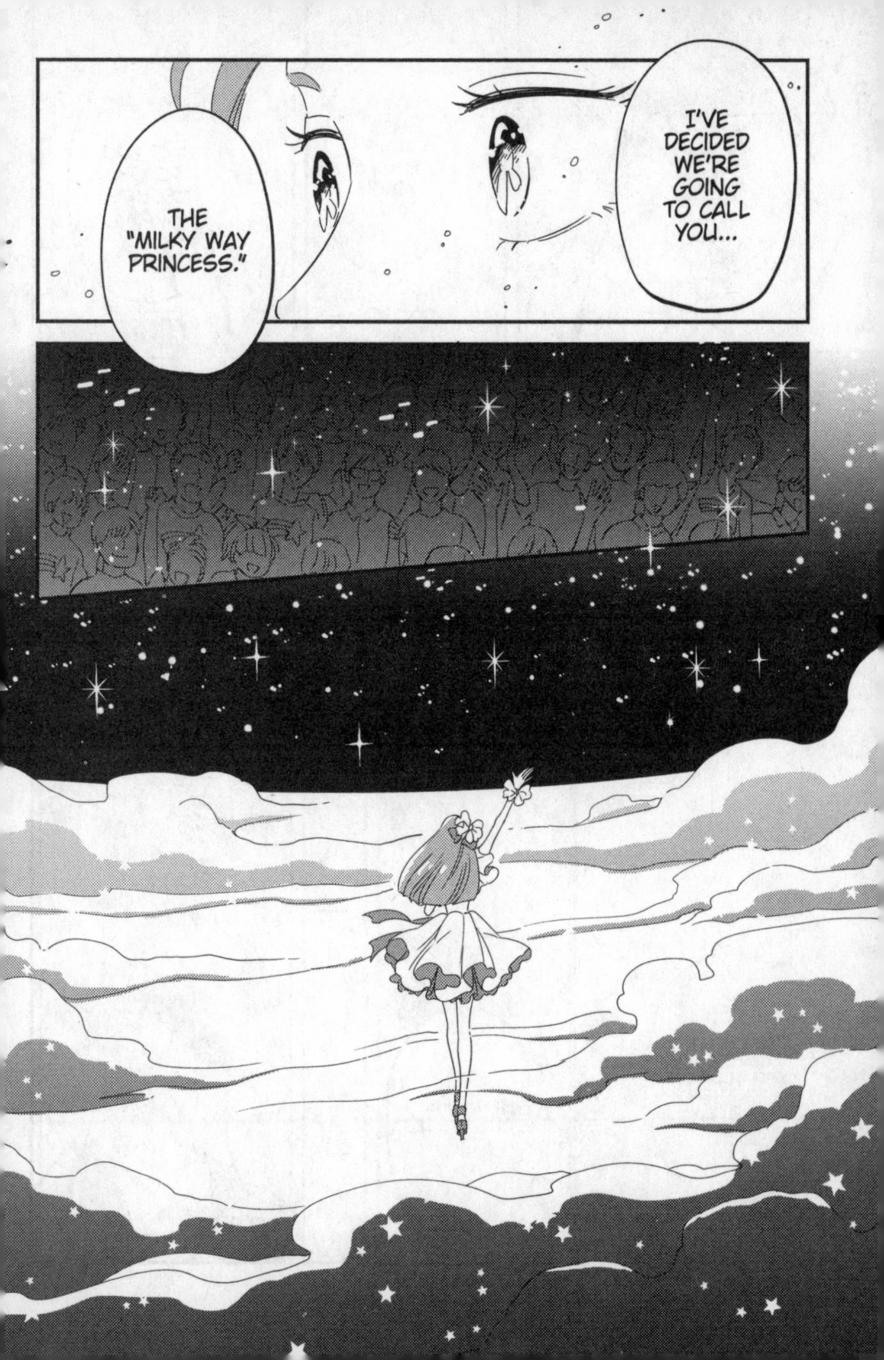
I'VE DECIDED WE'RE GOING TO CALL YOU...
THE "MILKY WAY PRINCESS."

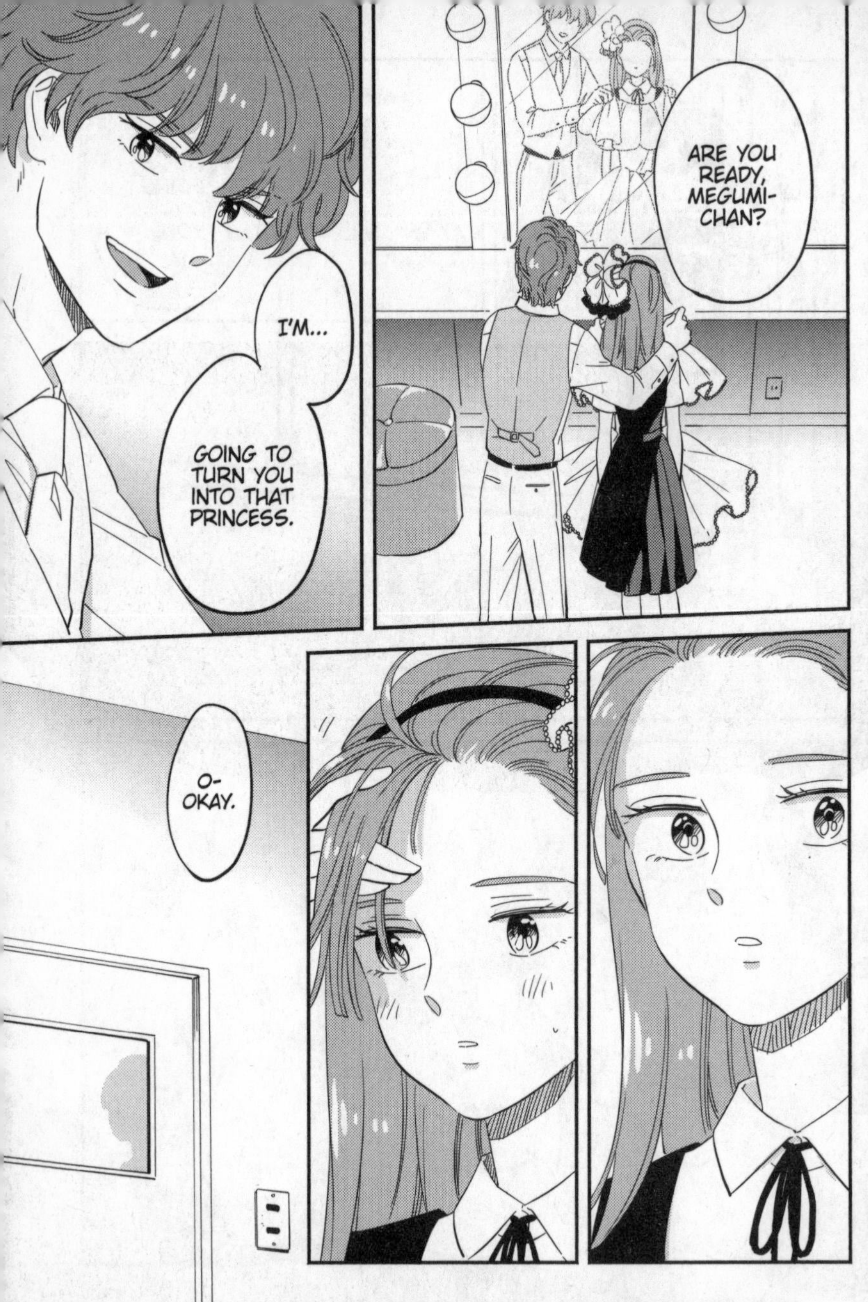
ARE YOU READY, MEGUMI-CHAN?
I'M...
GOING TO TURN YOU INTO THAT PRINCESS.
O-OKAY.

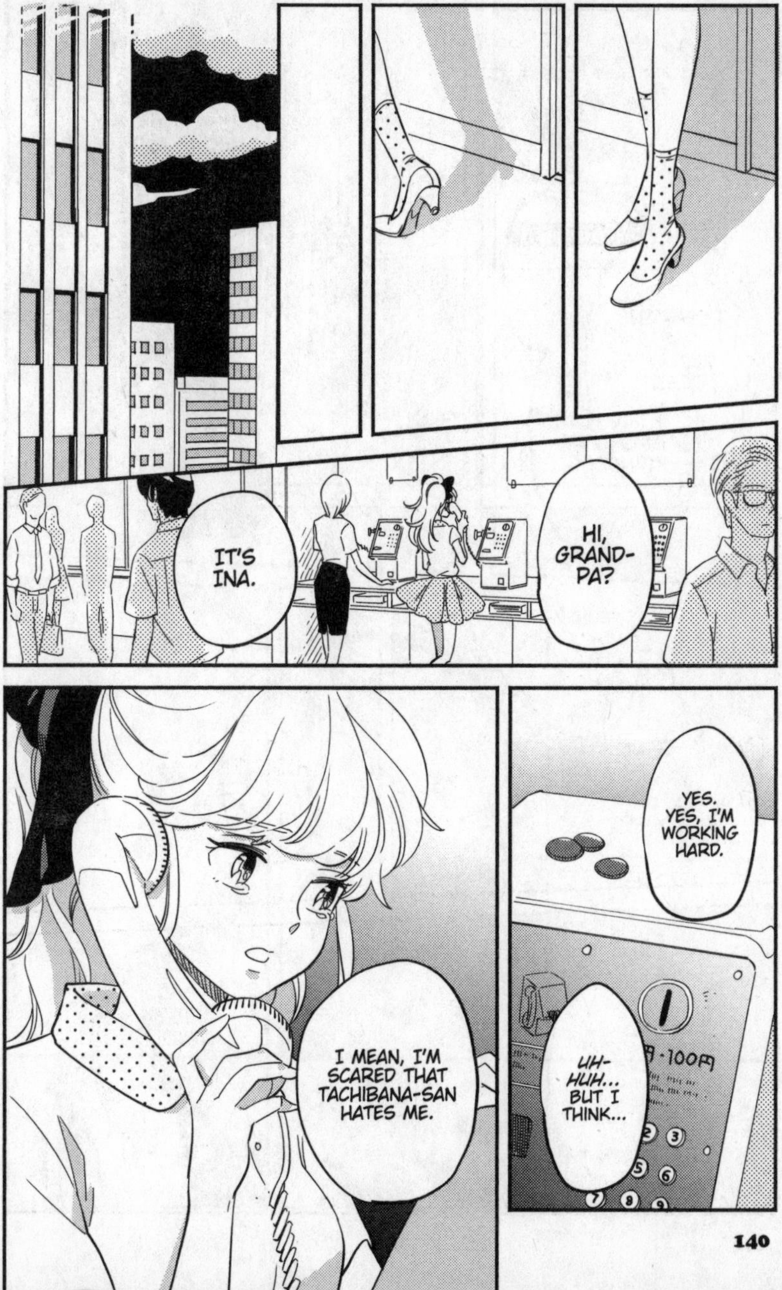
HI, GRANDPA?
IT'S INA.
YES. YES, I'M WORKING HARD.
UH-HUH... BUT I THINK...
I MEAN, I'M SCARED THAT TACHIBANA-SAN HATES ME.

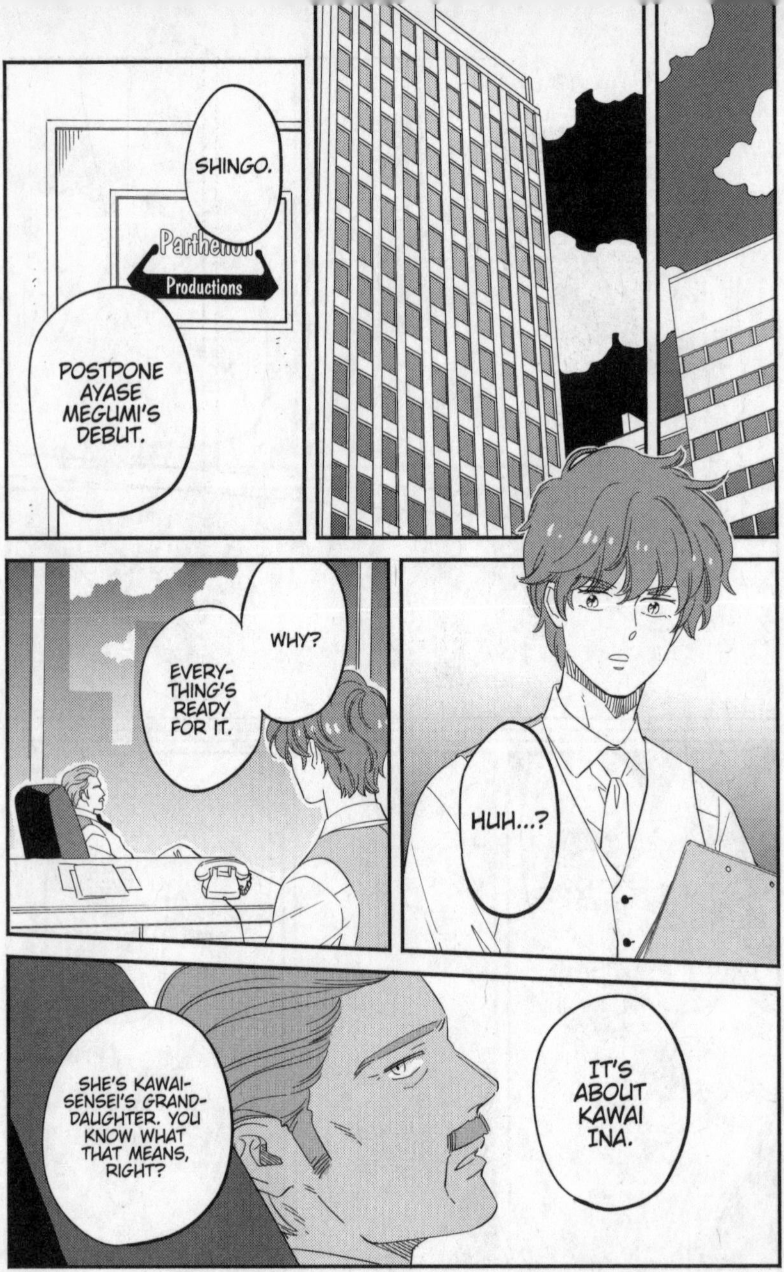
SHINGO.
Parthenon Productions
POSTPONE AYASE MEGUMI'S DEBUT.
HUH...?
WHY?
EVERYTHING'S READY FOR IT.
IT'S ABOUT KAWAI INA.
SHE'S KAWAI-SENSEI'S GRANDDAUGHTER. YOU KNOW WHAT THAT MEANS, RIGHT?

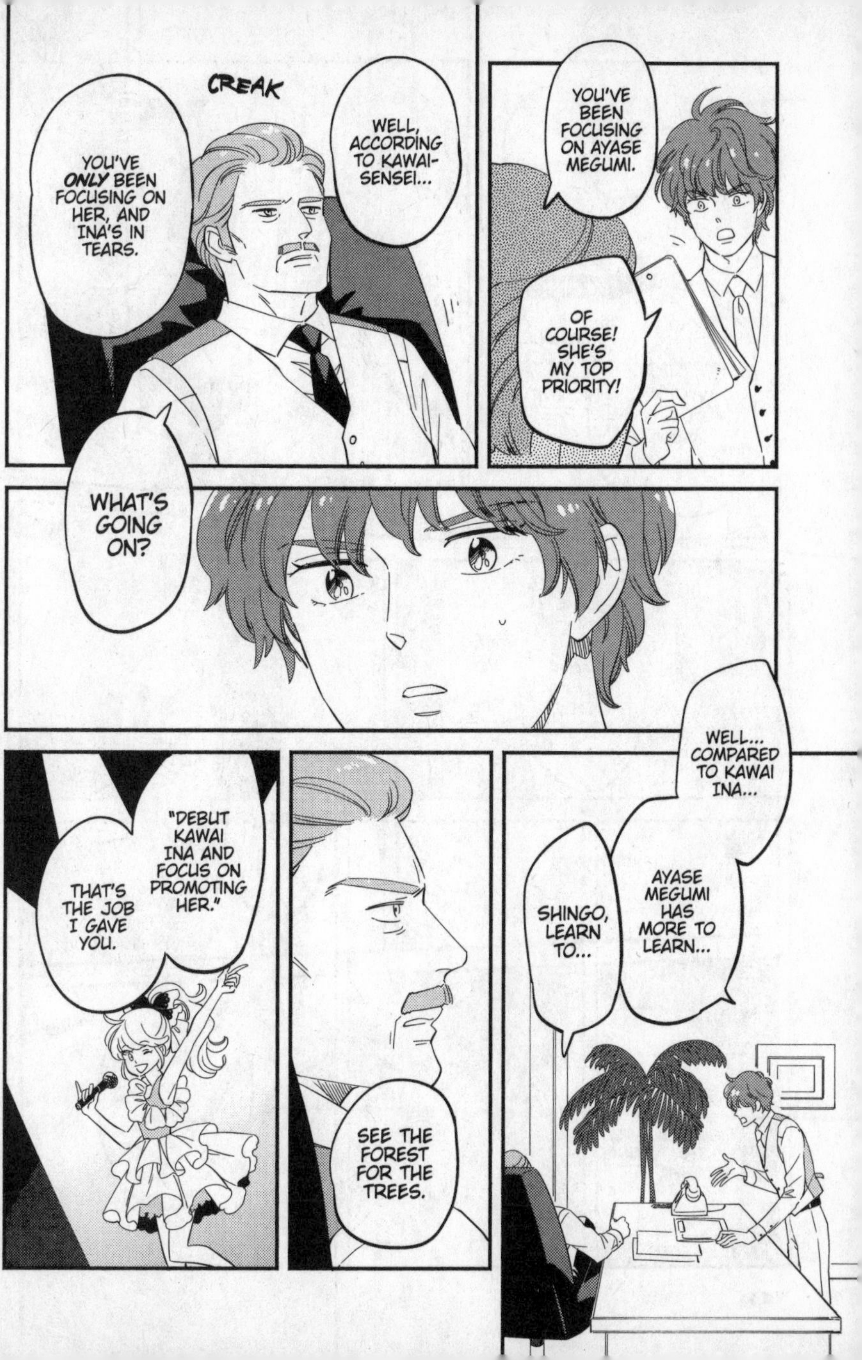
YOU'VE BEEN FOCUSING ON AYASE MEGUMI.
OF COURSE! SHE'S MY TOP PRIORITY!
WELL, ACCORDING TO KAWAI-SENSEI...
CREAK
YOU'VE *ONLY* BEEN FOCUSING ON HER, AND INA'S IN TEARS.
WHAT'S GOING ON?
WELL... COMPARED TO KAWAI INA...
AYASE MEGUMI HAS MORE TO LEARN...
SHINGO, LEARN TO...
SEE THE FOREST FOR THE TREES.
"DEBUT KAWAI INA AND FOCUS ON PROMOTING HER."
THAT'S THE JOB I GAVE YOU.

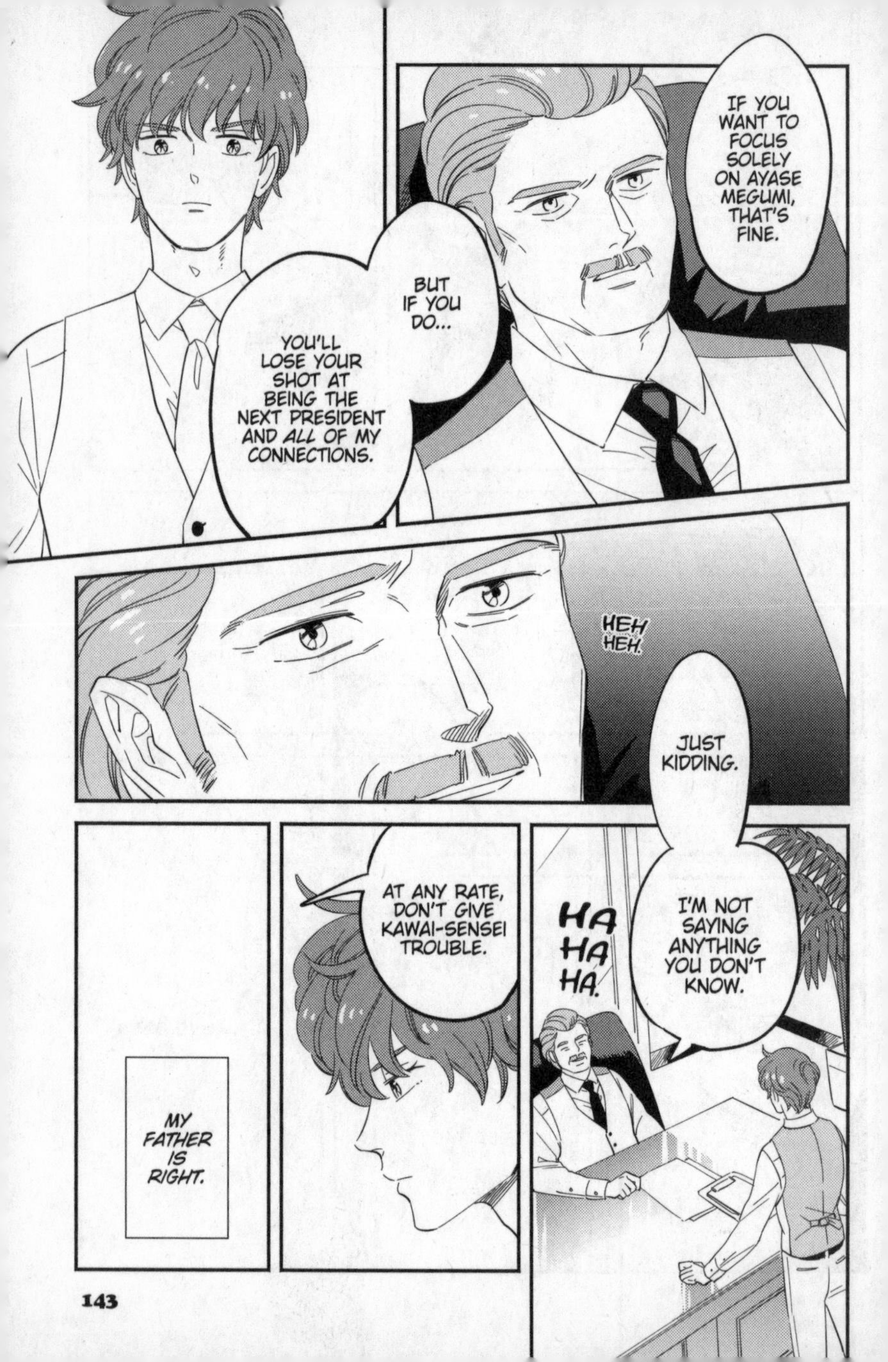
IF YOU WANT TO FOCUS SOLELY ON AYASE MEGUMI, THAT'S FINE.
BUT IF YOU DO...
YOU'LL LOSE YOUR SHOT AT BEING THE NEXT PRESIDENT AND *ALL* OF MY CONNECTIONS.
HEH HEH.
JUST KIDDING.
I'M NOT SAYING ANYTHING YOU DON'T KNOW.
HA HA HA.
AT ANY RATE, DON'T GIVE KAWAI-SENSEI TROUBLE.
MY FATHER IS RIGHT.

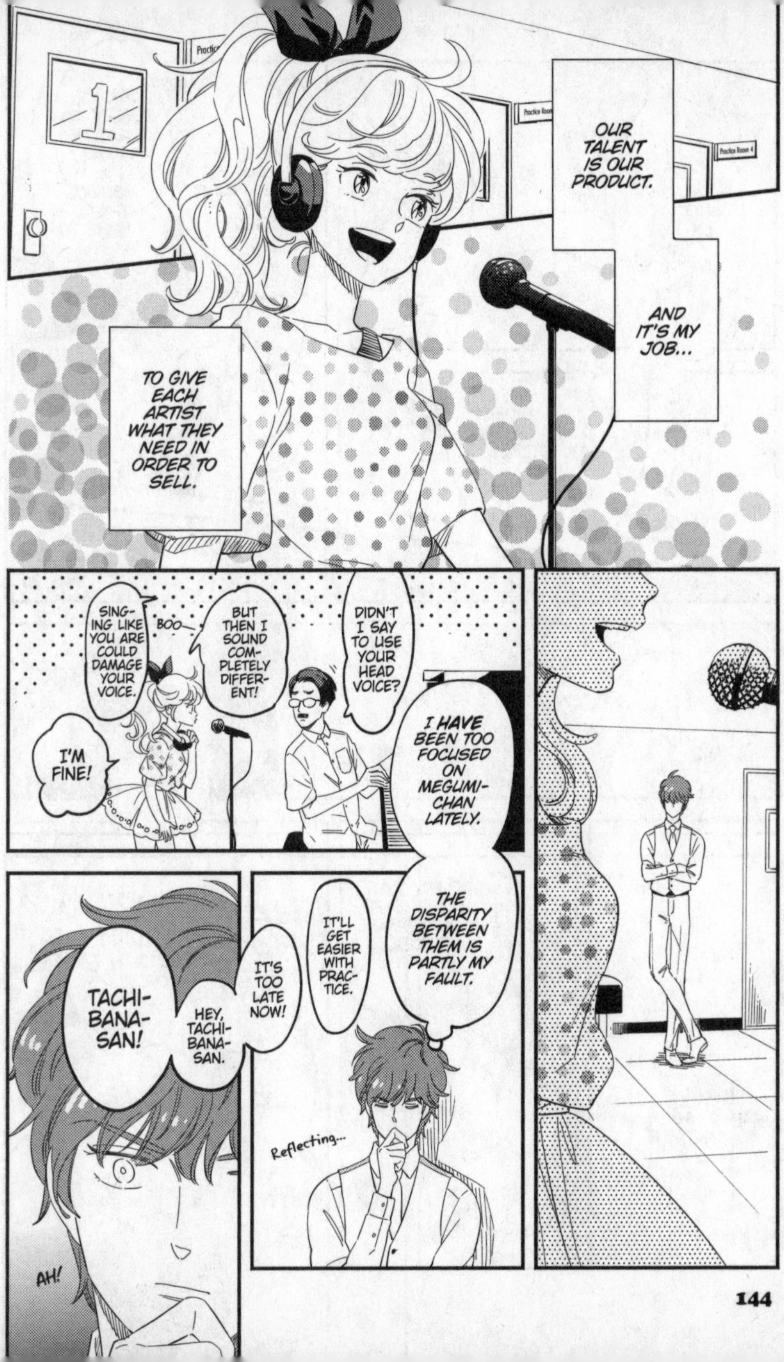
OUR TALENT IS OUR PRODUCT.
AND IT'S MY JOB...
TO GIVE EACH ARTIST WHAT THEY NEED IN ORDER TO SELL.
DIDN'T I SAY TO USE YOUR HEAD VOICE?
BUT THEN I SOUND COMPLETELY DIFFERENT!
BOO
SINGING LIKE YOU ARE COULD DAMAGE YOUR VOICE.
I'M FINE!
I HAVE BEEN TOO FOCUSED ON MEGUMI-CHAN LATELY.
THE DISPARITY BETWEEN THEM IS PARTLY MY FAULT.
IT'LL GET EASIER WITH PRACTICE.
IT'S TOO LATE NOW!
HEY, TACHIBANA-SAN.
Reflecting...
TACHIBANA-SAN!
AH!

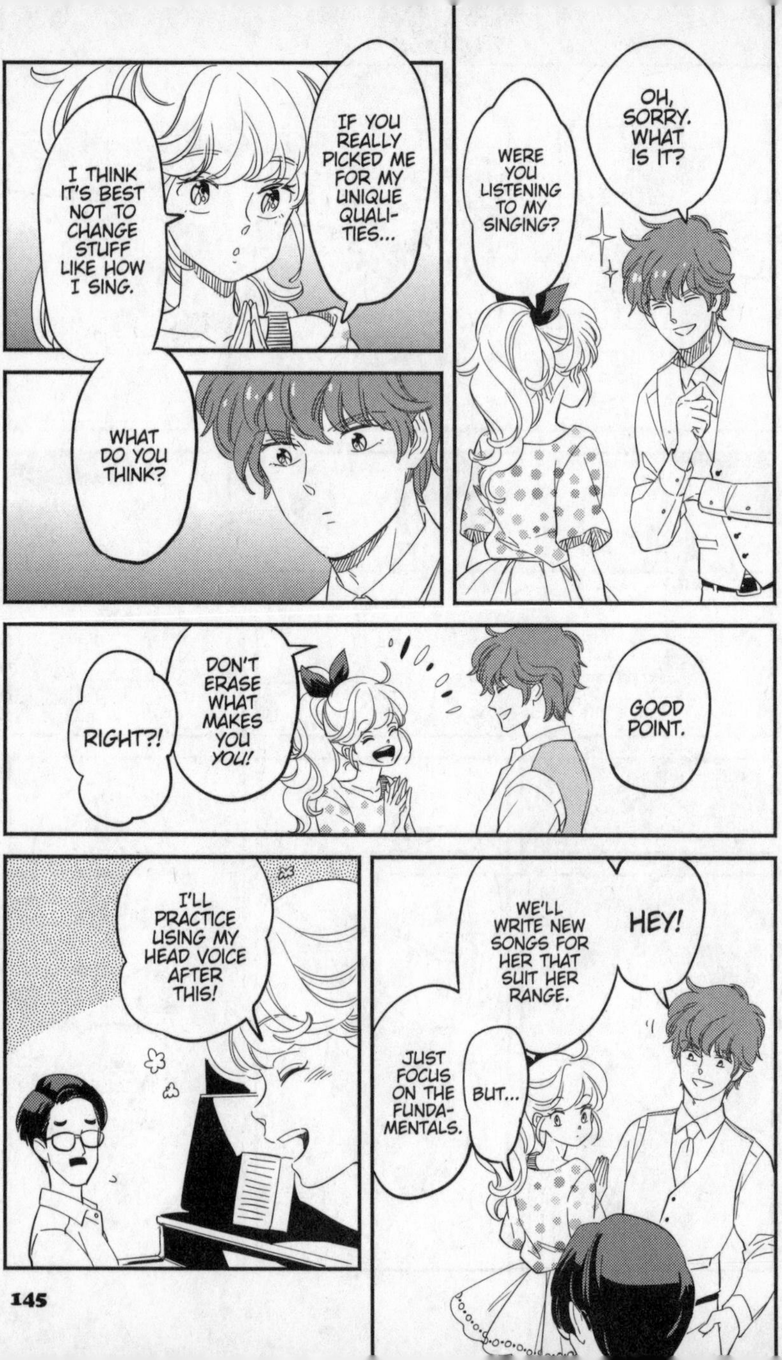

OH, SORRY. WHAT IS IT?
WERE YOU LISTENING TO MY SINGING?
IF YOU REALLY PICKED ME FOR MY UNIQUE QUALITIES...
I THINK IT'S BEST NOT TO CHANGE STUFF LIKE HOW I SING.
WHAT DO YOU THINK?
GOOD POINT.
DON'T ERASE WHAT MAKES YOU YOU!
RIGHT?!
HEY!
WE'LL WRITE NEW SONGS FOR HER THAT SUIT HER RANGE.
BUT...
JUST FOCUS ON THE FUNDAMENTALS.
I'LL PRACTICE USING MY HEAD VOICE AFTER THIS!

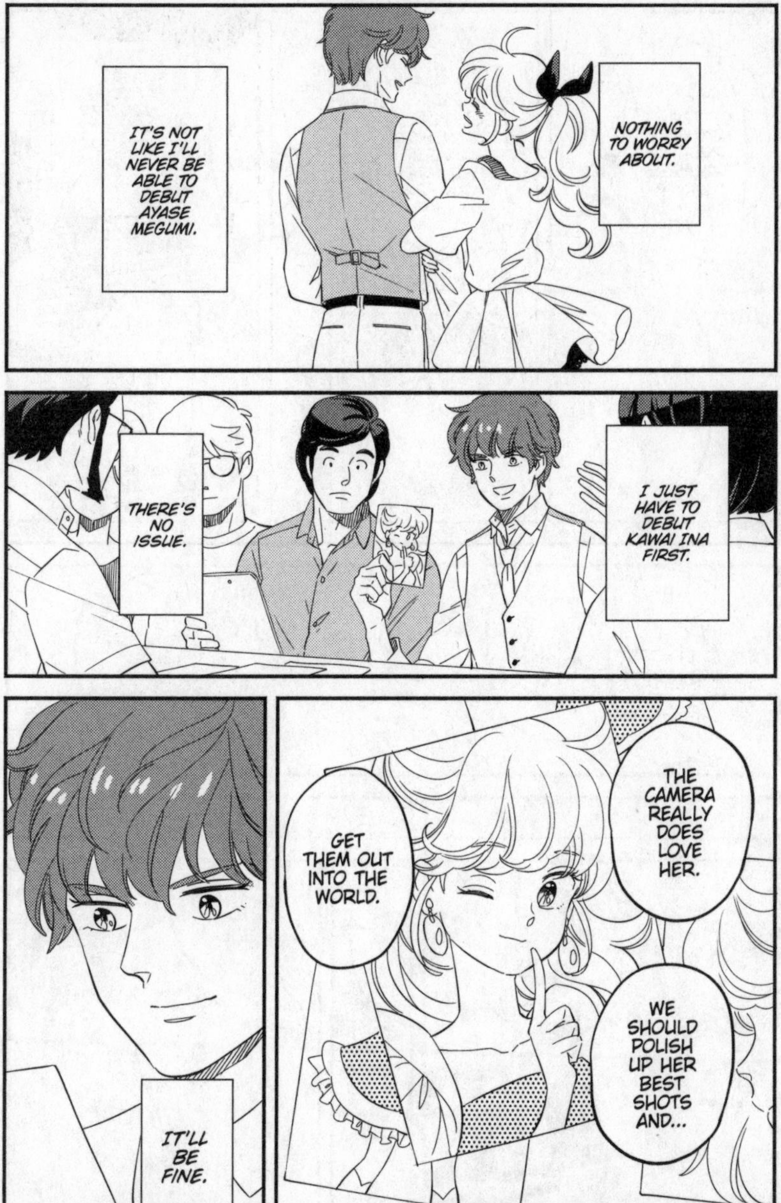
NOTHING TO WORRY ABOUT.
IT'S NOT LIKE I'LL NEVER BE ABLE TO DEBUT AYASE MEGUMI.
I JUST HAVE TO DEBUT KAWAI INA FIRST.
THERE'S NO ISSUE.
THE CAMERA REALLY DOES LOVE HER.
WE SHOULD POLISH UP HER BEST SHOTS AND...
GET THEM OUT INTO THE WORLD.
IT'LL BE FINE.

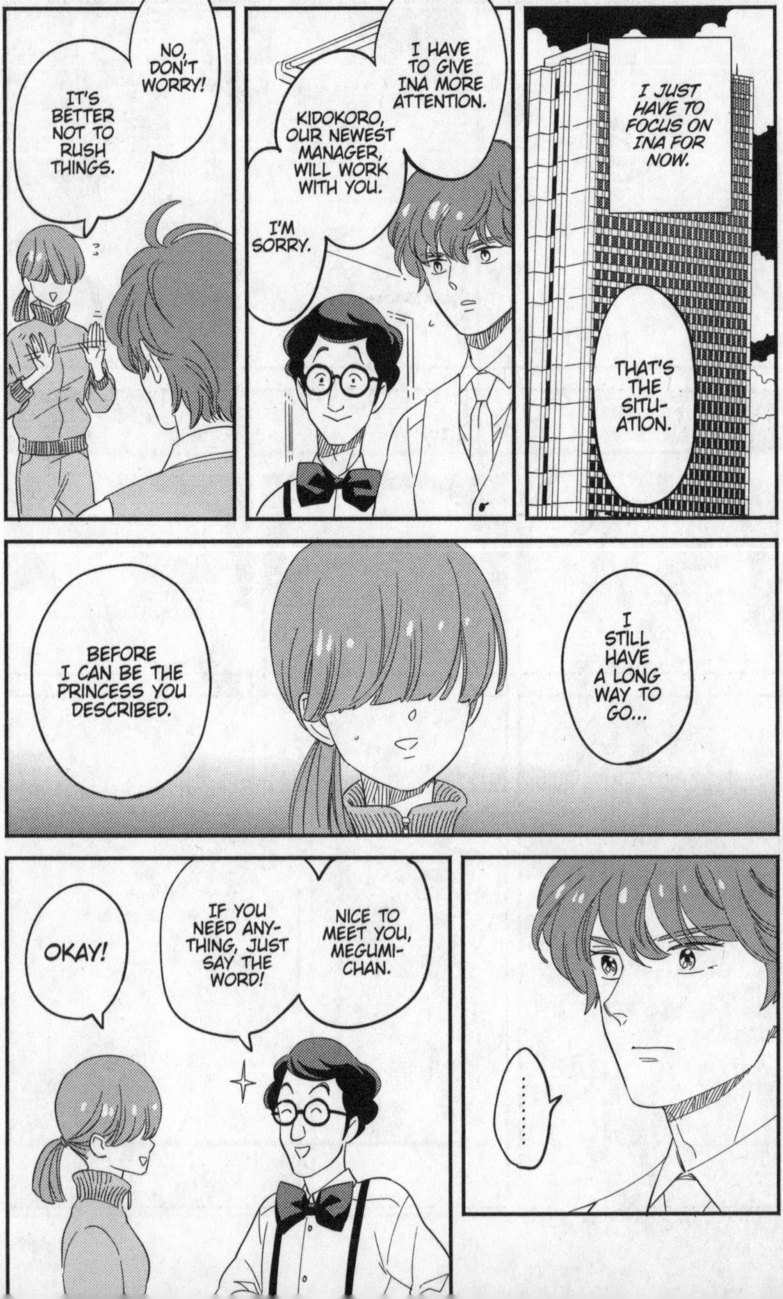
I JUST HAVE TO FOCUS ON INA FOR NOW.
THAT'S THE SITUATION.
I HAVE TO GIVE INA MORE ATTENTION.
KIDOKORO, OUR NEWEST MANAGER, WILL WORK WITH YOU.
I'M SORRY.
NO, DON'T WORRY!
IT'S BETTER NOT TO RUSH THINGS.
I STILL HAVE A LONG WAY TO GO...
BEFORE I CAN BE THE PRINCESS YOU DESCRIBED.
......
NICE TO MEET YOU, MEGUMI-CHAN.
IF YOU NEED ANYTHING, JUST SAY THE WORD!
OKAY!

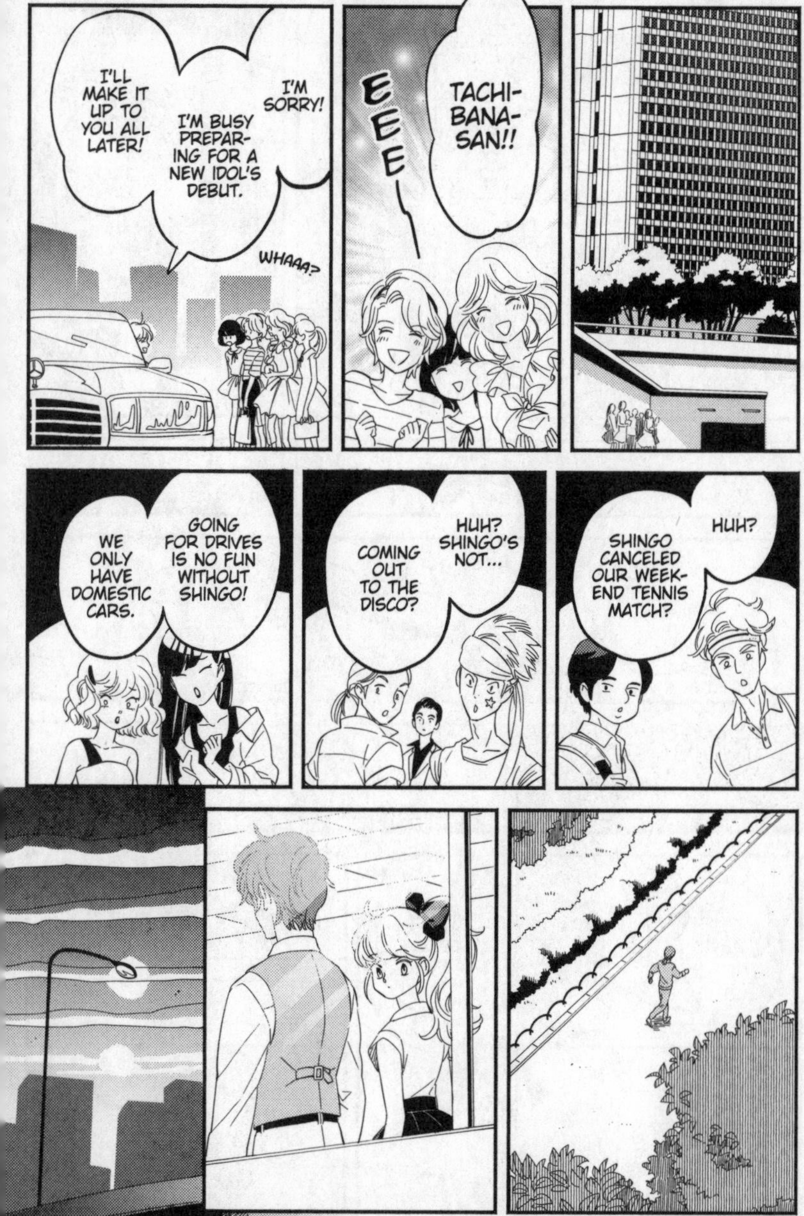
TACHI-BANA-SAN!!
EEE
I'M SORRY!
I'M BUSY PREPAR-ING FOR A NEW IDOL'S DEBUT.
I'LL MAKE IT UP TO YOU ALL LATER!
WHAAA?
HUH?
SHINGO CANCELED OUR WEEK-END TENNIS MATCH?
HUH? SHINGO'S NOT...
COMING OUT TO THE DISCO?
GOING FOR DRIVES IS NO FUN WITHOUT SHINGO!
WE ONLY HAVE DOMESTIC CARS.

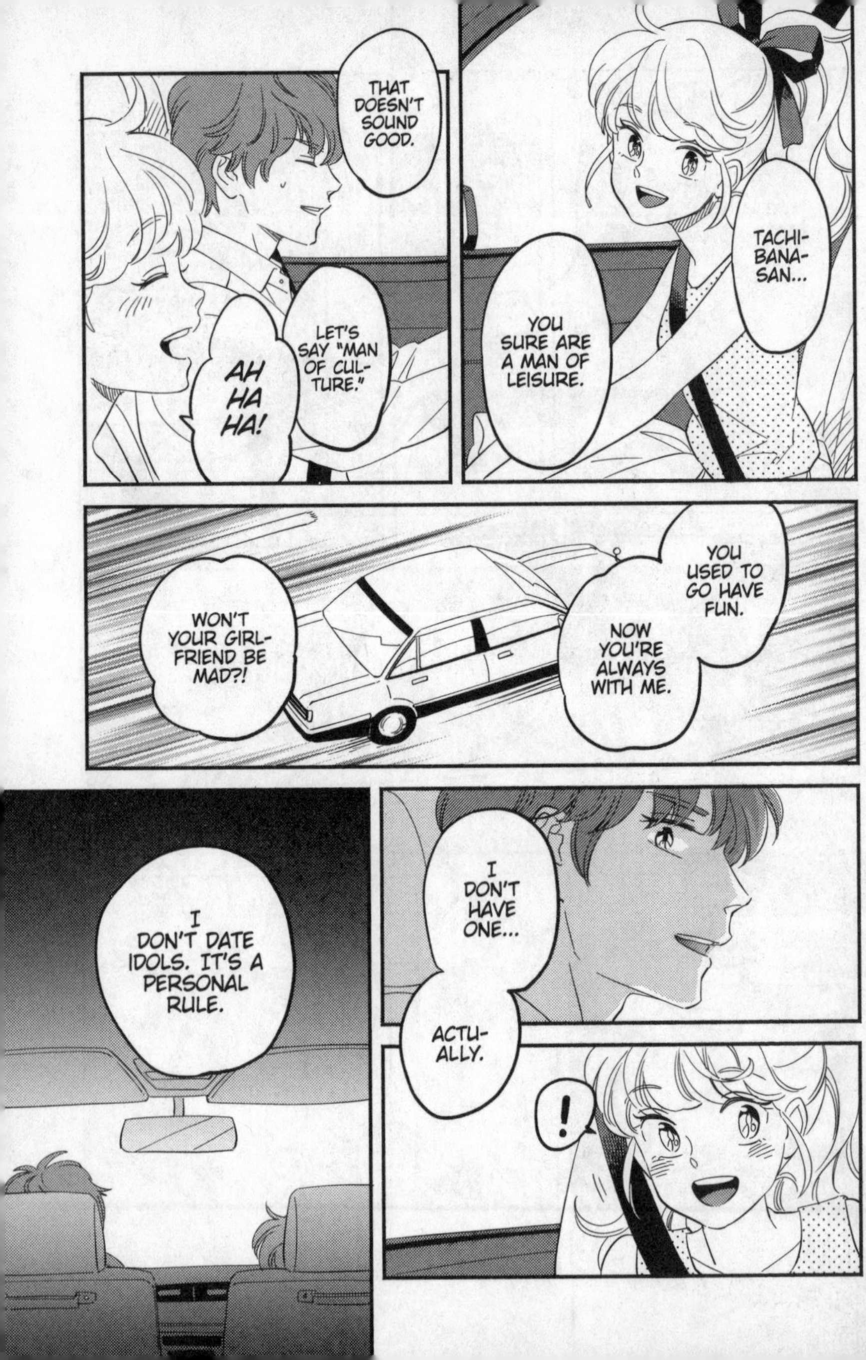
TACHIBANA-SAN...
YOU SURE ARE A MAN OF LEISURE.
THAT DOESN'T SOUND GOOD.
LET'S SAY "MAN OF CULTURE."
AH HA HA!
YOU USED TO GO HAVE FUN.
NOW YOU'RE ALWAYS WITH ME.
WON'T YOUR GIRLFRIEND BE MAD?!
I DON'T HAVE ONE...
ACTUALLY.
!
I DON'T DATE IDOLS. IT'S A PERSONAL RULE.

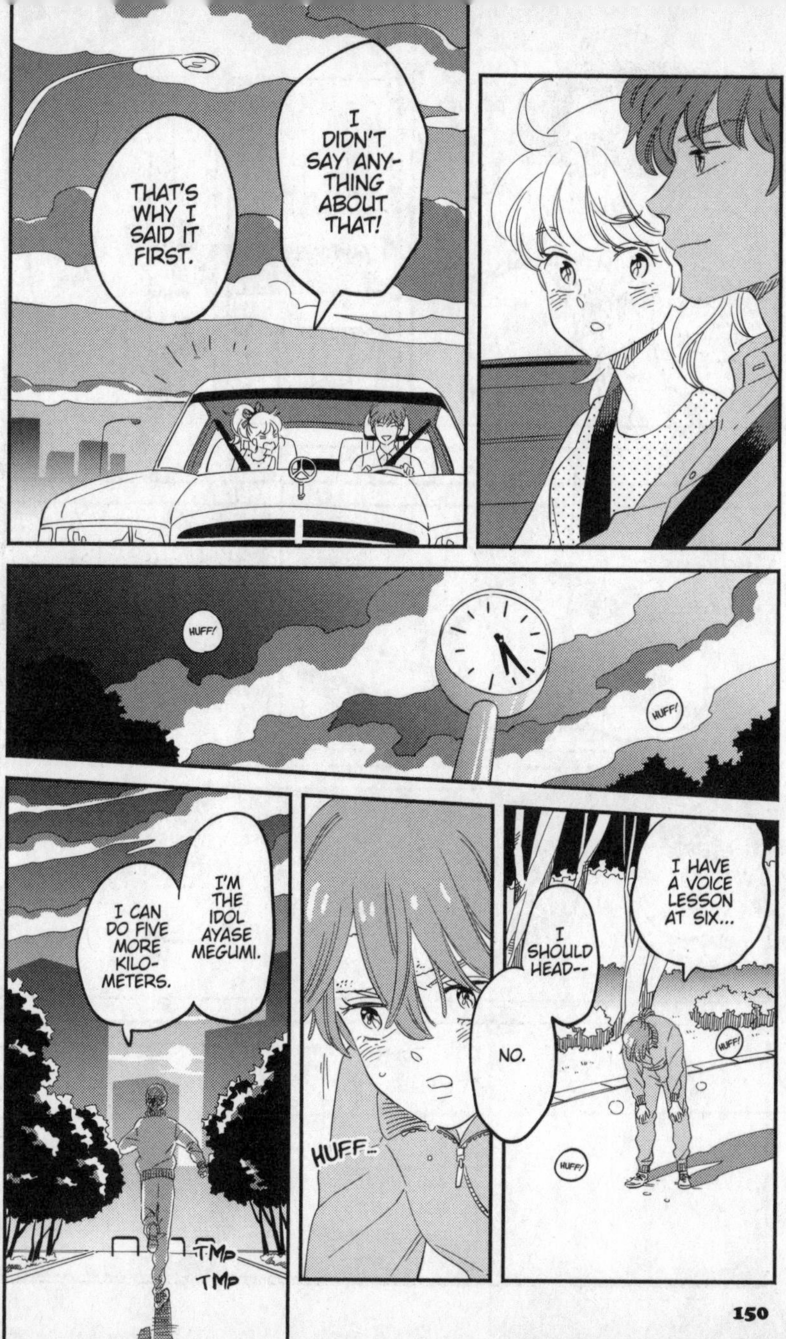
I DIDN'T SAY ANY-THING ABOUT THAT!
THAT'S WHY I SAID IT FIRST.
HUFF!
HUFF!
I HAVE A VOICE LESSON AT SIX...
I SHOULD HEAD--
HUFF!
HUFF!
NO.
HUFF...
I'M THE IDOL AYASE MEGUMI.
I CAN DO FIVE MORE KILO-METERS.
TMP
TMP

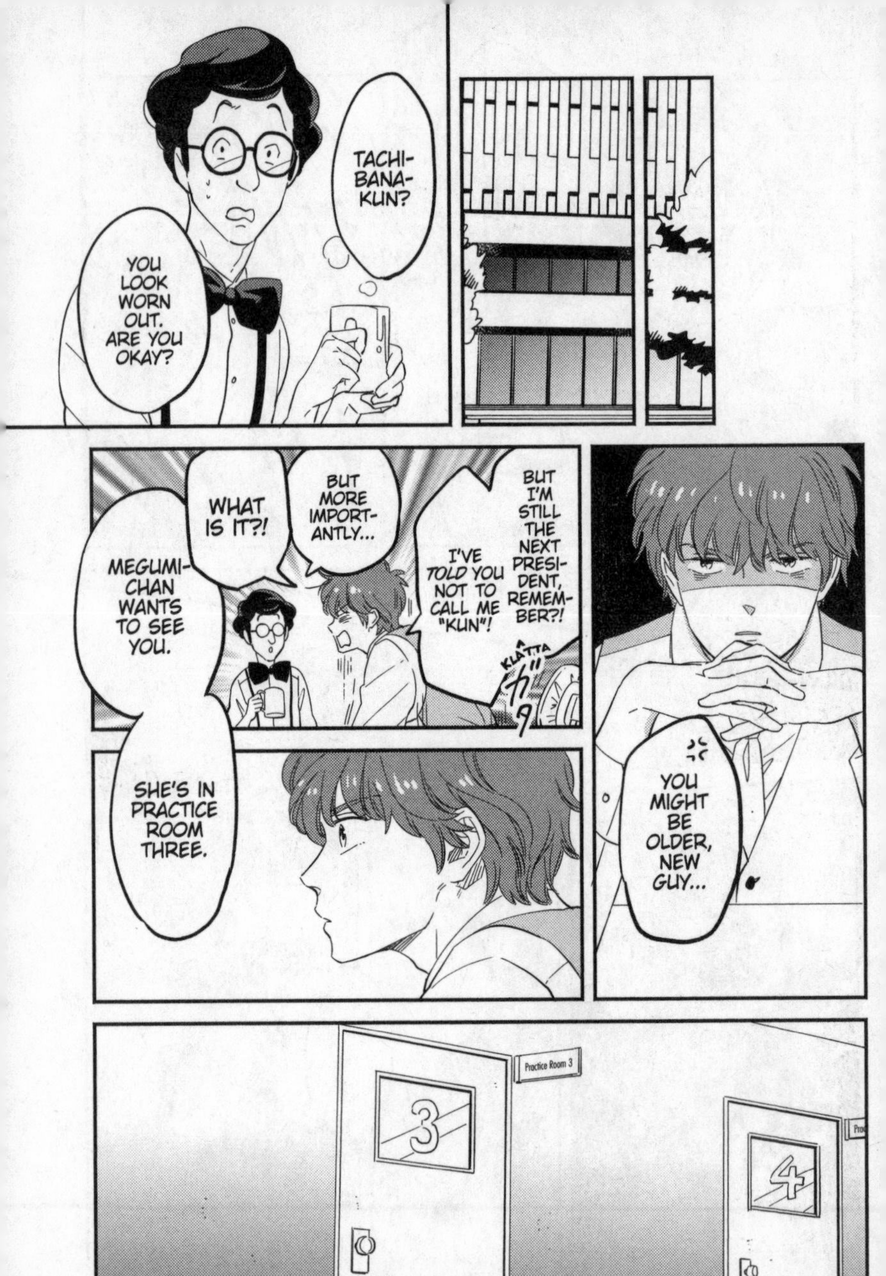
TACHI-BANA-KUN?
YOU LOOK WORN OUT. ARE YOU OKAY?
YOU MIGHT BE OLDER, NEW GUY...
BUT I'M STILL THE NEXT PRESI-DENT, REMEM-BER?!
I'VE TOLD YOU NOT TO CALL ME "KUN"!
KLATTA
BUT MORE IMPORT-ANTLY...
WHAT IS IT?!
MEGUMI-CHAN WANTS TO SEE YOU.
SHE'S IN PRACTICE ROOM THREE.
Practice Room 3
3
4

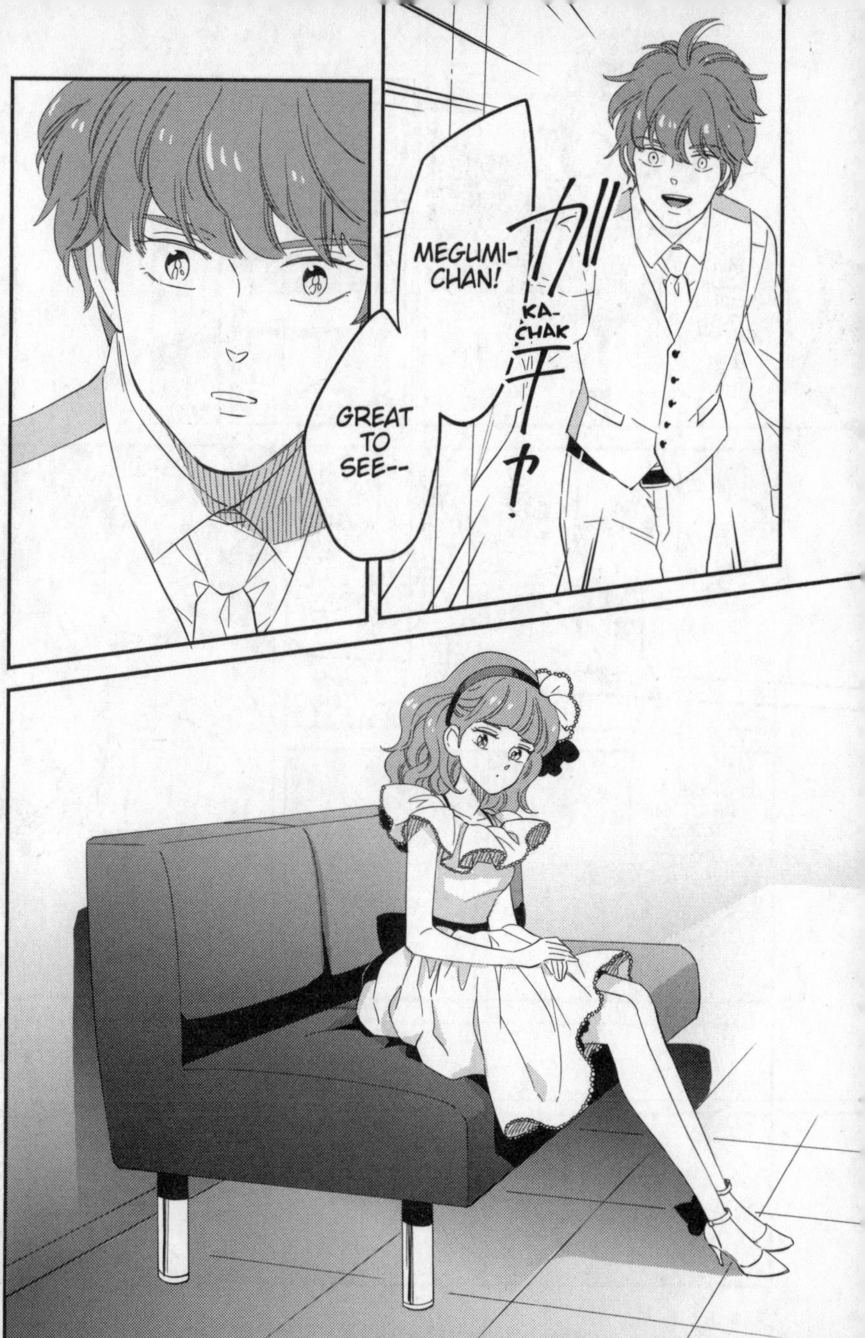
ガチャ!
KA-CHAK
MEGUMI-CHAN!
GREAT TO SEE--

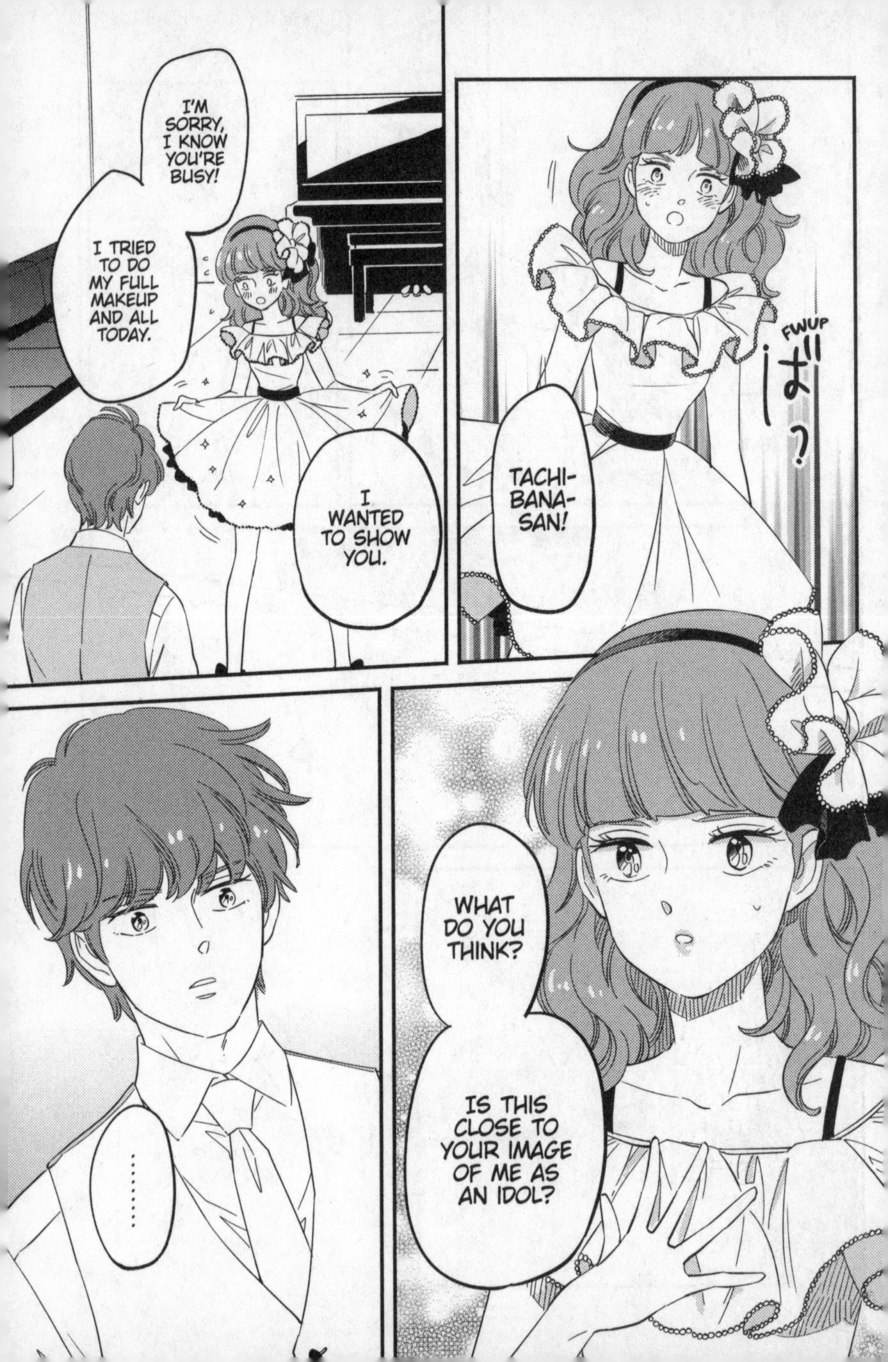
TACHIBANA-SAN!
FWUP
ばっ
I'M SORRY, I KNOW YOU'RE BUSY!
I TRIED TO DO MY FULL MAKEUP AND ALL TODAY.
I WANTED TO SHOW YOU.
WHAT DO YOU THINK?
IS THIS CLOSE TO YOUR IMAGE OF ME AS AN IDOL?
......

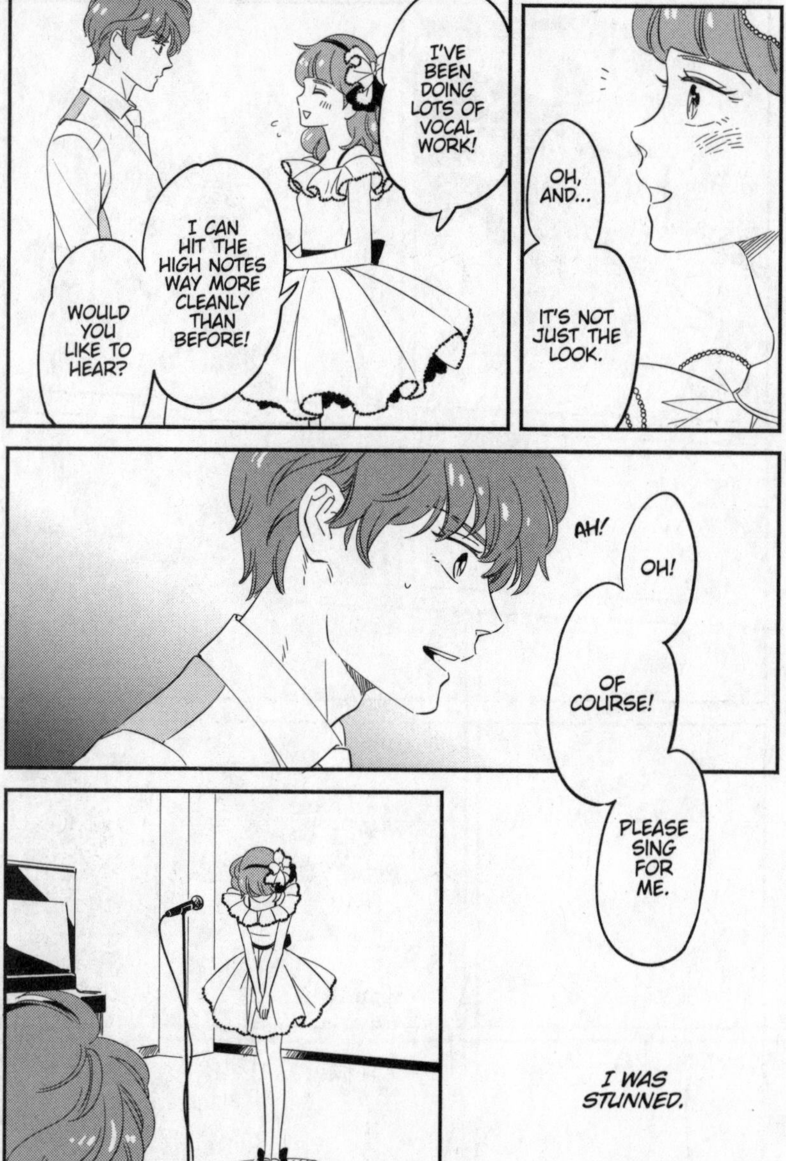
OH, AND...
IT'S NOT JUST THE LOOK.
I'VE BEEN DOING LOTS OF VOCAL WORK!
I CAN HIT THE HIGH NOTES WAY MORE CLEANLY THAN BEFORE!
WOULD YOU LIKE TO HEAR?
AH!
OH!
OF COURSE!
PLEASE SING FOR ME.
I WAS STUNNED.

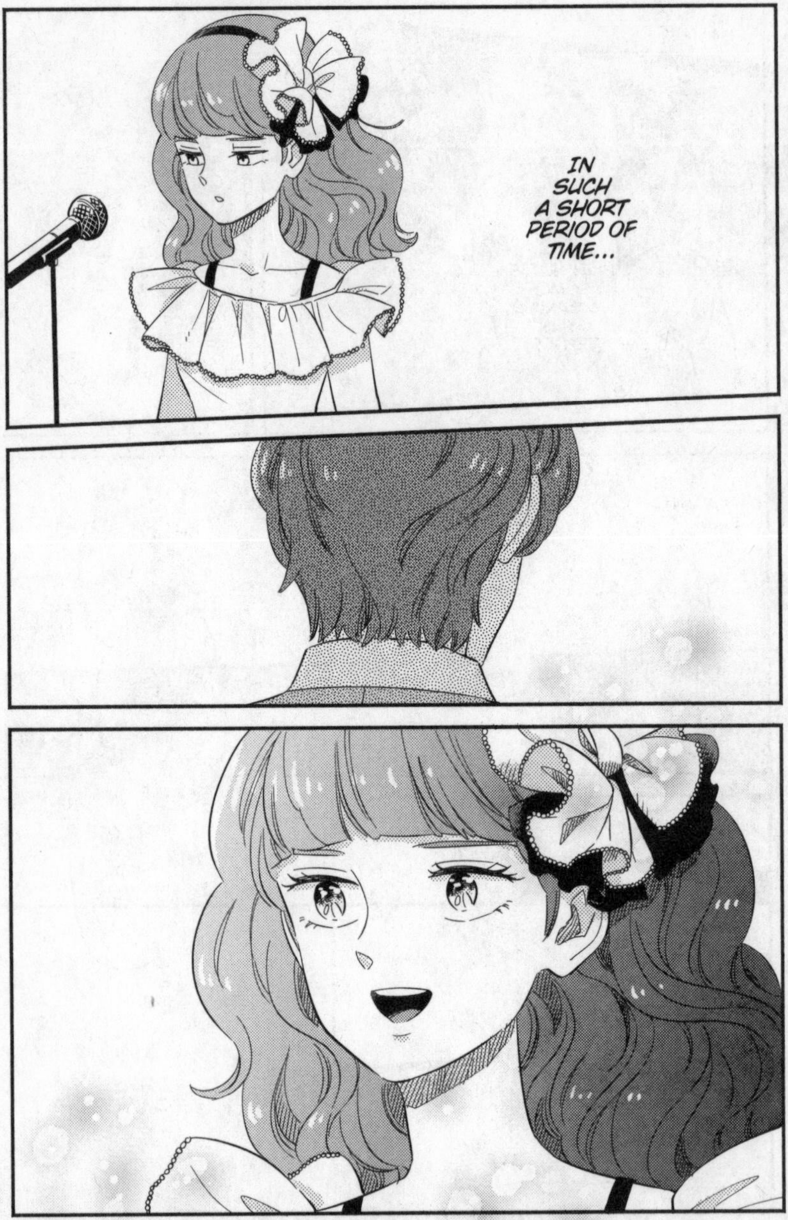
IN SUCH A SHORT PERIOD OF TIME...

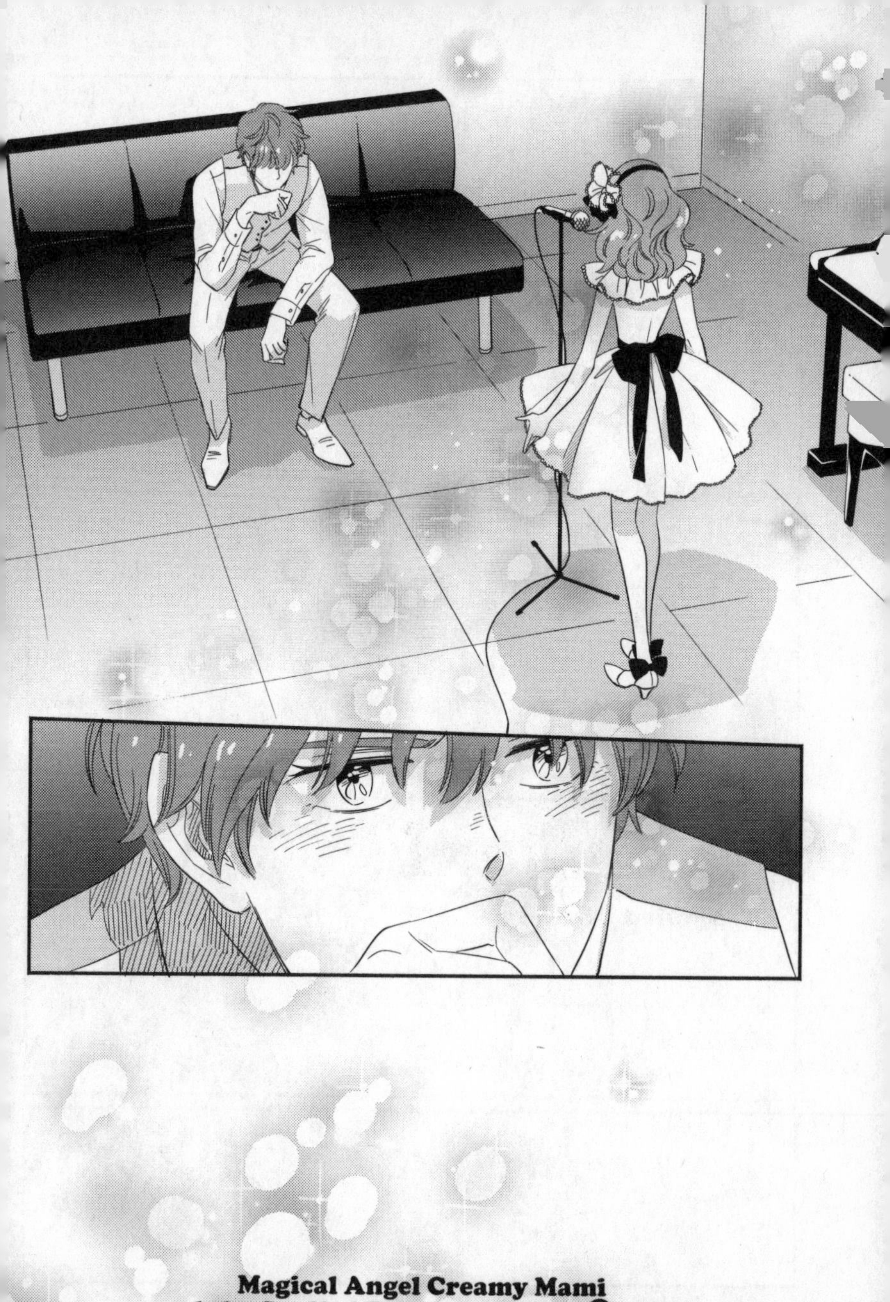

Magical Angel Creamy Mami
and the Spoiled Princess Volume ② / End

Magical Angel

Creamy Mami

and the

Spoiled Princess

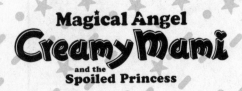

Afterword

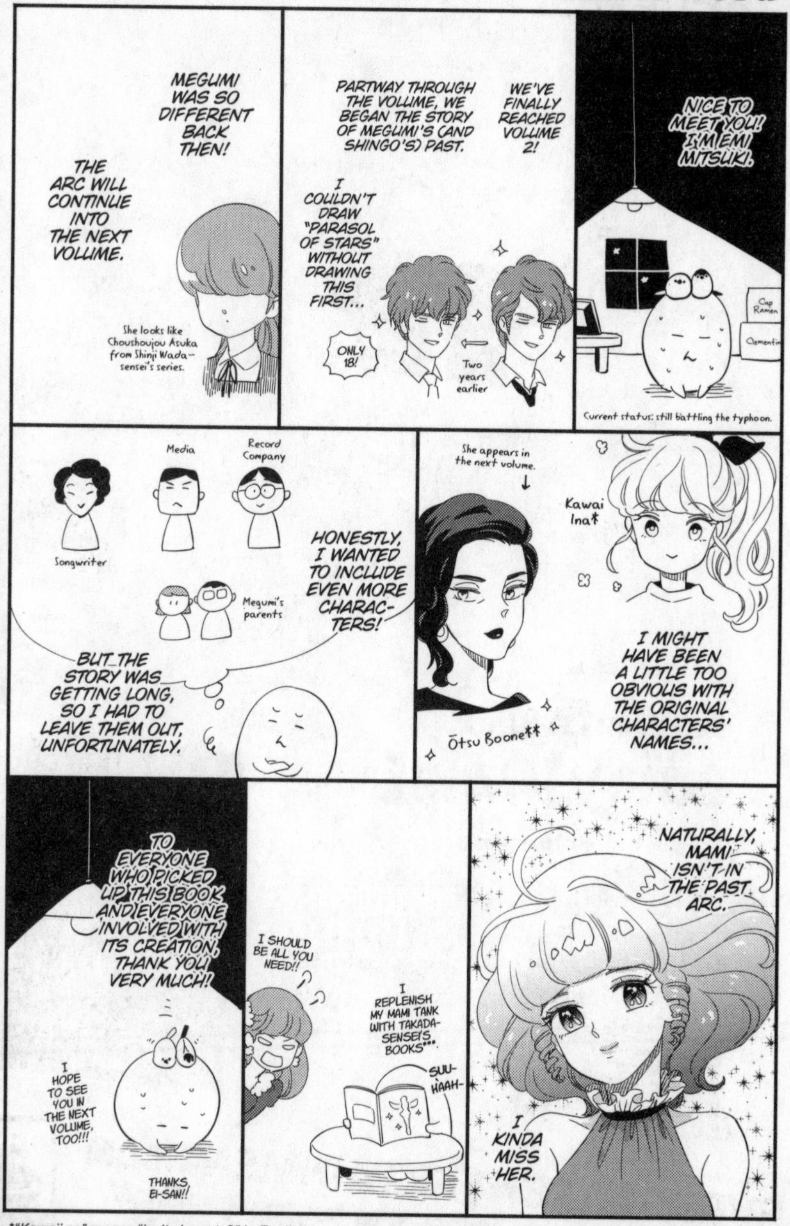
NICE TO MEET YOU! I'M EMI MITSUKI.
Cup Ramen
Clementin
Current status: still battling the typhoon.
WE'VE FINALLY REACHED VOLUME 2!
PARTWAY THROUGH THE VOLUME, WE BEGAN THE STORY OF MEGUMI'S (AND SHINGO'S) PAST.
I COULDN'T DRAW "PARASOL OF STARS" WITHOUT DRAWING THIS FIRST...
Two years earlier
ONLY 18!
MEGUMI WAS SO DIFFERENT BACK THEN!
THE ARC WILL CONTINUE INTO THE NEXT VOLUME.
She looks like Choushoujou Asuka from Shinji Wada-sensei's series.
Kawai Ina*
She appears in the next volume.
I MIGHT HAVE BEEN A LITTLE TOO OBVIOUS WITH THE ORIGINAL CHARACTERS' NAMES...
Ōtsu Boone**
Record Company
Media
Songwriter
HONESTLY, I WANTED TO INCLUDE EVEN MORE CHARACTERS!
Megumi's parents
BUT THE STORY WAS GETTING LONG, SO I HAD TO LEAVE THEM OUT, UNFORTUNATELY.
NATURALLY, MAMI ISN'T IN THE PAST ARC.
I KINDA MISS HER.
I SHOULD BE ALL YOU NEED!!
I REPLENISH MY MAMI TANK WITH TAKADA-SENSEI'S BOOKS***.
SUU-HAAH-
TO EVERYONE WHO PICKED UP THIS BOOK AND EVERYONE INVOLVED WITH ITS CREATION, THANK YOU VERY MUCH!
I HOPE TO SEE YOU IN THE NEXT VOLUME, TOO!!!
THANKS, EI-SAN!!

*"Kawaii na" means "isn't she cute?" in English.
**A play on the word "otsubone," which is slang for an older woman in an office who looks after younger staff members.
***Akemi Takada, the character designer for Creamy Mami, has released art books for the series.